Egor Kovalevsky

A Journey to Inner Africa

Translated from the Russian by
Anna Aslanyan

Copyright © 2020 by Sergey Glebov
Some rights reserved

This work is licensed under the Creative Commons Attribution-NonCommercial 4.0 International License. To view a copy of this license, visit http://creativecommons.org/licenses/by-nc/4.0/ or send a letter to Creative Commons, PO Box 1866, Mountain View, California, 94042, USA.

Published in the United States of America by
Amherst College Press
Manufactured in the United States of America

DOI: http://dx.doi.org/10.3998/mpub.12093663

ISBN 978-1-943208-16-6 (paper)
ISBN 978-1-943208-17-3 (OA)

Library of Congress Control number: TK

https://acpress.amherst.edu/

Originally published as E. P. Kovalevskii, *Puteshestvie vo vnutrenniuiu Afriku* (St. Petersburg: I. I. Glazunov, 1872).

As to the sources of the Nile, not one [. . .] professed to know anything, except the scribe of the sacred treasury of Athene at the city of Saïs in Egypt. To me however this man seemed not to be speaking seriously when he said that he had certain knowledge of it.

—Herodotus, book II, 28

The sources of the Nile are in paradise.

Fountain in Constantinople

Contents

A Wanderer on Land and Sea:
The Life of Egor Petrovich Kovalevsky ~ xi
David Schimmelpenninck

Introduction from a North African Perspective ~ xxix
Mukaram Hhana and Michal Wasiucionek

PART I: EGYPT AND NUBIA

Chapter I: Alexandria ~ 3

Chapter II: The First Impression Made upon Us by the Sight of the Desert: The Nile and Cairo ~ 15

Chapter III: Mohammed Ali and the Pyramids ~ 27

Chapter IV: Our Departure from Cairo and Voyage down the Nile to Minya ~ 39

Chapter V: From Minya to Esneh ~ 51

Chapter VI: *Almehs* in Esneh and, Generally, Women in the East ~ 59

Chapter VII: Nubia along the Nile ~ 71

Chapter VIII: The Great Nubian Desert ~ 79

Chapter IX: From the Great Nubian Desert to the
Confluence of the White Nile and the Blue Nile ⁓ 97

Chapter X: Khartoum and Sennaar ⁓ 109

Chapter XI: Three Varieties of the Palm-Tree
and the Baobab: Roseires ⁓ 119

PART II: THE LAND OF THE NEGROES

Chapter I: New Vistas ⁓ 127

Chapter II: Benishangul and Kamamil ⁓ 137

Chapter III: Farther into Africa Than Anyone Else ⁓ 145

Chapter IV: The Sources of the Nile in Studies,
from Herodotus to the Present Day ⁓ 155

Chapter V: The Second Expedition to the Mountains ⁓ 171

Chapter VI: Jebel Doul and Its Entertainments ⁓ 179

Chapter VII: The Negroes ⁓ 187

Chapter VIII: Our Return Journey: Diseases ⁓ 205

Chapter IX: The Lesser Nubian Desert and Meroë
with Its Pyramids: Dongola ⁓ 219

Chapter X: Giraffe- and Ostrich-Hunting:
Ipsambul and Thebes ⁓ 231

Chapter XI: Return to Alexandria: Mohammed Ali,
Ibrahim Pasha, and Their Families ⁓ 241

Addendum: Geographical Aspects of the Basin of the Nile:
Gold Deposits of Inner Africa ⁓ 251

Illustrations

Fountain in Constantinople ~ vi
Caravan in the Great Nubian Desert ~ 2
View of Alexandria ~ 4
Abyssinian female slave ~ 24
Jellab, a slave trader ~ 25
Mosque in Cairo ~ 49
Obelisk ~ 57
Portrait of Sève (Soliman Pasha) ~ 68
Visit to the *melek* of Uru Taor ~ 126
Lion-hunting ~ 128
Sphinx situated near pyramids ~ 146
Egyptian plough ~ 183
Sphinx, near Meroë ~ 222
Portrait of Ibrahim Pasha ~ 243
Portrait of Mohammed Ali ~ 247
Table of Barometric, Thermometric, and Psychrometric Observations ~ 268
Map of East Sudan and Abyssinia ~ 274

A Wanderer on Land and Sea

The Life of Egor Petrovich Kovalevsky

David Schimmelpenninck

A lively spirit invincible,
Always true to himself and everywhere,
A lively flame, often without smoke,
Burning in suffocating surroundings . . .
Unabashedly championing truth,
He battled vulgarity all life long.

—Fedor Tiutchev

As obscure today in Russia as he is abroad, Egor Petrovich Kovalevsky was well known to his 19th-century contemporaries.[1] Explorer, diplomat, and author—his collected works total five volumes—Kovalevsky

---

1 Unless noted otherwise, translations in this chapter are my own.
  Kovalevsky merited only one proper biography, as well as a briefer survey, Vladimir L'vovich Vilenkin, *Stranstvovatel' po sushe i moriam* [A traveler on land and sea], Zamchatel'nye Geografy i Puteshetvenniki (Moscow: Mysl', 1969). A contemporary who knew him well wrote a lengthy obituary, see Pavel Vasil'evich Annenkov, *Egor Petrovich Kovalevsky* (St. Petersburg: Tipografiia Imperatorskoi Akademii Nauk, 1868). Kovalevsky's service record up to 1856 is in Arkhiv vneshnei politiki Rossiikoi imperii (hereafter AVPRI), fond. Departament lichnogo sostava i koziastvennykh del, opis' 464, delo 1722, list 1–13, and is reproduced as an appendix to Egor Petrovich Kovalevsky, "Sobranie sochinenii. Vol. 1. Stranstvovatel' po sushe i moriam v 4-kh chastiakh," Priatnaia kompaniia, February 12, 2017, http://www.litres.ru/pages/biblio_book/?art+10423386.

even merited an epitaph by the poet Fedor Tiutchev. While it was his travel accounts that made him famous, he also played an important role in tsarist foreign affairs at a particularly sensitive time. Meanwhile, as an official with progressive views who was equally at home in the company of senior statesmen and as in that of radical writers, Kovalevsky's views provide an interesting insight in the world view of Russia's educated public during the reigns of Emperors Nicholas I (1825–55) and Alexander II (1855–81).

Egor Kovalevsky entered the world in 1811 (or 1809, according to some sources) as the youngest member of a large gentry family of modest means in Iaroshevka, a village near Kharkov in northeastern Ukraine. As his name suggests, Kovalevsky's ancestors were Russified Poles who had settled in the area in the 1650s, just as Ukraine's Cossack ruler pledged submission to the Russian tsar. After an upbringing typical of his caste, in 1825 Egor enrolled in Kharkov's new university, which his uncle, Vasilii Karazin, had founded 20 years earlier. Kovalevsky enrolled in the Faculty of Philology, although he was particularly interested in geography and also took many courses in the sciences.

A contemporary, the literary critic Pavel Annenkov, points out that Kovalevsky's generation was the first in Russia for which a university education was practically obligatory for a civil service career.[2] The decade after the Napoleonic Wars was also a time of considerable intellectual turmoil among Russian students, who were well acquainted with the ideas that had led to revolution in France a little over 20 years earlier. Indeed, toward the end of 1825 a group of militant guards officers, the Decembrists, tried to seize power in the wake of Emperor Alexander I's death. While the attempted coup was quickly put down and the archconservative Nicholas I acceded to the throne, radical thought continued to percolate among the empire's educated youth.[3] Egor Kovalevsky would not prove to be entirely immune to such notions.

Like most ambitious graduates in Imperial Russia, upon completing his university education in 1829, Kovalevsky moved to St. Petersburg to

---

2   Annenkov, *Kovalevsky*, 2–3.
3   For a good intellectual portrait of the generation, see Pavel Vasil'evich Annenkov, *The Extraordinary Decade: Literary Memoirs* (Ann Arbor: University of Michigan Press, 1968).

seek a career. He quickly found it in the government's Mining and Salt Department, which also employed his older brother Evgraf. Egor took to his job and eagerly broadened his knowledge of geology by auditing courses at the Mining Cadet Corps and working at its museum. When Evgraf was promoted to head of the mining works in Western Siberia's Altai Mountains the following year, Egor joined him there as his office manager.

The young mining engineer did not stay bound to his desk. He participated in many surveys of the region's mineral resources. By 1831, Kovalevsky was already leading expeditions to find gold in the northern Altai, and over the next few years, he began exploiting four deposits of the precious metal. Four years later, he again accompanied his brother, this time to the Urals, an ancient mountain range that had already been mined for well over a century. When in 1836 his department was absorbed into the army, Kovalevsky was given the rank of captain. In addition to prospecting for gold, iron ore, and other metals, he also helped modernize steel production. Meanwhile, he did not shy away from criticizing social conditions by arguing that using serf labor in the Urals' metallurgical works was inefficient.[4]

Kovalevsky had already began publishing in the *Gornyi zhurnal* (Mining journal) in the Altai. In addition to making important contributions to geology, the articles also brought him to the attention of his superiors back in the capital. They no doubt played a role in an important assignment that would entirely change the trajectory of his future.

Hemmed in by the Habsburg and Ottoman empires on the Adriatic, Montenegro's Orthodox Slavs looked to their mighty Russian coreligionists for help in maintaining their precarious independence. The nation's hereditary *vladika* (prince-bishop)[5] was no stranger to St. Petersburg. On one visit in 1837, Petar II Njegoš, then the vladika, added a special request to his usual appeals for economic support. According to legend, his realm's mountains had been mined for gold in Roman times. Perhaps the Russian tsar might send one of his specialists to relocate the source. The choice naturally fell on the ambitious young

---

4 Vilenkin, *Stranstvovatel'*, 9.
5 Since Orthodox bishops are not allowed to marry, succession went from uncle to nephew.

mining engineer who had already made his name by helping develop Siberia's deposits of the metal.

Captain Kovalevsky set off for Montenegro in spring 1837.[6] Since the isolated bishopric was only regularly accessible by sea, from the Austrian port of Trieste, the journey entailed a stop in Vienna, where Kovalevsky met the Russian ambassador to the Habsburg court, Dmitrii Tatishchev. When the captain arrived in Montenegro's capital, Cetinje, Vladika Petar laid on a lavish welcome for his Russian guest. Crowds cheered and warriors fired a loud salute—a gesture typically reserved for heads of state.

Kovalevsky duly spent the summer months conducting a thorough geological survey of the little land. There was very little gold, although the mountains did have deposits of iron ore, manganese, lead, and copper. Near Podgorica, Kovalevsky even found the ruins of Doclea (the Roman emperor Diocletian's birthplace), where he carried out some archaeological digs. Much to his disappointment, looters had emptied the town's treasury long ago.

Toward the end of his stay, Kovalevsky found himself in an unusual predicament. Habsburg troops had just invaded, and the vladika turned to him for help. Kovalevsky was hardly eager to become involved in an international incident and protested that he was a mining engineer; his epaulettes certainly were not those of an officer in the combat arms. Nevertheless, Petar's appeals to his sense of Slavic solidarity convinced the reluctant subaltern to join the beleaguered warriors in the mountains for, as his nephew put it, "a Romantic Byronic adventure."[7]

Although badly outnumbered, the small Montenegrin force managed to beat the Austrian interlopers. In the subsequent negotiations, the commander of the defeated troops would only accept the signature

---

6 Kovalevsky published an account of his trip four years later. See Egor Petrovich Kovalevsky, *Chetyre mesiatsa v Chernogorii* [Four months in Montenegro] (St. Petersburg: Tip. A. A. Pliushar, 1841). It also inspired a novel, Volodymyr Sinenko, *Gornyi kapitan. Istoricheskii Roman* [Mining captain. A historical novel] (Moscow: Sovetskii pisatel', 1958).

7 P. Kovalevsky, "Vstrechi na zhiznennom puti" [Encounters on the path of life], *Istoricheskii vestnik* (February 1888): 370–92. Egor himself describes the episode in Egor Petrovich Kovalevsky, "Epizod iz voini cherngortsev s avstriitsami" [An episode of the Montenegrans's war with the Austrians], http://www.vostlit.info/Texts/Dokumenty/Serbien/XIX/1820-1840/Kovalevskij_E_P/text1.phtml?id=9440.

of a Russian officer on the peace treaty. After some hesitation, Kovalevsky complied, even affixing his family seal to the document.

The news that a mere subaltern had negotiated an international agreement on behalf of the Russian government caused a furor in the Viennese press. Meanwhile, the Austrian ambassador in St. Petersburg lodged a formal protest, since Russia had signed a treaty with Austria five years earlier pledging to maintain the status quo in the Balkans. Tsar Nicholas was not amused, and he stripped Kovalevsky of his Russian nationality.

Now in Italy, Kovalevsky turned to a Russian diplomat (and future foreign minister), Prince Aleksandr Gorchakov, for advice. The prince suggested that he write a long letter *en bon français* to Ambassador Tatishchev to explain himself. Fortunately, it had the desired effect. When it finally reached the tsar, he noted in the margin, "Le Capitaine Kowalesky a agi en vrai russe."[8] All was forgiven. He was allowed to return to Russia, and Nicholas even invited him for a small reception at Anichkov Palace along with his foreign minister, Count Karl Nesselrode, to thank him for his services. Years later, when he was a senior diplomat, Kovalevsky kept a pair of pistols with silver settings from Petar inscribed "To Captain Kovalevsky from the people of Montenegro, for the campaign" in his office at the Choristers' Bridge.[9]

The writer Mikhail Saltykov-Shchedrin suggests that Kovalevsky's Montenegrin escapade was the most important event of his life, for it marked the beginning of a series of more extensive travels on three continents over the next 15 years.[10] The next journey came about as the result of a request by the emir of Bukhara, Nasrullah Khan. In January 1839, the emir's envoy presented the foreign minister with a letter requesting "an expert in precious stones."[11] Nesselrode could hardly ignore the request. At the time, Bukhara was one of the small independent

---

8 "Captain Kovalevsky behaved like a true Russian." P. Kovalevsky, "Vstrechi na zhiznennom puti," 375.
9 N. I. Khitrova, "Diplomaticheskaia deiatel'nost' E. P. Kovalevskogo V 30-X—50-X Godax," in *Portrety Rossiiskikh diplomatov*, ed. A. V. Ignat'ev (Moscow: Institut Istorii SSSR, 1991), 116–19; P. Kovalevsky, "Vstrechi na zhiznennom puti," 373–76.
10 Mikhail Evgrafovich Saltykov-Shchedrin, "Nekrolog. Egor Petrovich Kovalevsky," *Otechestvennye zapiski* 180 (October 1868): 273.
11 Naftula Aronovich Khalfin, *Rossiiai Khanstva Srednei Azii* (Moscow: Nauka, 1974), 262.

states separating Russia from Britain's possessions in India that had become objects of fierce contention between the two imperial powers in their Great Game for primacy in Central Asia. Here was a golden opportunity to strengthen Russia's influence in the emirate. With little hesitation, Kovalevsky was entrusted with the delicate mission.[12] The foreign ministry gave him detailed instructions. Not only did it ask him to carry out a geological survey, but Kovalevsky was also to study the possibilities for exports and, if possible, free Russian slaves.

Kovalevsky set out from Orenburg on October 30, accompanied by Staff Captain A. R. Gerngross and some miners.[13] It was a hazardous expedition. Nomads loyal to the khan of Khiva had been attacking Russian caravans on the steppes they would be traversing with alarming frequency. Meanwhile, Orenburg's military governor, Adjutant General Count Vasilii Perovskii, was launching a punitive expedition to the khanate. Within a fortnight of crossing into what is now Kazakhstan, the small party found itself held captive by a group of hostile tribesmen. Not only would they likely be robbed of all their possessions, but they also faced the distinct possibility of being sold into slavery. But when a sandstorm intervened on the night on November 22, Kovalevsky and his comrades made good their escape. For two and a half days they rode, covering some 300 kilometers until they reached a tsarist outpost at Ak-Bulak.

Kovalevsky's tribulations were not over. At the end of December, some 3,000 Kyrgyz surrounded the position. Although about half of the 300-man garrison was sick, the Russians withstood the siege until they were relieved. Within a few weeks, Kovalevsky was back in Orenburg. He had little time to rest, however; in March 1840, he set out for Bukhara again, this time by a different route. Kovalevsky had better luck with his second attempt. Together with another article in the *Gornyi zhurnal*, the voyage yielded the first volume of his travelogue, *Stranstvovatel' po sushe i moriam* (A wanderer on land and sea).[14]

---

12 Ibid., 256–68.
13 His route journal for the voyage is in AVPRI, f. SPB. Glavnyi arkhiv, II-10, op. 48, 1838–39 gg., d. 2, ll. 115–37 and is reproduced in Kovalevsky, "Sobranie sochinenii."
14 Egor Petrovich Kovalevsky, *Stranstvovatel' po sushe i moriam*, 3 vols. (St. Petersburg: Tip. P. P. Bocharova, 1843–45).

Sometime in the early 1840s, Kovalevsky also traveled to Xinjiang, Afghanistan, and Kashmir. However, aside from a few chapters in the second volume of *Stranstvovatel' po sushe i moriam*, he left few records of these peregrinations.[15] We do know more about his second trip to the Balkans, which he undertook in 1843 and 1844 on behalf of a gold-mining company in St. Petersburg.[16] This new journey took him through the Carpathian Mountains to the lower Danube. Much like his earlier journey to Montenegro, Kovalevsky's sympathies for its Slavic population, then still under Ottoman rule, were evident: "The Slavs ceaselessly fought against their [Turkish] enemies; it was the war of gladiators. They were defeated everywhere. But they were never slain. When the gladiator was worn out, he fell. But it was only to trick his enemy. At the earliest opportunity, he would rise again, if not with new forces, at least with the same courage."[17]

The books Kovalevsky wrote about his trips were popular among Russian readers and garnered positive reviews. In his critique of the first two volumes of *Stranstvovatel' po sushe i moriam*, the literary critic Vissarion Belinskii wrote, "Every page grabs your attention right away, and in three or four quick strokes, [the author] portrays the customs and character of the people he met," adding that the stories "remind one of Alexandre Dumas's travel accounts."[18]

The newly founded Imperial Russian Geographical Society also took note of the intrepid wanderer, electing him to membership in 1847, the third year of its existence. While ostensibly a private organization, its honorary president was one of the emperor's sons, Grand Duke Konstantin Nikolaevich, and many of its members were senior military officers. It was not uncommon for the Geographical Society to join with the army's general staff to sponsor expeditions to areas of strategic interest, such as the empire's Asian borderlands. At times, its missions

---

15 Ibid., 2:26–29.
16 Kovalevsky, "Sobranie sochinenii."
17 Ibid.
18 Vissarion Grigor'evich Belinskii, "Stranstvovatel' po sushe i moriam," *Otechestvennye zapiski* 29, no. 8 (1843): 45–47. For reviews of the other volumes, see *Finskii vestnik* 3 (1845): 27–31; *Sovremennik* 15 (1849): 227–30.

therefore served the dual masters of geographical science and military intelligence.[19]

Kovalevsky came to play an important role in the Geographical Society. He served as secretary to its president for eight years, from 1857 to 1865, and upon retiring from this position, he was rewarded by being voted an honorary member. At the same time, as director of the foreign ministry's Asian Department, Kovalevsky also helped plan several expeditions to Central Asia.

Kovalevsky's ties to the Geographical Society proved useful the same year he joined it, when he was asked to provide his gold-mining expertise to Egypt's viceroy, Mohammed Ali Pasha. Still nominally a vassal to the Ottoman sultan, Mohammed Ali ruled virtually independently as Egypt's self-declared khedive. He was also an energetic reformer who did much to modernize his fiefdom's economy and army. However, because he was suspicious of British and French ambitions in the Near East, the khedive preferred to turn to more disinterested powers for their advice. For this reason, when Mohammed Ali sought to develop gold mines on the lower Nile River, it was only natural for him to turn to another power, especially one that had expertise in extracting the precious metal.

It did not take much to convince Kovalevsky to agree to the khedive's request. He had long wanted to travel to Africa. Twice—in 1843 and again in 1846—he had asked the foreign ministry for permission to undertake a trip on the continent, but was turned down on both occasions.[20] As with his earlier expeditions, Kovalevsky had much more in mind than geology. One of the most controversial questions among geographers at the time was finding the source of the Nile, Africa's longest river, a quest that also intrigued him. As the first European in modern times who would travel so deeply into its watershed, he also hoped to make discoveries about the continent's fauna and flora. Together with the Geographical Society, Kovalevsky drew up a detailed plan for the expedition.[21]

---

19 David Schimmelpenninck van der Oye, "Reforming Military Intelligence," in *Reforming the Tsar's Army*, ed. David Schimmelpenninck van der Oye and Bruce W. Menning (New York: Cambridge University Press, 2004), 143–44.
20 Vilenkin, *Stranstvovatel'*, 32.
21 Petr Petrovich Semenov, *Istoriia poluvekovoi deiatel'nosti Imperatorskago Russkago geograficheskago obshchestva*, 3 vols. (St. Petersburg: Tip. V. Bezobrazova, 1896), 1:30.

Unlike in Montenegro 10 years earlier, Kovalevsky succeeded in his primary goal. After sightseeing in Alexandria and Cairo as well as an obligatory trip to the pyramids, in early February 1848, the expedition reached Khartoum, where the Nile splits into two: the White Nile and Blue Nile. Since Mohammed Ali had only added Sudan to his domains some 25 years earlier, Kovalevsky was now entering largely unmapped terrain. He paid particular attention to the basin of the Tumat River, a tributary of the Blue Nile on the Ethiopian border. It was here that Kovalevsky discovered deposits of gold as well as ironstone.

Kovalevsky's Soviet biographers were not being disingenuous when they portrayed him as having progressive views. In his description of "the Land of the Negroes" (southern Sudan), he indignantly disagrees with the notion of some Europeans that Africans are racially inferior:

> There are some who still, even now, . . . put the negro on the lowest rung of mankind, the one that serves as an intermediate step between men and apes . . . overwhelmed with self-respect and pride, are willing altogether to throw the negro off the ladder atop which they have determined their own place. Generally speaking, this ranking of human beings is no prerogative of man, nor is it compatible with the idea of brotherhood bequeathed to man by the words of the Gospels; it does nothing but demonstrate the relentless egotism and complacent fallacy of those who believe themselves to be the privileged caste of mankind.

The notion that they are less intelligent that the white man was entirely wrong, Kovalevsky maintained: "The negro, even in his savage state, not being alien to any human ideas, shall sooner be reasoned with than a Belorussian in our land or a French peasant living far from the high road and the city."

Such ideas would not have raised any hackles in St. Petersburg at the time. During the 19th century, attitudes toward blacks among educated Russians tended to be less racist than in the West.[22] But tsarist censors

---

22 See, among other, Eli Weinerman, "Racism, Racial Prejudice and Jews in Late Imperial Russia," *Ethnic and Racial Studies* 17, no. 3 (2010): 442–95; Alison Blakely, *Russia and the Negro: Blacks in Russian History and Thought* (Washington, DC: Howard University Press, 1986).

were far less tolerant of any critiques of their own social order. As Kovalevsky contemplated a group of shackled slaves his Arab host in Doul had asked to dance for his benefit, he likened their lot to serfs back home, "Yet what amusements! What a life! And there are so many, especially in our land, in boundless Russia, who are doomed to such a life."

When in 1849 Kovalevsky published these words in his account of the trip, *A Journey to Inner Africa*, Dmitrii Buturlin's notorious committee for censorship informed the emperor that the book contained "inadmissible outbursts." For a second time, Kovalevsky was in disgrace with the autocracy. Nicholas angrily ordered that he be given "the sternest reprimand for these senseless and impertinent outbursts, locked up in a guard room for eight days, and henceforth be put under the strictest supervision."[23]

Carrying out the tsar's command proved impractical, since Kovalevsky was already making his way to Beijing with the 13th Ecclesiastical Mission for another lengthy journey. By the time he returned the following year, Nicholas' anger had abated. The tsar now limited his punishment to asking the explorer to sign a document promising to be more careful in the future. At the same time, Nicholas decorated Kovalevsky with the Order of St. Anne, 2nd degree, for the successful completion of his Egyptian mission.

Aside from the censors, *A Journey to Inner Africa* proved a success among its readers. Osip Senkovskii, whose acid pen could be devastating, was fulsome in his praise: "When you read [Kovalevsky's] descriptions, you forget that you live in St. Petersburg, on the marvelous Neva's banks; no, it seems that you are in fact Mehemet Ali's guest. On every page, you intensely feel that you are in Africa, safely on a camel's back, overcome by unbearable heat and menaced by the *khamsin* . . . No one who writes about Africa can better acquaint you with this region as clearly and as palpably as Mr. Kovalevsky."[24] Academician Karl von Baer, a distinguished scientist who had helped found the

---

23 Khitrova, "Diplomaticheskaia deiatel'nost'," 121. The radical socialist Nikolai Chernyshevskii fully shared Kovalevsky's sentiments in this regard. Vilenkin, *Stranstvovatel'*, 49.
24 Osip Ivanovich Senkovskii, "Puteshestvie Vo Vnutrenniuiu Afriku," *Biblioteka dlia chteniia* 95 (1849): 87. A *khamsin* is a dry, hot, sandy wind blowing from the south, common to North Africa and Arabia.

Geographical Society, was equally complimentary: "The author writes neither like a tourist nor like a geographer. He entertains his reader, but it is edifying entertainment."[25]

Unlike his previous assignments, Kovalevsky had been sent to the Middle Kingdom on a purely diplomatic assignment. The Treaty of Kiakhta in 1727 had regularized trade with China on the East Siberian border, but there was no analogous agreement to the west. It was up to Kovalevsky, by now a colonel, to negotiate one. Since he would be traveling overland through largely uncharted Inner Asian terrain, the Geographical Society also took great interest in the voyage. Von Baer gave Kovalevsky detailed instructions about collecting plant and animal specimens along the way.

The Ecclesiastical Mission the colonel accompanied was a venerable institution. Formally established by the Treaty of Kiakhta, its ostensible purpose was to minister to the souls of a small group of Cossacks who had entered into the service of the Qing emperor at the end of the 17th century. Roughly every decade, the Russian Orthodox Church would send some clergy to preach among their coreligionists as well as a few seminarians who studied Chinese. Unofficially, the mission also played an important diplomatic role for St. Petersburg at a time when the Qing disdained formal relations with any other nation.

Led by Archimandrite Palladii (Kafarov), the mission traveled overland from Kiakhta in East Siberia via Mongolia, arriving in the Chinese capital at the end of September 1849. Kovalevsky was unable to conclude a new commercial agreement with the Qing, and he spent about seven months there largely studying Chinese science and buying books for the Russian Academy of Sciences. However, the colonel did manage to convince his hosts to allow Russian merchants to travel from Siberia by a more convenient route.

Kovalevsky had better luck in 1851, when he was sent to East Turkestan (now Xinjiang) to resume the talks he had begun the previous year in Beijing. After more grueling negotiations, on July 25, he finally convinced I Shan, the region's military governor, to sign the Treaty of Kulja. The pact's most important provisions opened Kulja (now Yining)

---

25 Quoted in Vilenkin, *Stranstvovatel'*, 44.

and Chuguchak (Tacheng) to Russian trade and allowed the foreign ministry to set up consulates in both towns. The results were almost immediately felt. Over the next three years, the value of trade between Russia and East Turkestan quadrupled.[26]

For his trouble, the emperor granted Kovalevsky an annual pension of 600 rubles. The colonel's travels to the Far East also resulted in another popular travel account, *Puteshestvie v Kitai* (A journey to China).[27] Most important, his successful negotiations with the notoriously difficult Qing cemented Kovalevsky's reputation as an expert on Asia.[28]

The beleaguered Slavs of Southeastern Europe were still Kovalevsky's first love. In the fall of 1853, at a time of growing tensions with the Sublime Porte, Foreign Minister Nesselrode sent the colonel back to the Balkans to study the possibility that their Christian population might support Russia in a war. Like many Pan-Slavs of his day, Kovalevsky firmly believed that it was his nation's historical mission to free the Slavs from the "heathen Turk." Should it come to a clash with the Ottomans, he hoped to convince the Montenegrins to take up arms along with the Serbians and Herzegovinians, join the tsar's army on the Danube, and liberate Bulgaria. His ultimate goal was a federation of Balkan nations united by blood and faith and governed by a parliament in either Constantinople or Sofia.[29]

On the pretext of delivering financial aid, Kovalevsky made his way to Cetinje in November. By this time, war had already broken out, and he soon found himself on the staff of Adjutant General Prince Mikhail Gorchakov in the Danubian campaign. After Turkey's French and British allies landed on Crimea, Gorchakov's troops were redeployed on the peninsula, where many of them participated in the defense of Sevastopol. Kovalevsky took part in the siege until illness forced him to return to St. Petersburg in September 1854. This adventure eventually yielded

---

26 William Frederick Mayers, *Treaties between the Empire of China and Foreign Powers* (Shanghai: North-China Herald, 1877), 97–99; B. P. Gurevich, *Mezhdunarodnye otnosheniia v Tsentral'noi Azii v XVII-pervoi polovine XIX v* (Moscow: Nauka, 1979), 279–83.
27 Egor Petrovich Kovalevsky, *Puteshestvie v Kitai*, 2 vols. (St. Petersburg: V tip. Koroleva i Kº, 1853).
28 Galen B. Ritchie, "The Asiatic Department during the Reign of Alexander II, 1855–1881" (New York: Columbia University, 1970), 285.
29 Khitrova, "Diplomaticheskaia deiatel'nost'," 125–26.

yet another book, *Voina s Turtsiei i razryv s zapadnymi derzhavami v 1853 i 1854 godakh* (The war with Turkey and the rupture with the Western powers in 1853 and 1854).³⁰

Russia's defeat in the Crimean War the following year had profound consequences, as its humiliation laid bare the empire's many shortcomings. Meanwhile, Nicholas's death in February 1855 saw the accession of his son, Alexander II. The new sovereign had a distinctly different political outlook, and he set out on a series of major transformations to rejuvenate his realm, including the abolition of serfdom. Collectively known as the "Great Reforms," they focused entirely on the domestic order.

The success of Alexander's ambitions at home hinged on avoiding any more complications abroad. His new foreign minister, Prince Aleksandr Gorchakov, fully shared his master's desire to remain at peace. Over the coming 20 years, the prince would steadfastly counsel moderation at the Choristers' Bridge in a policy that came to be known as "recueillement" (reflection).³¹

Prince Gorchakov had clearly taken a liking to the young subaltern he had advised back in Italy almost 20 years earlier, for shortly after Alexander named him his foreign minister in 1856, the prince tapped Kovalevsky to head his Asian Department. Established in 1819, this section had a broad geographical mandate that basically extended to the entire extra-European world (and even included the Balkans).³² Appointing Kovalevsky to the post proved to be astute. Major General Mikhail Veniukov, a military geographer with considerable expertise in Asia, wrote that "there was no better manager of Russia's Eastern politics than Egor Kovalevsky during the foreign ministry's entire existence."³³

---

30 Egor Petrovich Kovalevsky, *Voina s Turtsiei i razryv s zapadnymi derzhavami v 1853 i 1854 godakh* (n.p., 1868).
31 From the prince's famous remark, "La Russie en boude pas, mais elle se receuille" (Russia is not sulking, it is merely giving itself to reflection). Barbara Jelavich, *A Century of Russian Foreign Policy* (Philadelphia: J. B. Lippincott, 1964), 134.
32 As Kovalevsky's nephew put it, "Although [the department] is called Asian, it is also African, American, Australian, Slavic, Greek, etc." P. Kovalevsky, "Vstrechi na zhiznennom puti," 387. A thorough study of its operations in these years is in Ritchie, "Asiatic Department."
33 Quoted in N. S. Kiniapina, M. M. Bliev, and V. V. Degoev, *Kavkaz i Sredniaia Aziia vo vneshnei politiki Rossii vtoraia polovina XVIII–80e gody XIX v* (Moscow: Izd-vo Moskovskogo universiteta, 1984), 258.

The new director understood that restoring Russia's damaged prestige in the East was a top priority. Given his Pan-Slav leanings, he continued to pay particular attention to the Balkans. In Kovalevsky's opinion, the lot of the Slavs under Ottoman rule was nothing short of "slavery that would have been shameful even in the Middle Ages,"[34] and he worked hard to support them within the constraints of Gorchakov's cautious diplomacy.

One headache was Bulgaria, where some nationalists were beginning to turn to the West rather than Russia to support their efforts for emancipation from the Turks. To combat its influence, Kovalevsky arranged scholarships for Bulgarian youth and set up the Slavic Benevolent Committee, which promoted public support for Russia's Slavic brethren. At times, his zeal alarmed the foreign minister, who suggested that he refrain from forwarding consular reports about the plight of the Balkan Slavs to the emperor lest they distress him unduly.[35]

Kovalevsky also endeavored to advance Russia's interests further east. In Central Asia, where his country was still actively involved in the Great Game with Britain, the director's feelings about the right move were clear—strike Britain in India, "then the English will moderate their voice."[36] While he understood that his chief strongly opposed any such adventures, Kovalevsky did sponsor three expeditions through the Geographical Society (where he was now the president's secretary) to sway the region's khans and emirs to his side as well as to gather intelligence.

Despite their occasional differences, Gorchakov and Kovalevsky remained on friendly terms and were not averse to socializing together.[37] By all accounts the emperor also valued his services. When General Nikolai Murav'ev, under Kovalevsky's watch, annexed 600,000 square kilometers of Chinese territory to East Siberia by the Treaty of Aigun

---

34 N. I. Khitrova, "Rossiia Sosredotochivaetsia," in *Istoriia Vneshnei Politiki Rossii. Vtoraia polovina XIX veka*, ed. V. M. Khevrolina et al. (Moscow: Mezhdunarodnye otnosheniia, 1997), 61.

35 Viktoriia Maksimovna Khevrolina, *Rossiiskii Diplomat Graf Nikolai Ivanovich Ignat'ev* (Moscow: Institut rossiiskoi istorii, 2004), 103.

36 Khitrova, "Diplomaticheskaia deiatel'nost'," 132.

37 Aleksandr Vasil'evich Nikitenko, *Dnevnik*, 3 vols. (Moscow: Zakharov, 2005), 2:253.

in 1858, Alexander rewarded Kovalevsky with 3,300 hectares of land in the Government of the Samara.[38] However, Kovalevsky's career did not remain immune from the vicissitudes of politics. The student disturbances of 1861 that resulted in his brother Evgraf's dismissal as minister of education also led to Egor's removal from his post. To ease the pain, the tsar made the former director a senator with a seat on the State Council for foreign affairs.

In the last decade of his life Kovalevsky increasingly devoted himself to literature. He had tried his hand at drama and poetry early on. Already at the age of 21, shortly after he had begun his career in mining, Kovalevsky published a play about a 15th-century rebel against Muscovite autocracy, *Marfa-Posadnitsa*. Inspired by his work in the Altai, that year also saw a book of his verse, *Dumy o Sibiri* (*Thoughts about Siberia*).[39] Deciding that he might be better at prose, during the following decade Kovalevsky went on to write short stories and a novel, *Peterburg dnem i nochiu* (St. Petersburg by day and night), often under a pseudonym. Many of the former were published in Senkovskii's thick journal *Biblioteka dlia chteniia*, although censors held up the novel because of its critical portrayal of poverty in the Russian capital.[40]

By the 1860s, Kovalevsky limited himself to historical works, such as his history of the Crimean War and a biography, *Graf Bliudov i ego vremia* (Count Bludov and his times), which focused on reaction during the latter years of Tsar Alexander I's reign.[41] Yet while no longer writing prose, he remained active in St. Petersburg's literary circles and actively promoted other writers. Fyodor Dostoyevsky fondly recalled the senator's encouraging words about his new novel *Crime and Punishment*.[42] And he also knew many other authors, ranging from Nikolai Chernyshevskii and Nikolai Nekrasov to Fedor Tiutchev, Count Lev Tolstoi,

---

38 Annenkov, *Kovalevsky*, 17.
39 Egor Petrovich Kovalevsky, *Marfa-Posadnitsa, ili Slavianskie zheny* (St. Petersburg: V tip Pliushara, 1832); Kovalevsky, *Dumy o Sibiri* (St. Petersburg: V tipografiia Pliushara, 1832).
40 The novel did appear in German translation: Egor Petrovich Kovalevsky, *Petersburg Am Tage Und Bei Nacht*, trans. Philipp Löwenstein (Stuttgart: Carl Spindler, 1847).
41 Egor Petrovich Kovalevsky, *Graf Bliudov i ego vremia* (St. Petersburg, 1866).
42 Fyodor Dostoyevsky, *A Writer's Diary. Volume 1: 1873–1876*, trans. Kenneth Lantz (Evanston, IL: Northwestern University Press, 1997), 146.

and Ivan Turgenev.⁴³ One indication of their respect was Kovalevsky's election in 1859 as president of a new charitable organization, the Society for Aid to Writers and Scholars.

When Kovalevsky died in 1868, the obituaries were full of praise and affection.⁴⁴ In a lengthy eulogy to the Geographical Society, Pavel Annenkov spoke of Kovalevsky's "severe, somewhat stern, and apparently cold appearance which nevertheless poorly masked the unquenchable ardor of his spirit."⁴⁵ But his entry in the *Russian Biographical Dictionary* puts it best:

> Never closing himself off in bureaucratic formalities and keeping a lively interest in the urgent social questions of the day, Kovalevsky always used his influence and his government position to support everything that was sensible, even if it had no relevance to his primary responsibilities.⁴⁶

References

Annenkov, Pavel Vasil'evich. *Egor Petrovich Kovalevsky*. St. Petersburg: Tipografiia Imperatorskoi Akademii Nauk, 1868.

———. *The Extraordinary Decade: Literary Memoirs*. Ann Arbor: University of Michigan Press, 1968.

Belinskii, Vissarion Grigor'evich. "Stranstvovatel' po sushe i moriam." *Otechestvennye zapiski* 29, no. 8 (1843): 45–47.

Blakely, Alison. *Russia and the Negro: Blacks in Russian History and Thought*. Washington, DC: Howard University Press, 1986.

Dostoyevsky, Fyodor. *A Writer's Diary. Volume 1: 1873–1876*. Translated by Kenneth Lantz. Evanston, IL: Northwestern University Press, 1997.

Gurevich, B. P. *Mezhdunarodnye otnosheniia v Tsentral'noi Azii v XVII-pervoi polovine XIX v*. Moscow: Nauka, 1979.

---

43 Some of Turgenev's letters to Kovalevsky were reproduced in I. S. Turgenev, "Ivan Sergeevich Turgenev v ego pis'makh k Egory Petr. Kovalevskomu," *Russkaia Starina* 42 (May 1884): 397–402.

44 Saltykov-Shchedrin, "Nekrolog," 273–74; M. S. Saltykov-Shchedrin, "Nekrolog. Egor Petrovich Kovalevsky," *Vestnik Evropy*, no. 10 (1868): 894–96; "Nekrolog. General-Leitenant Egor Petrovich Kovalevsky," *Voennyi sbornik* 64 (1868): 11, 34–37.

45 Annenkov, *Kovalevsky*, 20.

46 *Russkii biograficheskii slovar'*, vol. 9, s.v. "Kovalevsky, Egor Petrovich."

Jelavich, Barbara. *A Century of Russian Foreign Policy*. Philadelphia: J. B. Lippincott, 1964.
Khalfin, Naftula Aronovich. *Rossiiai Khanstva Srednei Azii*. Moscow: Nauka, 1974.
Khevrolina, Viktoriia Maksimovna. *Rossiiskii Diplomat Graf Nikolai Ivanovich Ignat'ev*. Moscow: Institut rossiiskoi istorii, 2004.
Khitrova, N. I. "Diplomaticheskaia deiatel'nost' E. P. Kovalevskogo V 30-X—50-X Godax." In *Portrety Rossiiskikh diplomatov*, edited by A. V. Ignat'ev, 115–37. Moscow: Institut Istorii SSSR, 1991.
———. "Rossiia Sosredotochivaetsia." In *Istoriia Vneshnei Politiki Rossii. Vtoraia polovina XIX veka*, edited by V. M. Khevrolina et al., 49–84. Moscow: Mezhdunarodnye otnosheniia, 1997.
Kiniapina, N. S., M. M. Bliev, and V. V. Degoev. *Kavkaz i Sredniaia Aziia vo vneshnei politiki Rossii vtoraia polovina XVIII-80e gody XIX v*. Moscow: Izd-vo Moskovskogo universiteta, 1984.
Kovalevsky, Egor Petrovich. *Chetyre mesiatsa v Chernogorii*. St. Petersburg: Tip. A. A. Pliushar, 1841.
———. "Epizod Iz Voini Cherngortsev C Avstriitsami." http://www.vostlit.info/Texts/Dokumenty/Serbien/XIX/1820-1840/Kovalevskij_E_P/text1.phtml?id=9440.
———. *Graf Bliudov i ego vremia*. St. Petersburg, 1866.
———. *Marfa-Posadnitsa, ili Slavianskie zheny*. St. Petersburg: V tip Pliushara, 1832.
———. *Petersburg Am Tage Und Bei Nacht*. Translated by Philipp Löwenstein. Stuttgart: Carl Spindler, 1847.
———. *Puteshestvie v Kitai*. 2 vols. St. Petersburg: V tip. Koroleva i K°, 1853.
———. *Dumy o Sibiri*. St. Petersburg: V tipografiia Pliushara, 1832.
———. "Sobranie sochinenii. Vol. 1. Stranstvovatel' po sushe i moriam V 4-kh chastiakh." Priatnaia kompaniia, February 12, 2017. http://www.litres.ru/pages/biblio_book/?art+10423386.
———. *Stranstvovatel' po sushe i moriam*. 3 vols. St. Petersburg: Tip. P. P. Bocharova, 1843.
———. *Voina s Turtsiei i razryv s zapadnymi derzhavami v 1853 i 1854 godakh*. N.p., 1868.
Kovalevsky, P. "Vstrechi na zhiznennom puti." *Istoricheskii vestnik* (February 1888): 370–92.
Mayers, William Frederick. *Treaties between the Empire of China and Foreign Powers*. Shanghai: North-China Herald, 1877.
"Nekrolog. General-Leitenant Egor Petrovich Kovalevskii." *Voennyi sbornik* 64 (1868): 11, 34–37.
Nikitenko, Aleksandr Vasil'evich. *Dnevnik*. 3 vols. Moscow: Zakharov, 2005.
Ritchie, Galen B. "The Asiatic Department during the Reign of Alexander II, 1855–1881." New York: Columbia University, 1970.
Saltykov-Shchedrin, Mikhail Evgrafovich. "Nekrolog. Egor Petrovich Kovalevsky." *Otechestvennye zapiski* 180 (October 1868): 273–74.

———. "Nekrolog. Egor Petrovich Kovalevsky," *Vestnik Evropy*, no. 10 (1868): 894–96.
Schimmelpenninck van der Oye, David. "Reforming Military Intelligence." In *Reforming the Tsar's Army*, edited by David Schimmelpenninck van der Oye and Bruce W. Menning, 133–50. New York: Cambridge University Press, 2004.
Semenov, Petr Petrovich. *Istoriia poluvekovoi deiatel'nosti Imperatorskago Russkago geograficheskago obshchestva*. 3 vols. St. Petersburg: Tip. V. Bezobrazova, 1896.
Senkovskii, Osip Ivanovich. "Puteshestvie Vo Vnutrenniuiu Afriku." *Biblioteka dlia chteniia* 95 (1849): 83–114.
Sinenko, Volodymir. *Gornyi kapitan. Istoricheskii Roman*. Moscow: Sovetskii pisatel', 1958.
Turgenev, I. S. "Ivan Sergeevich Turgenev v ego pis'makh k Egory Petr. Kovalevskomu." *Russkaia Starina* 42 (May 1884): 397–402.
Vilenkin, Vladimir L'vovich. *Stranstvovatel' po sushe i moriam*. Zamchatel'nye Geografy i Puteshetvenniki. Moscow: Mysl', 1969.
Weinerman, Eli. "Racism, Racial Prejudice and Jews in Late Imperial Russia." *Ethnic and Racial Studies* 17, no. 3 (2010): 442–95.

Introduction from a North African Perspective

Mukaram Hhana and Michal Wasiucionek

In a stunning victory under the command of Count Aleksei Orlov, the Russian fleet destroyed the sultan's navy off the waters of Çeşme in the summer of 1770. While the battle's strategic importance was relatively small and quickly overshadowed by other Russian victories on the Danube, it nonetheless served as potent sign of Russia's growing military reach into the heartland of Ottoman domains and, more broadly, its entry into the Mediterranean. Pitted against the Sublime Porte in Southeastern Europe and the Caucasus, Russian imperial policies constituted the center of what came to be known the "Eastern Question," a geopolitical quagmire that created constant concerns among in diplomatic cabinets of many an imperial center across Europe and beyond. Meanwhile, within the halls of the *bab-i 'ali*, the High Porte, Russian territorial expansion and the subsequent loss of Crimea prompted the Porte to introduce a wide-ranging set of naval, and later military and governmental overhauls under the auspices of Abdul Hamid I and Selim III.

Because of their intertwined histories, no scholar of the Ottoman Empire would deny the profound impact of Russian territorial expansions on the historical trajectory of the sultan's "well-protected domains" throughout the 19th century. However, in practice, Ottomanists' engagement with the Russian Empire has stayed relatively limited, focusing almost exclusively on the scope of geopolitical, military, and diplomatic relations between the two land-based imperial giants. This is not for sheer oversight on the part of historians but rather due to the nature of archival sources and the barriers of languages.

This is to say that while most Anglophone, Turkophone, and Arabic-language scholarship of the Ottoman Empire has embedded the Sublime Porte within the geopolitical constellations of its European rivals, many specialists are hindered from accessing Russian sources directly, forcing us to rely on a handful of (oftentimes poorly) translated documents instead.

One of the most obvious examples is the controversy over the interpretation of the 1774 Treaty of Küçük Kaynarca. The treaty, which sealed the disastrous Ottoman losses of the Russo-Ottoman War of 1768–74, was often cited as a case of "Russian skill and Turkish imbecility" because of the clauses that secured Catherine II's right to intervene on behalf of the Orthodox subjects of the sultan. However, as Roderic Davison has noted, this stipulation—supported by English and French translation—was not included in either the original Ottoman or Russian documents. Rather, the concessions made by the Porte were far more modest than had previously been believed.[1] If we take into consideration that the 1774 constitutes one of the crucial documents for Russian-Ottoman relations in this period, the extent of the difficulties posed by the language barrier become blatantly evident.

The situation has been changing in recent decades, with notable contributions by Lale Can, Michael Reynolds, Victor Taki, and others.[2] However, even when important studies by a new generation of scholars are taken into account, our knowledge of the Russian imperial presence

---

1 Roderic H. Davison, "'Russian Skill and Turkish Imbecility': The Treaty of Kuchuk Kainardji Reconsidered," *Slavic Review* 35, no. 3 (1976): 463–83.
2 See Lale Can, "Connecting People: A Central Asian Sufi Network in Turn-of-the Century Istanbul," *Modern Asian Studies* 46, no. 2 (2012): 373–401; Michael Reynolds, *Shattering Empires: the Clash and Collapse of the Ottoman and Russian Empires* (Cambridge: Cambridge University Press, 2011); Victor Taki, *Tsar and Sultan: Russian Encounters with the Ottoman Empire* (London: Bloomsbury, 2016).

in the 19th-century Middle East and North Africa still remains relatively small in comparison to the enormous number of studies devoted to British and French encounters with the region.

This is not entirely a matter of the accessibility of sources but also owes much to the character of Russian historical experience in the Arabic-speaking domains of the Ottoman sultan, which differed greatly from that of maritime empires of Western Europe. Although the Russians made significant territorial gains in the Balkans and the Caucasus, the Middle East and North Africa proper played a secondary role in the Russian Empire's grand strategy. With the vast expanses of its Eurasian empire, St. Petersburg was predominantly concerned with controlling the Black Sea—securing the passage of its ships through it and the Dardanelle Straits into the Mediterranean. This stands in sharp contrast to the direct control that first France and later Britain sought in the Arab provinces of the Ottoman Empire. Moreover, as Kovalevsky notes, Russian presence in the region was much smaller than either its British of French counterparts. These two forces taken together lead to the appearance, at least on the surface, that the Russian influence in the region was historically interpreted as limited and its importance negligible.

However, this conclusion is far from conclusive. In fact, Russian sources constitute a treasure trove—still largely untapped—for students of 19th-century Middle East and North Africa. Throughout the century, numerous Russian officials, scholars, merchants and pilgrims ventured across the region and frequently wrote down and published their travelogues and memoirs. Nevertheless, only a handful of them have attracted the attention of Western scholars. When approached in their own right, Russian accounts of sojourns in the Ottoman Middle East provide an alternative and, in many respects, unique perspective on the region. Far from being a source of purely factual data, they offer a distinct perspective on the 19th-century realities of the region, filtered through their authors' own experiences of the Russian continental empire.

Egor Kovalevsky's account of a mining expedition into Sudan fits well into this trend, providing invaluable information on Mohammed

Ali's policies in the recently acquired territory as well as providing a distinct perspective on Egypt and Sudan as seen from the standpoint of an official and scholar with ample experience in Russia's own imperial project. In this sense, both his narrative and the mission stem from three parallel developments: Mohammed Ali's expansion into Sudan, the governor's attempts to harness the human and natural resources of his domains, and the growing involvement of St. Petersburg in the Ottoman Middle East.

Mohammed Ali, the Conquest of Sudan, and the Quest for Fazoglu Gold

In many respects, the rise of Mohammed Ali at the beginning of the 19th century overturned the balance of power within the sultan's imperial domains. Born in Kavala, he arrived in Alexandria in 1801 as a lowly quartermaster for a contingent of Balkan troops sent to oust Bonaparte's army from Egypt. Despite his relatively modest beginnings, the young officer quickly managed to secure power by forming a political alliance with Albanian troops stationed in the province. This alliance, along with his position as quartermaster, propelled his career in the postinvasion chaos of Bonaparte's Egypt. His powerbase and his political acumen allowed him to dominate the politics of the province and consolidate political hegemony by 1805.

In the years following his quick rise as *vali*, his prestige further increased. After massacring his rivals at the citadel and eliminating any serious opposition to his rule, the *vali*, on the behest of Mahmud II, managed to wrest control of the Hijaz and the holy cities of Mecca and Medina in a series of destructive campaigns against Abdullah bin Saud's forces.

However, Mohammed Ali's ambitions went far beyond the boundaries of Egypt and the Red Sea. Instead, he engaged in a multipronged political strategy to expand his possessions in the region while still maintaining his political relationship with the Ottoman Porte. To secure the resources necessary, the *vali* engaged in a general overhaul of the province's military and naval fleet, as well as far-reaching administrative and economic reforms designed to bring more revenue to the treasury, including the expansion of irrigation infrastructure, as well as early attempts at industrialization.[3]

This focus on increasing Egypt's resources also played into Mohammed Ali's decision to launch his campaign for Sudan in 1820. While still part of the Ottoman Empire's "well-protected domains," Egypt was now building an empire of its own, and Mohammed Ali's forces remained in Khartoum until 1885.

However, the Egyptian conquest of Sudan failed to provide resources that Mohammed Ali hoped to secure, and the administration of such an extensive province constituted a serious challenge for the new administration. Short on man power, the governor's troops were hit with frequent bouts of illness, revolts, and unreliable communications. This was especially true for those tasked with one of the Egyptian *vali*'s most important projects: the establishment of gold-mining and extraction facilities.

Finding gold deposits constituted one of the main objectives of a fact-finding mission led by Selim Qapudan in 1820, and further attempts were made in the following years with the employment of European prospectors in the 1820s and 1830s.[4] However, the results remained disappointing for Mohammed Ali, as the establishment of the mines in Fazoglu region produced only meager amounts of gold.[5] In 1837, a Piedmontese engineer in Egyptian service named Carlo Boreani was sent to evaluate the viability of the mines. His findings resulted in a pessimistic report, and he advised the *vali* to abandon the project altogether.

Despite these difficulties, Mohammed Ali forged ahead and, in 1838–39, undertook a long journey to Fazoglu to inspect the mines. Boreani's report was dismissed in favor of a much more optimistic

---

3 On the expansion of the Egyptian irrigation system, see Alan Mikhail, *Nature and Empire in Ottoman Egypt: An Environmental History*, Studies in Environment and History (Cambridge: Cambridge University Press, 2011). For the discussion regarding the efficiency of Mohammed Ali's economic policies, see Laura Panza and Jeffrey G. Williamson, "Did Muhammad Ali Foster Industrialization in Early Nineteenth-Century Egypt?," *Economic History Review* 68, no. 1 (2015).
4 Eve M. Troutt-Powell, *A Different Shade of Colonialism: Egypt, Great Britain and the Mastery of Sudan* (Berkeley: University of California Press, 2003).
5 Ibid.

account produced by Joseph von Russegger.[6] Following his return to Egypt, the *vali* stepped up his attempts to bring Sudan under his effective control by co-opting local powerholders and tying them to his imperial enterprise. Further, the governor renewed attempts to revive the project by recruiting engineers and miners from Europe, this time turning to St. Petersburg for assistance. The request, passed to the Russian government by way of the general consul in Egypt, Aleksandr Medem, resulted in a report on gold-mining techniques employed in Russia, a leading exporter of the precious metal in this period, that was presented to the Egyptian governor.

In 1843, Mohammed Ali issued another request, this time asking for experienced engineers and miners to revive the Fazoglu project. However, his request was rejected by the tsarist government. The argument was that the booming mining industry in Russia made it impossible to spare skilled workmen. However, in order not to alienate the *vali*, St. Petersburg agreed to employ two Germany-educated Egyptian engineers, Ali Muhammad Ibrahim and Issa al-Dashuri, to observe the mining techniques employed in the Ural Mountains.[7] Throughout the Egyptians' stay in the Urals, Egor Kovalevsky was tasked with their supervision. His performance was praised by the governments in St. Petersburg and in Cairo; following Ali Muhammad and al-Dashuri's returns, Kovalevsky received a personal gift from Mohammed Ali himself—an encrusted tobacco box—which he reciprocated by sending a collection of minerals to Egypt.

The Egyptian engineers' sojourn in the Ural Mountains laid the groundwork for further cooperation between the Russian state and the Egyptian governor. In 1847, Mohammed Ali renewed his request for engineers. The Russian Ministry of Foreign Affairs complied. Due to his experience in Montenegro and Central Asia, as well as his previous contacts with the Egyptian *vali*, Kovalevsky was a natural choice to serve as the leader of the expedition. Having recruited two experienced foremen from the Zlatoust' mine—Ivan Borodin and Ivan Fomin—the

---

6 Richard L. Hill, *A Biographical Dictionary of the Sudan*, 2nd ed. (London: Frank Cass, 1967), 322.

7 Aleksei V. Antoshin, *Zoloto Sennara: Egipet i Sudan glazami ural'skogo mastera zolotodobychi XIX veka* (Moscow: IV RAN, 2013), 19–42.

expedition set out for Egypt by way of Istanbul. It is this context that paved the way for Egor Kovalevsky's Alexandrine docking.

Russia's Involvement in Northeast Africa in the Mid-19th Century

Mohammed Ali's modernization of Egypt and his imperial expansion into Sudan corresponded with the growing involvement of Russia in the Middle East and Egypt itself. The Russo-Ottoman wars of the 18th and early 19th centuries as well as Alexander I's victory over Napoleonic France confirmed the position of Russia as a global power, and the opening of the Black Sea straits greatly expanded the empire's interests in the Mediterranean. The rising importance of the region was reflected in the rising status of Russia's consuls in Egypt. At the beginning of the 19th century, consular functions were performed by local merchants and go-betweens in Alexandria. However, starting in the 1830s, the post was occupied by high-ranking Russian officials with ample government experience, such as Aleksandr O. Dugamel'. This reflected the priorities of St. Petersburg and stemmed from geopolitical concerns as well as Russia's status as a multicultural continental empire, which included the growing economic ties between Russia and Egypt.

The decline of Mediterranean corsairing and the development of warm water ports in the Black Sea increased Russia's commercial presence in the region, including Egypt. This trend continued despite the bouts of conflict that accompanied the War of Greek Independence that engulfed the region throughout the 1820s. For example, in 1820, only 10 Russian ships dropped anchor in Alexandria; by 1827, this number almost quadrupled, showing the growing commercial exchange between the Black Sea and Egypt. Pilgrimage and religious ties constituted another important facet of Russia's connections with the region. In the late 18th century, Russia claimed the right of patronage over the Orthodox Christian population of the Ottoman Empire. This was further enhanced by Nicholas I, who embraced Sergei Uvarov's formula of "Orthodoxy, Autocracy, and Nationality" as state ideology in the 1830s and 1840s. This policy was exemplified by the activity of Porfirii

Uspenskii and the establishment of an ecclesiastical mission in Jerusalem in 1843, which aimed at providing support for Orthodox pilgrims in the Levant.[8]

However, Orthodox Christians were by no means the only Russian subjects to engage Middle Eastern pilgrimages. Recent scholarship has demonstrated that Muslim subjects of the tsar likely outnumbered their Orthodox counterparts because of hajj.[9] The Muslim subjects' role in shaping Russian policies toward the region was by no means negligible in the 19th century, in large part due to their ties with Ottoman domains. The existence of these cross-imperial confessional ties constituted a serious source of concern for the Russian authorities, especially in Crimea and the Caucasus.

Russian-Egyptian Ties

Mohammed Ali's relationship with the Russian Empire was a complex and changed significantly throughout his reign. After all, Russia played a considerable role in thwarting the *vali*'s expansionist designs in the Mediterranean in the late 1820s and early 1830s during the War of Greek Independence. In October 1827, the Russian navy participated in the destruction of Mohammed Ali's newly built fleet in the Battle of Navarino, effectively cutting off supplies for the Egyptian troops and contributing to Ibrahim Pasha's eventual withdrawal. The subsequent escalation of hostilities led to a new war between the Sublime Porte and Russia, bringing further territorial losses for the Ottoman state.

Further, Mohammed Ali's invasion of Syria in 1831 and the following conflict with the Sublime Porte again pitted Russian and Egyptian interests against one another. As Egyptian troops under Ibrahim Pasha overran Syria and entered Anatolia, the panicked authorities in Istanbul turned to Russia for assistance in exchange for commercial and political concessions in the sultan's domains. The Russian deployment of troops

---

8 Theofanis G. Stavrou, "Russian Interest in the Levant 1843–1848: Porfirii Uspenskii and Establishment of the First Russian Ecclesiastical Mission in Jerusalem," *Middle East Journal* 17, 1–2 (1963).

9 See, for instance, Elena I. Campbell, "The 'Pilgrim Question': Regulating the Hajj in Late Imperial Russia," *Canadian Slavonic Papers* 56, nos. 3–4 (2014): 239–68.

and the Treaty of Hünkâr İskelesi (1833) forced Mohammed Ali to seek an agreement with Sultan Mahmud II, bringing the hostilities to a halt and possibly saving the Sublime Porte. Yet again, St. Petersburg's policy prevented the *vali* from reaching his objectives.

After the 1831–33 conflict, relations between Russia and Egypt warmed significantly, creating a favorable climate for future cooperation. In his attempts to garner international support for his modernizing efforts, Mohammed Ali saw the Russian Empire as a potential ally, one less intrusive than Great Britain or France. In turn, the government at St. Petersburg clearly recognized the *vali*'s influence, both in the Middle East and among Russian Muslims. As Ilya Zaytsev and A. Kroll point out, it is likely that during the 1831–33 crisis, Mohammed Ali used hajj networks to foment dissent among Muslim subjects.[10]

In his reports, the governor-general of Crimea reported that rumors circulated among local Tatars that—following the capture of Istanbul—Mohammed Ali would liberate Crimea from Russian rule. In the following years, Mohammed Ali corresponded with Imam Shamil, the leader of anti-Russian rebellion against the tsarist regime in the Caucasus. Taking into consideration Mohammed Ali's prestige in the Islamic world, it comes as no surprise that post-1833 St. Petersburg sought to establish amicable ties with the Egyptian *vali*. At the same time, this fit into the wider pattern of the tsarist empire during this period, which aimed to expand its role in the Middle East after the agreements reached with the 1833 Ottoman Empire and the cessation of hostilities with Qājār Persia through the Treaty of Turkmenchay (1828).[11]

This détente set the stage for Kovalevsky's mission and the presence of Egyptian engineers in the Ural mines. However, it is important to note that this intellectual exchange between Russia and Egypt under Mohammed Ali was by no means one-sided. Seven years prior to Kovalevsky's departure to Egypt, a graduate of the Cairene al-Azhar, Sheikh Muhammad Ayyad al-Tantawi (1810–61) arrived in St. Petersburg and

---

10 Ilya Zaytsev and A. A. Kroll, "'Vrazhi rifmy': Pervyi egipetskii krizis, hadzh iz Kryma i egipetskaia propaganda sredi krymskikh tatar v 1832 g.," *Vostok* 5 (2016): 91–104.
11 For the dynamics of Russian-Qājār relations, see Moritz Deutschmann, *Iran and Russian Imperialism: The Ideal Anarchists, 1800–1914* (London: Routledge, 2017).

served as a lecturer at the Asian Department of the Ministry of Foreign Affairs and the Department of Oriental Studies at the University of St. Petersburg. In this capacity, he contributed to the development of Middle Eastern studies in Russia, publishing numerous works and producing his own account of Russia in the Arabic language.

It is against this background of intensifying Russian-Egyptian contact that Egor Kovalevsky began his expedition. The political realities of the period and his own experiences in the Ural Mountains and Central Asia all played a role in the way he recounted and interpreted the state of affairs in Egypt and Sudan. In effect, it makes his memoirs an invaluable source for both Mohammed Ali's imperial project in Africa and the Russian perception of the region.

Kovalevsky's Mission and Its Accounts

Kovalevsky's mission to Sudan has been known to Western scholars, and his biographical note was included in the *Biographical Dictionary of the Sudan*, the basic reference work for the region's history.[12] However, his activity in Fazoglu has been overlooked or disregarded. Richard L. Hill claims, "As a geographer the Russian gives an impression of naivety and arrogance."[13] In his perception of Kovalevsky's ineptitude as a scholar, he refers to the criticisms launched against him by his contemporary P. Tremaux, who claimed that the engineer's work included numerous geographical mistakes and had limited value as a scholarly contribution.[14]

However, Hill's critical judgment of Kovalevsky's writings is rather surprising when we consider his report of the expedition as presented in this edition. While he did not shy away from moments of self-aggrandizement, Kovalevsky nonetheless creates the impression of being a keen observer of his surroundings and gives no indication of professional ineptitude. Moreover, Hill's harsh remarks were based on

---

12 Hill, *Biographical Dictionary of the Sudan*, 207.
13 R. L. Hill, "An Unpublished Fragment of a Manuscript concerning Events in the Sudan, 1843–1848," *Sudan Notes and Records* 36, no. 2 (1955): 112–22.
14 P. Tremaux, "Notes sur la localité où sont situées les principales mines d'or . . . et observations critiques sur le récit du Colonel Kovalevski," *BSGP* 13 (1850): 201–32.

a single source—namely, the French translation of the lecture the engineer delivered at the Geographical Society of St. Petersburg—rather than his whole body of work. Again, we experience the necessity of utilizing Russian sources for the study of 19th-century Middle East and Africa.

Apart from Kovalevsky's work, two other sources have been published regarding the expedition to Fazoglu. Unfortunately, the account of Ivan Borodin, a foreman who accompanied Kovalevsky in Fazoglu, has been published only in Russian, which renders it similarly inaccessible to Western scholarship.[15]

The other account is a fragment of the chronicle of Sudan, translated and published in English by Richard Hill in 1956. The anonymous author, who accompanied the expedition to the Tumat valley and produced an account of political events in French, is replete with grammatical mistakes.[16] The bombastic style of the source contrasts starkly with the much soberer and to-the-point literary strategy employed by Kovalevsky, whose arrival to Cairo—as the author claims—overjoyed Mohammed Ali: "The Viceroy saw in him the Mahdi of the Muslims and the Messiah of the Jews. Honors, emoluments, and facilities surpassing those rendered to the highest personage in any European court were lavished on the polar bear from Siberia and his companions."[17]

Literary decorum aside, the chronicle published by Hill provides a much shorter and shoddier narrative. However, it provides some complementary information that Kovalevsky—who addressed his account to a general audience—decided to omit, such as details regarding the technique of prospecting. Thus, from our perspective, while the anonymous chronicle provides some interesting details, it constitutes an inferior source regarding the events surrounding the mission, as well as lacks details regarding the Russian's discussions with Mohammed Ali and Ibrahim Pasha.

In this sense, Kovalevsky's account constitutes the central source for Mohammed Ali's last attempts to revive the Fazoglu gold-mining

---

15 Antoshin, *Zoloto Sennara*, 7–11. Unless noted otherwise, translations in this chapter are my own.
16 Hill, "An Unpublished Fragment," 112.
17 Ibid., 114.

project and, consequently, one of the main aspects of Egyptian imperial policies in Sudan. In the following sections, I will discuss the topics that Kovalevsky focused on during his sojourn in Egypt and Sudan, as well as the interpretative framework he applied to analyze them.

Kovalevsky and Mohammed Ali's Egypt

In many respects, Kovalevsky follows Orientalist tropes regarding Egyptian history. He focuses on antiquity and ignores virtually all of the country's Islamic history, only deeming to mention the conqueror of Egypt, 'Amr ibn al-'As, and then Saladin, who himself is only referenced when discussing the very prominent Citadel of Cairo. Particularly striking is the almost complete erasure of Ottoman history, though the lands, upon Kovalevsky's travels, still constituted a formal a part of sultan's "well-protected domains." Indeed, the only reference to the Sublime Porte that makes it into the account is Kovalevsky's description of Mohammed Ali's rise to power at the beginning of the 19th century.

This stands in sharp contrasts with extensive descriptions of ancient Egyptian and Nubian monuments that the author visited, complemented with Herodotus's comments on the country and its people. Kovalevsky's propensity to ignore Islamic history is exemplified in his account of Alexandria: after mentioning the city's grandeur in antiquity and at the eve of Arab conquest, Kovalevsky quickly moves on to the Napoleonic period and the reign of Mohammed Ali, claiming that the *vali* took over Alexandria in a "most miserable state." In this sense, the author creates an impression that the "golden age" of Egyptian antiquity was followed by a millennium of decline, which ended only with the French invasion in 1798 and the emergence of Mohammed Ali. In this sense, Kovalevsky is very much a man of his time.

Kovalevsky impressions of the cities of Egypt were overwhelmingly negative. He claimed that—with the exceptions of Cairo and Alexandria—every single one of them "is worse than the one preceding it." While he praised Alexandria's European style boulevards and architecture, his perception of Cairo was much more reserved. On the one hand, he was certainly impressed by the extent of the city, as well as the abundance of antiquities, but simultaneously decried the decay of numerous buildings, the lack of hygiene, and considered the new Levantine-style edifices disagreeable.

The Ottoman erasure further highlights the role of the *vali*, whom Kovalevsky identifies as the modernizer of Egypt and the driving force behind the imperial expansion into Sudan. However, his portrayal of the elderly ruler was written in an ambiguous and somewhat melancholic fashion:

> Mohammed Ali is not tall; shriveled by age and illness, he seemed diminutive, his tiny hands and head matching his entire figure; his thin white beard and small mustache did not conceal his face, once handsome but now pale and wrinkled, although not in the least unpleasant, as it can often be said of old men—on the contrary, it made you respect and trust him, whilst his light-brown, deep-set eyes, quick and alive, still glinting, illuminated his figure in a peculiar way, evidence that he was still sparkling with vitality and possessed of a rebellious spirit, just as active today as he had been 20 years ago. Only from time to time could we hear some terrible exclamation that seemed to erupt from the ailing man's deepest soul, all of a sudden, through no effort of his own. It frightened us, but the others were accustomed to it, for Viceroy's illnesses had always been accompanied by similar cries, which neither his strong will nor the efforts of doctors could eliminate. They say it occurred in consequence of the extreme moral stress that he had suffered during the war with the Wahhabis.

In Kovalevsky's eyes, Mohammed Ali presented himself as a shrewd and forceful ruler who pursued his goals with ruthlessness and determination, paying scant attention to the human and financial costs of his enterprises. This is particularly salient in his discussion of irrigation system, which the *vali* greatly expanded by conscripting local peasantry as corvée. Kovalevsky discusses Mohammed Ali's style of governance in the context of the construction of the Mahmoudiyah Canal, which linked Alexandria to the Nile. As he points out, while the canal was finished within 10 months, disease and the lack of provisions took an enormous toll on the workers.

Similar traits manifested with regard to the Fazoglu project. For example, Mohammed Ali offered to send 10,000 workers right away, a plan that startled Kovalevsky, as the infrastructure was not yet set up. While the engineer clearly enjoyed his discussions with the *vali*, he nonetheless remarks that Mohammed Ali had grown increasingly reclusive with age and distrustful of those outside his immediate circle. These points, coupled with the governor's low tolerance for dissent, inspire Kovalevsky to write, "Everyone wanted, in their turn, to cheer the old Pasha, as if he were a spoilt child."

Nonetheless, Kovalevsky appreciated Mohammed Ali's achievements and saw the ailing *vali* in a generally positive light, valuing his determination, praising his modernization of the Egyptian economy and attempts to uproot the administrative abuse that impoverished the population. This last point, as per Kovalevsky, was hampered by the prevalent corruption among officials and not the heavy hand of the pasha. Kovalevsky was equally unimpressed with the character traits among Egyptians, who allegedly "have no self-confidence whatsoever, neither will-power nor character, not a shade of personal dignity or self-respect."

Kovalevsky argued that this was the basis for the virtual exclusion of Egyptians from the sphere of administration. However, administrative positions were historically occupied by Turks, Circassian, and Albanians, which further limited the upward mobility for the local population. This struggle between Mohammed Ali's efforts to reform Egypt and the administrative inertia of the state apparatus is best exemplified in Kovalevsky's dim hopes for his own mining project in Fazoglu. According to the Russian, the determination of the *vali* was the only thing that kept the project alive. With his eventual abdication of power, the whole enterprise was doomed to fail. He writes,

> Bearing in mind the close-minded stubbornness and superstitions of the present-day Governor-General, Khalid Pasha, who is able to destroy but not to create. Mohammed Ali, who dreamed of the discovery of gold

(that favorite idea of his whole life), who spent several million piasters on the business over 20 years, undertaking a most dangerous journey to the Sudan, where he was struck by an illness due to his complete disappointment in the success of the matter—Mohammed Ali was not destined to see this enterprise realized, even though he still talks, dimly and unconsciously, of the search for gold.

In the Russian's narrative, Mohammed Ali appears as a tragic figure in many respects: a forceful, but ultimately unsuccessful reformer increasingly engulfed in by crippling senility.

The news of Ibrahim Pasha's succession reached the expedition on the way back to Alexandria. The Russian had a chance to meet the regent in Alexandria, prior to the latter's departure for Istanbul. Ibrahim Pasha struck Kovalevsky with his unassuming behavior, greeting him in a European fashion and strolling by foot along the streets to buy candleholders. Ibrahim expressed great interest in the expedition's findings, including its geographical and ethnographical surveys, and made plans for securing the frontier with Ethiopia. While Ibrahim Pasha definitely impressed the author with his way of life, modesty, and military fame, Kovalevsky nonetheless remarks that the son is not as brilliant as the father.

In general, Kovalevsky steers away from discussing international politics, with the single exception of the news regarding the revolutionary wave that swept through Europe in 1848. Instead, European penetration can be seen in Kovalevsky's everyday situations and encounters with other imperial agents. The flurry of activity accompanying the arrival of Indian mail to el-Aft or the sorry state of the Catholic mission led by Bishop Cozzolani and Father Rillo—who, during their stay in Khartoum, failed to convert a single soul—provide us with insights into the Russian's understanding of his imperial rivals. Kovalevsky also provides us with other details regarding the Russian presence in the region, including the presence of a consular agent in Keneh, whose task was to assist Russian subjects performing hajj, further evidence of Islam's role in Middle Eastern–Russian ties. In these nuances, we can glean insights into Kovalevsky's intended audience in St. Petersburg.

Kovalevsky and the Egyptian-Sudanese Imperial Experience

In late January 1848, Kovalevsky and his mission embarked from Cairo toward their final destination in Sudan. From the very beginning, the Russian engineer highlights enormous difficulties associated with Egypt's Sudanese expansion, most important of which were unreliable communication, long supply lines, and Egypt's lack of sufficient administrative capacity. The sections of the route from Cairo and Khartoum, where the party had to disembark and cross the desert, proved to be particularly trying for the engineer, who suffered from extensive heat and thirst. For Kovalevsky, the Nubian Desert constituted a tomb devoid of life and water.

Further challenges focused on the lack of proper administration. Kovalevsky describes the Sudanese system, which centered around a governor-general in Khartoum and the *mudirs* of the provinces (Dongola, Taka, Kordofan, Khartoum, Sennar, Fazoglu.) Kovalevsky argued that the weak administrative structure meant administrative boundaries mattered little in actual governance and that the distribution of power only created further challenges for proper authority. In fact, with his control of vast provincial resources, and at a safe distance from Cairo, Governor-General Ahmed Pasha Abudan exercised considerable power and used it enhance his own position vis-à-vis Mohammed Ali. According to Kovalevsky, Abudan looked to follow the example of Mohammed Ali and break off his relations with the metropole.

In order to secure his base of power, he replaced many of incumbent *mudirs*, inserted his clients into the army ranks, and established contacts with rival Ottoman governors via the port of Suakin. These actions raised Mohammed Ali's suspicion, but Ahmed Pasha was able to retain his position, promising to launch a campaign into Darfur, another region that the *vali* had been hoping to conquer. However, the campaign never materialized, and Ahmed Pasha finally committed suicide in 1845 in order to escape his looming arrest.

Subsequently, the *vali* tried to decentralize the system of governance by sending the comptroller Mohammed Pasha Melikhli to manage the province while enhancing the prerogatives of *mudirs*. However, this plan also failed. By 1847, Mohammed Ali was forced to revert to the previous arrangement and appointed Halid Pasha as the new governor-general. Kovalevsky deemed him superstitious and injudicious, which bode poorly for the pasha's Sudan enterprise.

Further troubles were posed by the climate and diseases, which took a serious toll on the *vali*'s troops from Cairo. High mortality rates among Egyptian troops forced local commanders to recruit locally, but Sudanese troops—which constituted 80 percent of Mohammed Ali's forces in the region—were not reliable. In Wad Medina, Kovalevsky mentions a failed revolt among the local troops, who conspired to kill the Egyptian soldiers and abandon their service altogether. Troubles were further exacerbated by a constant shortage of manpower and often lax discipline among the troops, not least due to considerable amounts of liquor consumed. Moreover, the lack of frontier garrisons opened the country to predatory raids from neighboring lands, most importantly by the Galla, who—according to Kovalevsky—enjoyed a reputation of being invincible.[18]

In spite of these challenges, Kovalevsky identifies Sudan as a fruitful resource for Mohammed Ali's administration, highlighting its human and natural assets. He considers Khartoum one of the best locations in Mohammed Ali's domains, second only to Alexandria and Cairo. Further, Kovalevsky points out opportunities for trade that could revive other spaces and, most importantly, Sennar. Upon his return to Alexandria, the Russian went so far as to propose a secured border with Ethiopia and the Galla, suggesting to Ibrahim Pasha to properly equip Sudanese units and station them at the garrisons along the frontier.

However, his main focus during his stay in Sudan remained geographical and ethnographic research. Kovalevsky provides detailed description of the tribes and ethnic groups inhabiting the province, with a special look at the region of Fazoglu and Sennar, providing interesting, although limited, analyzes of languages and indigenous beliefs. Even more precise are his descriptions of geological features of the country, its flora and fauna. Kovalevsky shows a somewhat amusing fascination

---

18 See M. Abir, "The Origins of the Ethiopian-Egyptian Border Problem in the Nineteenth Century," *Journal of African History* 8, no. 3 (1967): 443–61.

with particular species, which he mentions repeatedly: the camel (which he compares with the camels of Central Asia), crocodile, giraffe, and baobab. However, the topic he is most concern with is the location of the sources of the White Nile, hotly debating the topic throughout the text. His research, which is known through French translations of his work, constituted an important contribution to the discussion that was taking place exactly at this time, involving prominent geographers such as Antoine-Thomson d'Abbadie and Charles Tilston Beke.

The Russian Imperial Experience and Kovalevsky's Perception of Egyptian Sudan

By the time Kovalevsky arrived in Egypt, he was experienced as a military and mining engineer in the employ of the Russian Empire, with deployments in the Urals, the Altai, Montenegro, and Khiva. This experience as an imperial servant in Eurasia provided him with an interpretative grid, which he utilized when describing the Egyptian imperial experiment and ethnography of Sudan in a manner distinct from Western travelers.

This becomes apparent as soon as he begins describing his conversation with Mohammed Ali. In response to the *vali*'s remarks on the harsh climate of Sudan, the Russian lightheartedly points out that the conditions are not dissimilar from those in Siberia:

> Here, he said incidentally, you have to constantly change your underwear for perspiration, but in the Sudan, no sooner has it got wet than it dries and begins crackling like paper: crack, crack!
>
> I told him that a similar thing could happen in Siberia too: no sooner has your underwear got wet than it freezes, and then it also begins crackling like paper: crack, crack! He was much amused by my remark.

Of course, these comparisons are not limited to remarks on the speed of drying undergarments but abound throughout the narrative. For Kovalevsky, the great distances and harsh environmental conditions of Sudan corresponded to the Russian imperial experience in Siberia.

However, not all his comparisons with the Russian landscape are as gloomy. When arriving in Sudan, he is thoroughly impressed with the rich vegetation and vastness of the province: "Nature is sprawled widely, in a manner reminiscent of Russia; there is sufficient room for both man and wild beasts, and myriads of birds, and the various reptile creatures inhabiting these forests—indeed, man takes up the least space of all." This is especially the case for the nomadic population of Egypt and Sudan, whom he constantly compares with Central Asian nomads, most notably the Kyrgyz.

In a detailed comparison, he argues that while Bedouins are more resilient in bearing the harsh conditions of travel, they are generally more prone to flee and have only a limited grasp of the principles of navigation across the desert when compared with Central Asian pastoralists. In spite of these differences, however, their styles of life—including the principles of hospitality and loose attachment to religious prescription and their reliance on camels and horses for survival—show striking similarities. At the same time, he points out the rift dividing the Bedouins from *fellahs*, from whom the former differ in all respects.

While it cannot be proven, it is quite possible that Kovalevsky's origins and life in the Russian Empire contributed to his perception of race, which is quite distinct from those that were emerging in the West. In his discussion of the black population of Sudan, he strongly rejects the claims—inspired by Monboddo and Rousseau—of the inherent biological inferiority of Africans. Though, in line with 19th-century discourses, he refers to whiteness as the superior skin color and sees "lack of whiteness" as a defect, he insists that there is no biological grounds for racial theories. In this sense, he identifies nurture and social background as the defining features of one's mental capabilities and pointed out that the Sudanese, "not being alien to any human ideas, shall sooner be reasoned with than a Belorussian in our land or a French peasant living far from the high road and the city."

While there is little chance of exploring how Kovalevsky's views came to be, it is tempting to see this insistence on social environment and mode of life rather than physiological differences as a reflection of Russian imperial experience. Since the mid-16th century, the Grand

Duchy of Muscovy and its successor, Imperial Russia, faced the challenge of accommodating the wide array of ethnic and religious identities of its subjects. The administrative practice of cooptation resulted in an inclusive, composite elite, which included Orthodox Russian Muslims and Christians of various denominations and defined itself primarily along social rather than religious or cultural lines. This system was further reinforced during the reign of Catherine the Great, who drew on both traditional imperial models and Enlightenment ideals of religious toleration in order to support the muliticonfessional nature of the Russian autocracy.[19] Largely continued after the empress's death, these policies served as both the institutional framework and the mental grid for interpreting diversity.

At the same time, this horizontal inclusiveness existed within stark vertical hierarchies, as is most evident in the institution of serfdom, abolished only in 1861.[20] The centrality of serfdom as the defining feature of an individual's place in Russian society overrode religious differences, though it did not necessarily imply the existence of a racially defined difference between the aristocracy and its serfs. While we find isolated cases where such opinions were uttered, it seems that racial theories played only a limited role in justifying social hierarchies within the Russian imperial structure. More often there not, the deplorable state of the peasantry was interpreted in terms of ignorance rather than inherent biological capacities—a sharp divergence from that of their Western counterparts. Furthermore, as the 19th century progressed, an idealized vision of peasant community became in fact an object of aspiration for the intellectual and social elites as a means to remedy their own sense of alienation. In the generation that followed Kovalevsky's, the Slavophile movement positioned the Russian peasants

---

19   Robert D. Crews, *For Prophet and Tsar: Islam and Empire in Russia and Central Asia* (Cambridge, MA: Harvard University Press, 2006), 2. This commitment to tolerance sometimes undermined other goals of imperial policy in the religiously mixed provinces of the empire, as Mara Kozelsky points out, effectively providing religious minorities with a competitive advantage over their Orthodox counterparts. See Mara Kozelsky, *Christianizing Crimea: Shaping Sacred Space in the Russian Empire and Beyond* (DeKalb, IL: Northern Illinois University Press, 2009).

20   For the new approach to serfdom as a crucial institution of Russian social and political order, see Elise Kimmerling Wirtschaftler, *Russia's Age of Serfdom, 1649–1861* (Oxford: Wiley Blackwell, 2008).

as the caretakers of the "true Rus" heritage, as opposed to that of the cosmopolitan capitals of St. Petersburg and Moscow.[21] Needless to say, such juxtaposition would have been impossible if the peasantry was considered physiologically or racially inferior.

This complex and at times paradoxical attitude toward diversity and hierarchy arguably found its fullest expression in the writings of another Russian with ample firsthand experience of the Middle East. Born in 1831, Konstantin Leontiev, who worked as a consul in numerous postings within the Ottoman Empire during the 1850s and 1860s, owed his fame to his status as a social thinker. In contrast to the overwhelming sentiment of Russian public opinion, which pushed the tsarist authorities to support Southern Slavs against the Sublime Porte, Leontiev argued that the Ottomans should be left to rule in the Balkans, since they were a shield that protected the diversity of their domains against the onslaught of the equalizing liberal ideology.[22] While Leontiev's unusual stance, which favored diversity and distinctiveness, is far from the sober description of Kovalevsky, both men are the products of the centuries-long Russian experience with diversity and attempt to explain it through a cultural rather than a biological lens. In this sense, the realities of the Russian colonial enterprise in Eurasia and the Egyptian expansion in Sudan were much more similar than either were to French or British colonialism.[23]

The Importance of Kovalevsky's Account for the Study of Egypt and Sudan

Taken together, the aforementioned aspects of Kovalevsky's travel account provide a treasure trove for researchers studying Egypt and Sudan in the mid-19th century, elucidating on a number of topics. First,

---

21 The most comprehensive account of the Slavophile current in Russia remains Andrzej Walicki's *The Slavophile Controversy: History of a Conservative Utopia in Nineteenth-Century Russian Thought*, trans. Hilda Andrews-Rusiecka (Oxford: Oxford University Press, 1975).

22 Andrzej Walicki, *The Flow of Ideas: Russian Thought from the Enlightenment to the Religious-Philosophical Renaissance*, trans. Jolanta Kozak and Hilda Andrews-Rusiecka (Frankfurt am Mein: Peter Lang, 2014), 348–49.

23 For an English-language account of Russian Orientalism and its specificity in the 19th century, see Victor Taki, "Orientalism on the Margins: The Ottoman Empire under Russian Eyes," *Kritika* 12, no. 2 (2011): 321–51.

A Journey to Inner Africa provides an important contribution to the history of imperial explorations of the broader Sudan, both in terms of geographical discoveries and territorial expansion. While Kovalevsky's claims to novelty are to some extent exaggerated, he nonetheless provides ample information about Sudan and contributes to one of the greatest scholarly debates of the period: the location of the Nile's sources.

Even more importantly, for the history of the Middle East, he presents a vivid picture of Egypt's colonial project in Sudan, Mohammed Ali's quest for Sudanese gold, and the challenges that ultimately brought about the failure of the enterprise. This abortive endeavor formed the crux of the *vali*'s colonial ambition, his attempt to enhance the position of Egypt and modernize state infrastructure. Kovalevsky's detailed account as presented here easily surpasses other Western-language sources on the topic. In this sense, it constitutes a must-read for any scholar addressing Egyptian imperial policies in Sudan.

Finally, Kovalevsky's origin and career in the tsar's service accounts for a different way of seeing the region in the mid-19th century. The Russian vantage point—born from its own imperial experience, which differed from that of Western European empires—elucidates both similarities and differences between its own Eurasian domains and Egyptian possessions in Sudan. The presence of a nomadic population, the multiethnic character of the elite, and similar challenges posed by sparsely populated and environmentally adverse domains run like a red thread throughout Kovalevsky's account; taking into consideration the role Russia played in the region throughout the 19th century, the engineer's account is too important for students of the region to ignore.

Part I

Egypt and Nubia

Caravan in the Great Nubian Desert

Chapter I

Alexandria

Travelers reaching Alexandria look upon the sandy shores of Africa with sadness. Napoleon's soldiers, too, lost heart as they went ashore on the deserted land of Egypt. And prior to Napoleon's soldiers, the army of Cambyses rebelled against their commanders, who had brought them to this sun-scorched country; and prior to that, the slaves of the pharaohs cursed the land upon which they were building their pyramids—the pyramids that have since seen so many devastating epochs and so much great fame.

Alexandria made no extraordinary impression on me. The sight of palms, beautiful against the bright horizon, was familiar to me, coming as I had from Rhodes. A low, sandy shore appears too plain to an eye that, being used to Russian marsh banks, at times even gazes upon them with affection. As for the city itself, it is quite a decent sight not just by Oriental standards but indeed by Western ones. Alexandria is especially beautiful when viewed from the old port, where our steamboat was docked. On the left there are the palace of the Pasha, his *harem*, a garden, and a lighthouse; opposite to them are a fine arsenal building, some beautiful houses, a fortress, and more gardens. It is only on the right that a sandbar, protruding far into the sea, heralds the desert,

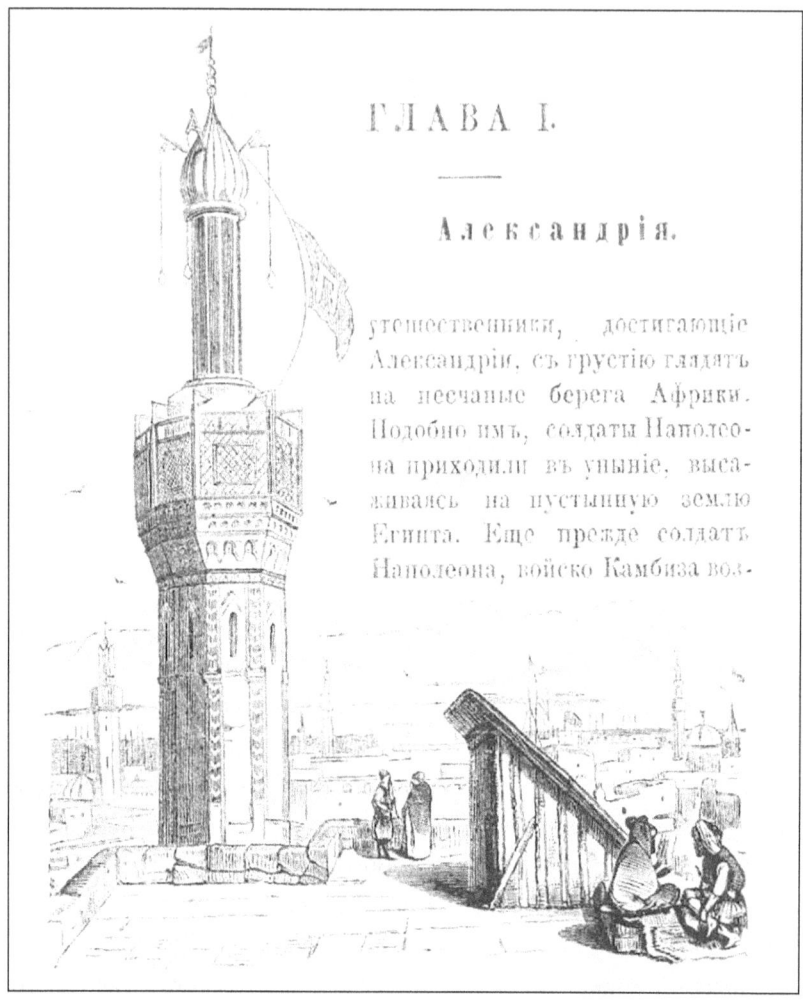

View of Alexandria

frightening to a traveler; scattered across it are some hovels, an unpleasant disturbance to the eye, whilst a large number of windmills, their wings spread, seem to be wishing to evict one and all from the place.

The port is excellent, whilst also being the only one along the entire African shore, from Tunis to Alexandria. On the opposite side, there is a new port, almost inaccessible to large vessels; the old one being so immense, however, that it could accommodate the entire European fleet.

The founding of Alexandria, similar to the founding of Constantinople, was accompanied by a miracle. In the East, there are miracles wherever you look, and in this respect, time has not changed its mores. Alexander the Great was struck by the advantageous position of a small village named Rhacotis. Having gone to sleep with the thought of a world-celebrated trading city, whence his name would easily reach every corner of the universe, he dreamed of an old man engulfed in light and flames (Constantine the Great was visited by an old woman), who—speaking in a prophet's voice, in the verses of Alexander's beloved *Odyssey*—indicated a spot for such a city: the very same village of Rhacotis. On the morrow, Alexander and the learned Dinocrates of Rhodes[1] commenced to draw a plan of the city which still bears Alexander's name, even though the ancient city built by him is no more.

It is odd that people can never recognize genius in things that they themselves would be able to achieve. In order to explain a great deed, they are willing to concoct a fairy-tale, to admit the influence of chance, the unavoidable nature of fate—anything but the excellence of man. And yet Napoleon saw Alexander's genius; the greatest of conquerors, he said that Alexander had covered himself in fame in the construction of Alexandria more than he had done in all his conquests. It is a pity that this marvelous idea came to Napoleon somewhat late. Like the ancient Greek hero, he, too—struck by the advantageous position of the city on the frontier of Asia and Africa, within sight of Europe—never doubted Alexandria's capacity to be the capital of the world; however, we should add: it can only ever be so in the hands of a commander such as Napoleon, for Alexandria, deprived of natural defenses, can be and indeed has been captured by the enemy with little effort, from the land and from the sea. Not so with Constantinople. It has the Bosphorus and the Dardanelles, spread like two mighty arms northward and southward—so as to join

---

All notes, unless otherwise indicated, are by the editor.
1　Dinocrates of Rhodes (4th century BCE), a Greek thinker and architect; designed plans for Alexandria.

together for peace and for trade, whilst also, like two mighty arms, always ready to defend it.

It was not until we arrived at Alexandria that we learned about a 10-day-long quarantine that everyone had to observe upon arrival here. You can imagine how the news affected us, having as we did so many reasons to hasten to our destination. We were separated from the other passengers and taken to a small palace, the residence of Ibrahim Pasha[2] in Alexandria, where we were soon left quite alone.

A spacious cross-shaped room had windows facing in all directions, every spot providing a view of the calm sea and the sky, lucid and edged with the bright-red horizon where the sun had just set—a sky the similar of which I had not seen in a long time. The night fell suddenly, dark despite a myriad of stars scattered across the sky. My footfalls echoed hollowly on the marble floor of the deserted, dimly lit palace . . .

Alexandria! Egypt! . . . What ample food for thought they provide. Alexandria, a source of enlightenment, wisdom, faith, and beliefs to the Greeks, who bequeathed them to the world. Egypt, a land abounding with Biblical deeds, drenched in the blood of the early martyrs, one which was among the first to receive the legacy of the Christian teaching . . . The land of the Nile and the pyramids, the land of fertility, abundant and evergreen! . . . What a wealth of memories, what a wealth of expectations, many of which, alas, were never to be fulfilled! Childhood beliefs are the brightest, the most radiant of all beliefs! Happy is he who will never part with them, whose bitter experience will never extinguish them along the way, nor replace them with another light, one in which things and people appear in a different guise! . . .

We were received with rare welcome and hospitality. In spite of that, our imprisonment was becoming ever harder to bear, and when the day of liberation came, we set off for the city ere daybreak.

In the time of Pliny,[3] Alexandria had 600,000 inhabitants, of whom 300,000 were citizens and 300,000 slaves. Upon capturing Alexandria,

---

2 Ibrahim Pasha (1789–1848), the eldest son of Mohammed Ali, the ruler of Egypt; in 1847–48, the regent ruling in his ailing father's stead.
3 Pliny the Elder (Gaius Plinius Secundus, 23–79 CE), Roman scholar and author of *Natural History*.

Amr[4] related to Omar[5] that there were 4,000 palaces, 4,000 baths, 400 theaters, and 12,000 shops in the city. At the time of Napoleon's expedition to Egypt,[6] Alexandria lay in ruins, the latter providing shelter to pirates; nevertheless, it had as many as 8,000 inhabitants. Apart from building some fortifications, Napoleon managed to do nothing for the city. Mohammed Ali[7] found Alexandria in a most miserable state; there were barely 4,000 or 5,000 people left there. Having learned his lesson from the landing of the English, still fresh in memory,[8] the Pasha hastened to restore the ancient wall that Saladin's[9] successors had built with a view to defending the city from the crusaders, and he also erected some new fortifications. Having completed the first of his tasks, he then turned to the city that was put on the map of the world by Alexander and Napoleon!

These days Alexandria resembles a European city not just from without but also from within, tinted with a dark Oriental hue that does not quite become her. It is clean and tidy, like most cities in Egypt, which is bound to catch the eye of any traveler, especially one familiar with Turkish cities. The original impelling reason for such a state was this. Unaccustomed to opposition, Mohammed Ali was defeated, time and time again, by the plague, which he fought most desperately. He put quarantine cordons not only along the shores but also around the inland areas of the country; he brought European doctors and inspectors there; he took the strictest measures—but all in vain: the plague kept recurring in Egypt, reaping a rich death harvest. Finally, one of the Europeans, I forget the name, gave him an idea, bearing in mind the mores of the East in general and, particularly, Mohammed Ali's own disposition. The European put his suggestions in the form of a well-known fable, in which a shepherd, having herded his sheep

---

4 Amr ibn al-'As (585–664 CE), Muslim military commander in charge of the conquest of Egypt.
5 Omar (also Umar) ibn al-Khattab (584–644 CE), Mohammed's companion, caliph; presided over a rapid expansion of the Arab caliphate.
6 1798–1801.
7 Mohammed Ali (1769–1849), the founder of the Khedive (viceroyal) dynasty ruling Egypt under the nominal suzerainty of the Ottoman Empire.
8 Alexandria expedition, led by General Alexander Mackenzie-Fraser in March–September 1807 as part of the Anglo-Ottoman War.
9 Saladin (An-Nasir Salah ad-Din Yusuf ibn Ayyub, 1137–93), the first Ayyubid sultan of Egypt and Syria; led the Muslims against the crusaders.

behind a solid fence, stands by the gate and guards them day and night, while the sheep keep perishing, for a wolf had got inside the pen even before the shepherd took his guard.

"So what is one to do?" Mohammed Ali asked. "Should one wait for the wolf to kill the shepherd himself!?"

"No, one has to destroy its lair completely."

"And where is it?"

"In the dirt that is piled up on the streets of every city, so much so that one cannot pass through."

That was enough for Mohammed Ali to set to work with all the energy which he alone possessed. Not only have the cities, whatever you say of them, been cleaned and swept ever since, but they have also been daily sprinkled with water, and so the plague, touch wood, has not returned to Egypt for nearly 10 years now!

Up until this year, Alexandria was believed to have 80,000 inhabitants; however, according to a census that is coming to a conclusion all across Egypt now, and which should give us a chance to obtain correct information about the country's population, there appear to be 145,000 people in Alexandria.

The city has a square, a fairly spacious one, with a fountain in the middle—albeit with no water, but one has to accustom oneself to such oddities in the East—and a very beautiful fountain it is. The square is laid out with the houses of European consul-generals: some owned by themselves, others by their governments, yet others rented from Ibrahim Pasha, for one side of the square is almost entirely taken up by his houses; there are also houses of rich merchants, built in the Italian taste, and a number of shops, hotels, and coffee houses. One has to note that consuls and rich merchants constitute Oriental aristocracy.

The square brings to mind squares in Italian cities: the same crowd of people, constantly moving and hustling, the same costumes, the same language, the same energetic, fitful manner in which people move when they walk or talk, very much like timid little animals rushing around ere the onset of a storm.

We visited the dutiful T., who had stayed behind as the deputy of the Russian Consul General, the latter having gone to Cairo, where the

Pasha's court also was. Accompanied by T., we set off to visit Artim Bey.[10] Artim Bey is the Egyptian Minister for Foreign Affairs and Commerce, which title obliges him to live permanently in Alexandria. Of Armenian descent, he was brought up in France and is very well educated. Having replaced Bogos Bey,[11] the renowned figure who had for many years been a confederate and the closest aide of Mohammed Ali, at his post, Artim Bey, in his turn, had managed to win the confidence of the old Viceroy, who was not too easily swayed by new people.

To find the East in Alexandria, reader, you have to go to her bazaars: they are as variegated, crowded, dark, and mysterious as the fairy-tales from *One Thousand and One Nights*. You shall be amazed by women's heavy clothes, each of them being shrouded, in all senses of the word, in a black satin *habara* and a black veil, *tarkha*; withal, falling across the bridge of her nose, a *burqu*[12] covers her face, shaped as a triangle, also of black fabric. The nose appears to be sunken; the cloth is not draped; the woman cannot control the veil lying upon her, as heavy as the burden of marital restraint. It is quite different in Constantinople. Light and snow-white, the veil is graciously wrapped round the wearer's head and face, and as her hands hold it from below, it parts slightly, as if stirred by an unconscious movement, so that you can frequently see not only her jet-black eyes but also her ivory cheeks and extremely well-shaped nose. Plain women pride themselves on never breaking Mohammed's commandment, and right they are to be proud, whatever the reason for their behavior.

Suburban houses, drowning in their gardens, are beautiful, especially along the Mahmoud-iya Canal;[13] not far from them, upon a hill, rises a magnificent pillar crowned with a capital in the composite order. We shall not dwell on the precise dedication of this pillar,

---

10 Artin Bey (1800–1859), Egyptian politician and scholar; minister of Foreign Affairs and Commerce under the Khedive dynasty in 1844–52.
11 Boghos Bey (Yusufian, 1775–1844), Egyptian politician; minister of Foreign Affairs of the Khedives.
12 *Al-habara* is the Egyptian form of the niqab; Kovalevsky refers here to the traditional long dress. *Tarkha* is the head cover, and *al-burqu* is the face cover worn by women.
13 Mahmoudiya Canal, constructed by Mohammed Ali between 1817 and 1820 to bring fresh water to Alexandria.

named after Pompey[14]—whether it be to himself, or to Diocletian[15] (whose name is on its top), or to the founder of Alexandria, as others believe; suffice it to say that the tomb of Alexander was not situated here, as many claim, and it was not his grave that this pillar stood over. Here they had a royal palace, temples, perhaps even the Temple of Serapis,[16] and the priests' dwelling. The body of Alexander is known to have been placed in a coffin of pure gold and transported by Ptolemy I[17] to the capital of his kingdom. Ptolemy Cocles[18] happened to be in need of gold, so he moved the great conqueror from the golden coffin to a crystal one and installed it at the opposite end of the city. We shall devote to the subject an article apart, in which we shall attempt to justify our words.

Some say that the original shape of this and many other similar pillars is borrowed from the cypress; others give a poetic interpretation to the ancient tale of closed lotus leaves, which they take for the prototype of the capital. In my opinion, columns with capitals have been revived as an imitation of the palm-tree with its flopped crown, whilst the minaret imitates the cypress. The first column ever was erected in the land of palms; the first minaret, in the land of cypresses.

On the embankment of the new harbor, near the gates, there are two obelisks, both brought from Memphis by the Greeks during their reign in Egypt. One stands on a slightly carved plinth, the other lies in the dust; both, however, have been seriously damaged, most of the hieroglyphs on one side of the standing obelisk rubbed off. They say it has been battered by sand during the *khamasin*[19] blowing in April and May, which is hard to believe unless you have yourself experienced the effect of the wind, and that is something still awaiting me. The hieroglyphs on the other sides, especially on the opposite one, are quite intact and very beautiful.

---

14 Pompey (Gnaeus Pompeus Magnus, 106–48 BCE), Roman statesman and general.
15 Diocletian (244–311 CE), Roman emperor.
16 A Greek-Egyptian syncretic deity of abundance.
17 Ptolemy I Soter (r. 305/304–282 BCE), the first ruler of Egypt and the founder of the Ptolemaic dynasty.
18 Kovalevsky is mistaken. There was no ruler in the Ptolemaic dynasty named "Cocles." Kovalevsky likely relies on another Russian travelogue, A. S. Norov, *Puteshestvie po Egiptu i Nubii v 1834–1835 gg.* (St. Petersburg, 1840), 48.
19 Khamsin, the hot and dry wind in the spring.

The obelisk is known as Cleopatra's Needle.

Both monoliths have been presented by Mohammed Ali, one to France, the other to England; but how magnificent soever they may be, neither country has taken them away yet, for transporting them would be extremely expensive.

From these obelisks on the embankment, one can look toward the sea and toward the city, including her dead part, the necropolis—a view so fine that one forgets what is behind: hovels inhabited by soldiers' wives and half-naked children, who cry for *bakshish*, or alms.

There are catacombs in Alexandria or, more precisely, beyond Alexandria; a traveler, unless he loses his way or suffocates in them, shall be extremely happy to emerge into daylight and breathe in fresh air. There are also the so-called Baths of Cleopatra, although why those creep-holes are called baths, let alone the Baths of Cleopatra, is a mystery to me.

Social life in Alexandria, like anywhere else in the East, is a thing unknown. There is theater, but it is poor and not attended by polite society; two or three houses open their doors to travelers.

Now, reader, you are cognizant with present-day Alexandria: one might even say, with her best aspects. We shall presently turn 2,132 years back and see what was here then. I shall not describe its buildings and monuments for you, as those dead signs are not as clear, their language not as comprehensible to the soul as life itself, the inner life of the city.

Alexandria is celebrating: Ptolemy Soter declares his son, Ptolemy Philadelphus, his co-ruler.[20] They are presently in a pavilion built for the occasion, a pavilion gleaming with gold, silver, Persian and Indian fabrics, precious stones, and rare minerals from every land. Finally, the procession commences to move. Marching at its head are flag-bearers of divers corporations. They are followed by Greek priests, lined up according to their hierarchy. The celebration is mainly Greek, expressing

---

20 Author's note: Kallixeinos of Rhodes.
    Editor's note: Callixeinus of Rhodes (also Callixeinos or Kallixeinos), Hellenist author, contemporary of the first rulers of the Ptolemaic dynasty. His works are no longer extant, but citations are collated in Felix Jacoby, "Kallixeinos von Rhodos (627)," in *Die Fragmente der Griechischen Historiker Part I–III*, ed. Felix Jacoby, accessed May 10, 2019, http://dx.doi.org/10.1163/1873-5363_boj_a627.

the most significant myths of Bacchus, and therefore innumerable priests take part in it, all riding in ornate chariots, performing various scenes from the god's life.

There follows a four-wheeled chariot, drawn by 60 people, carrying an enormous statue representing the city of Nisa. This last—dressed in a yellow, gold-embroidered tunic with a Laconic cloak over it—is holding a scepter in its left hand, its head decorated with ivy and vine leaves made of pure gold and precious stones. Operated by a clever mechanism, the statue can get up on its own, pour milk from a full cup, and sit down again.

Behind the statue, 100 people draw a chariot carrying a press. Sixty satyrs, led by Silenus, press grapes to the sounds of singing and flutes, a stream of sweet wine running in their wake all along the way.

Next comes a whole section with vases, urns, priestly paraphernalia of every kind, tripods, crockery, kitchen utensils, &c.—all of pure gold, of fine workmanship and extreme value. I shall forego a detailed description of all those objects, omitting the size and weight of each.

One thousand and six hundred children, dressed in white tunics, wreaths on their heads, follow those precious objects, carrying divers wine vessels and jugs, golden and silver.

One cannot help mentioning an enormous cage drawn by 500 people. Pigeons and doves constantly fly out of it, and people catch them by long ribbons wrapped round them. Two fountains, one gushing milk, the other wine, stand on the chariot itself, the latter surrounded by nymphs with golden crowns on their heads.

A special chariot carries things that Bacchus used on his journey back from India. A statue of Bacchus—colossal in size, all in purple, a golden wreath on its head, and golden shoes on its feet—rides a lavishly decorated elephant. In front of it, on the elephant's neck, there sits Satyr, whilst 120 satyrs and 120 girls with golden crowns lead the way; another 500 girls, dressed in purple tunics belted with golden cords, bring up the rear; and behind that suite of Bacchus's innocent followers comes a crowd of silenuses and satyrs wearing golden crowns, riding upon asses, also decorated with gold and silver. There follow 24 elephant-drawn chariots, another 60 drawn by goats, and a great many others, drawn by various animals, deer, wild asses, and finally, ostriches, all ridden by children in tunics, each chariot assigned a child playing the role of an assistant, holding a sword and a spear and wearing gold-embroidered dress.

Next come slow-moving chariots drawn by camels and, toward the end, by mules; there are enemy tents on them, and in those tents Indian women are kept, dressed as slaves. Next they bring various aromas: frankincense, iris, saffron, cassia, &c. Beside them walk Ethiopian slaves bearing divers gifts: ivory, ebony, gold-dust, &c. Hunters march in their wake, all gilded, with 2,400 dogs of various breeds; as many as 150 people carry enormous trees with a variety of animals and birds hanging from them: pheasants, pintados, parrots, peacocks, &c. Following numerous other departments, they drive along bulls and rams of divers breeds, which are, of course, intended to feed the people; they also lead leopards, panthers, tigers, lions, a polar bear, &c.

Women in rich dress, named after Ionia and other Greek cities, as well as a chorus consisting of 600 people, golden crowns on their heads, accompany a chariot with a colossal temple of pure gold, surrounded by statues and animals. Special chariots carry 3,200 golden crowns, one of them distinguished among the rest—a crown dedicated to sacrament and decorated with precious stones—as well as plenty of gold set into weapons and sewn into garments, two golden pools, jugs, cups, &c.

Finally, soldiers bring up the rear, among them 57,600 on foot and 23,200 on horseback, all in their finery.

Kallixeinos of Rhodes adds that he has described the most precious accoutrements of the procession only, omitting many other things, less significant in his view. In my turn, I have shortened the truthful historian's description.

Ancient writers cry in surprise: Could any other city, be it Persepolis or Babylon at the height of her fame, or any of the lands irrigated by the blessed Patroclus, ever display such treasures? Of course not! Egypt was the only one to be able to do so.

As I was finishing these notes, a whip cracked outside, making me look out of the window. An out-runner ran down the street, waving his whip this way and that, so that it touched pedestrians, many of them half-naked. He was followed by a small Viennese carriage, which halted at my entrance. Presently a man came in, dressed quite modestly, a *tarboosh*[21] on his head: that was Artim Bey, the Minister for Foreign Affairs and Commerce, the First Minister of the present ruler of Egypt, come to bid us farewell.

---

21 Male headgear, similar to the fez, made from felt.

CHAPTER II

The First Impression Made upon Us by the Sight of the Desert

The Nile and Cairo

We traveled to the pier in carriages. Suburban houses; gardens whose atmosphere—mild, moist, and sultry, fragrant with the blossom of jasmine- and lemon-trees—enveloped us; the bright greenery of the kind one can only see here in winter; the Mahmoud-iya Canal itself, brimming with water; further on, numerous people moving along the embankment, dressed to the nines on the occasion of a holiday; a number of carriages, rather dandy, with passengers looking out, wearing all manner of dress, as if at a carnival in an Italian city—all that made rather a pleasant impression upon us, marking our departure from Alexandria.

We accommodated ourselves on a small steamboat that towed a barque with our inseparable companions, Mustapha Bey,[1] the second son of Ibrahim Pasha, and his numerous entourage. After sailing for a quarter of an hour, we saw a completely changed view: the desert

---

1 Mustafa Fazil Pasha (1830–75), a prince in the Khedive dynasty.

of sands merged with the desert of waters—those of Lake Mareotis (Bahr-el-Maryut)—both equally bleak and melancholy.

Everything round us was dead. The very horizon, pale and lifeless, where the rays of the setting sun were fading, appeared nothing but the desert continued, and consequently there was no end to it in sight. The change from life to death was astonishing. The desert accompanied us all the way to the Nile, and even after we had reached the latter, it still remained true to itself in general, varying only in details.

The Mahmoud-iya Canal links Alexandria and the Nile over a stretch of 25 leagues. It was dug by Mohammed Ali in the early years of his rule, and cost many millions of rubles and as many as 30,000 men, who died during the works. The only object being to complete the canal as quickly as possible, at times they would gather up to 300,000 workers at once to dig the earth, literally speaking, with their fingernails and take it away in handfuls. The men all jostled together in a crowded space, in a stuffy, dusty atmosphere; they crushed each other as they collapsed the banks, carrying out the works in an ill-advised fashion; they perished of hunger and eye diseases, the latter having already been rife in the country. Add to that the plague, if only for a mere week, and you shall see what harvest it shall reap. On the other hand, the canal was finished in 10 months. Traces of that haste are still visible: the canal is all over the place, you can see that they worked at different points at the same time, with no preliminary consideration—indeed, consideration must have been the last thing they had in mind! Whenever Mohammed Ali had an idea, it would bother him constantly and haunt him like a nightmare, day and night, until realized (in which case it would be, for the most part, successful and useful) or until it fell to pieces altogether, proved impossible to achieve. To be sure that the latter was the case, however, Mohammed Ali would first have to make every attempt and every effort to succeed, for which he sometimes had to pay dearly. This is a man who allows no obstacles to stop him.

Near el-Aft, the canal ends, and there was a large Nile steamboat waiting for us. It was dark; it began to sprinkle fast with rain, which happens very seldom here. Suddenly el-Aft, where all had long been asleep, was alive with flickering lights, presently moving toward us. Soon there was shouting and noise, and then quite a crowd of half-naked people, driven by a whip, descended on the boat and seized our luggage. As we stood there perplexed, the crowd subsided, leaving us in the complete dark on the steamboat that it had emptied. Our situation was quite miserable.

"This way they'll steal everything," said one of us in desperation.

"I do not think so," replied someone from behind my back, speaking in a fairly good Russian. "It is true that Arabs are the worst thieves in the world, but they are dead afraid of Mohammed Ali."

"Are you Russian?" I asked, paying no heed to his none too comforting words but terribly glad to have found a man who could not only understand me but also took the trouble to answer.

"I . . . work here . . . making sure passengers have their things dispatched in an orderly fashion."

Orderly fashion indeed, thought I. "So why not do it in the same orderly fashion as they do in Europe?"

"I have tried."

"And?"

"It made matters worse: I nearly lost my post. So then I decided to leave things just as they are; it is not going too badly."

Then he volunteered to walk us to the steamboat docked on the Nile. He took us here and there, down alleyways and up little steps and above steep banks. He seemed to be eager to finish his story, but I had other things to worry about as I hastened to follow his long figure, which, wrapped in a wide *burnous*,[2] took strange, fantastic forms, now falling across the water in an infinite shadow, now half-disappearing in the darkness of narrow streets. Besides, I am so used to these adventurous types with their stories that I know them in advance, including what they are likely to tell you about themselves, portraying themselves as victims of unrelenting fate, as well as what they are likely to forego, being too kind to their own feelings and too respectful to you.

---

2 A woolen cloak with a hood, Berber in origin.

Approaching the steamboat, we heard a stream of horrible oaths, French with some Arabic additions, and soon discovered the man who was belching them forth. He was standing over a heap of things thrown on the ground haphazardly and—upon seeing our guide, who shyly huddled behind us—leapt up at him.

The Frenchman was evidently in charge here. "Where are our things?" I asked him.

"What do I care about your things!? The Indian mail is coming any minute now. Hurry up, otherwise the boat will leave without you; you can find your things later."

That was the last thing I wanted, that the boat waiting particularly for my arrival should leave without me! However, you never know: the phrase *Indian mail* has a magical effect here, and I should not be surprised if our boat had to leave the pier for its sake. The English know how to firmly establish themselves, here as well as anywhere.

It was still raining. I was no longer concerned about our things but rather about where to put myself up for the night as all the cabins were fully occupied. I went back to the Frenchman, who had one foot on the steamboat's gangway, ordering the crew to shove off, but this time, I claimed my rights with him.

"Listen," he said, learning that the boat had been put at my disposal, "no-one recognizes others' right here—you have to act by force. Go to any room, have a few strong words with whoever has taken it, and be sure to be strict with them, wave your fist if need be. That shall make them see that you definitely have the right, and they shall clear the room for you."

Well, thought I, *they seem to have their own rules here; let me try the Frenchman's remedy*. The very first attempt was a complete success.

Now the boat was going full steam ahead, true to the Egyptian custom, stumbling all the while over sandbars and oftentimes brushing against the shores. A long time had passed; it was already past midnight, and yet I could not go to sleep. The thought of being on the Nile—the Nile I once worshipped, whose mysteries, hidden from mere mortals, had been passed from Egyptian priests to the Greeks, who in their turn, having transformed them, as was their wont, into poetic images, had bequeathed them to us—this thought would not leave me alone. A childhood dream was beating inside my breast, but alas! These dreams, which hectic life had been unable to smother, were destined to collapse by themselves at the sight of the naked essence of things.

I rose before sunrise. The Nile flowed quietly and majestically. We had already left its Rosetta branch, and now the Nile presented us with its full width, nearly twice wider than the Neva by the Isaac Bridge. The banks of the Nile are gently sloping and desolate; palm-trees stand there in rows, one after another, like a stockade fringed with spikes. Even when there is a village to be glimpsed behind them, it is of the kind that makes you wish you could not see it at all. *So this is the Nile!* thought I. On the other hand, there are objects, just as there are faces, which the more you peer into, the more you study them, the more beauty and deep meaning you find in them. Perhaps the Nile is one of those, and undoubtedly it cannot be the same everywhere, stretching as it does over more than 3,000 versts,[3] which space we shall cover together, reader, if you can muster enough patience for that: you reposing in an armchair, in a cool room, or even in bed; I traveling, variously, by water, on camelback, on foot, or on a donkey, in the heat attaining 45 degrees Reaumur;[4] and yet, my position shall be no worse than yours, for I shall be seeing live nature, whilst you shall be reading the dead word.

I have deliberately omitted any description of that colossal project, the system of locks on the Nile, by the spot where its two branches merge. It requires a detailed and lengthy examination, which I shall deal with on our return journey. It would be worth noting here a habit travelers have of judging people and things so readily and confidently. Prince Pückler-Muskau[5] borrows a description from a work by

---

3 An obsolete Russian measure of length, about 0.66 mile. Three thousand versts is approximately 2,000 miles.
4 56°C.
5 Prince Hermann Ludwig Heinrich von Pückler-Muskau (1785–1871), Saxon and Prussian aristocrat and landscape gardener, well known for his travelogues. Kovalevsky cites his three-volume *Aus Mehemet Ali's Reich* (Stuttgart: Hallberger, 1844).

Clot Bey[6] (without, of course, quoting him) of a design to construct a system of locks on the Nile made by the engineer Linant Bey,[7] claiming that the works were carried out under the latter's supervision. Clot Bey was right, for at the time of his book's publication, the works were indeed being carried out by Linant Bey and according to his design. By the time Pückler-Muskau traveled to Egypt, however, those works had been abandoned and a new design, by Mujeau,[8] approved, based on different principles and indicating a different position for the construction of the locks.

Late on the same day, we moored by Ibrahim Pasha's palace. The view of Cairo, drowning in twilight and amidst the bright greenery of gardens, was picturesque. We spent the night on the boat and on the following morning went to the town.

Today Cairo remains the only typical city of the Mohammedan East—not the present-day East that grovels in ignorance or slavery, but the East of the past, reminiscent of the time of its fame, the time of the caliphs. Behold this mosque: how beautiful it is, how magnificent in all its graceful simplicity, how light, airy, and exquisite its minarets. They rise high from the ground, trying, as if of their own accord, to reach the sky, one chasing after another, higher and higher—you cannot be quick enough to follow them, nor to behold them. And these carved, chiseled balconies, covered with a very fine lattice as if with lace; and the windows of filigree workmanship, in which Oriental fantasies verily run wild; and the streets, covered now with canvas, now with timber, so as to protect one from the sun at the height of the day; and at night—oh, what mysteries these streets harbor at night. It is easy to believe that the adventures from *One Thousand and One Nights* could truly unfold in these streets. Yes, the first sight of Cairo greatly impresses a traveler who is sensitive to all things exquisite and tired of the cities of good old Europe, so alike in their aspect. But

---

6 Clot Bey (Antoine Barthelemy Clot, 1793–1868), French physician; directed the military medical school; was chief surgeon under Mohammed Ali.
7 Linant Bey (Louis Maurice Adolphe Linant de Bellefonds, 1799–1883), French engineer in charge of public works under the Khedive dynasty.
8 Kovalevsky is mistaken. The design was produced by Dieudonné Eugène Mougel (Mougel Bey, 1808–90), also known for his work on the Suez Canal.

alas! Mosques and minarets decay, maintained by no-one; houses are demolished to widen the streets or to be replaced with new ones, built in the Levantine taste, which constitutes an ugly mixture of European and Oriental architecture. Perhaps it is something Cairo can benefit from, although not to so great an extent as Alexandria has—the very city that has led others by her own example, Alexandria that has turned from a dirty little village into a large semi-European city—yet there can hardly be any benefit in the architectural sense, nor in the poetic sense. You might say, "But who cares about that today? One only needs things that are useful, essential, wholesome: straight, wide streets leave enough space for air, facilitate communication, and instill order"—an extremely prudent remark. Do you think, however, that in the past, they could not be just as prudent, and that people who still carried in their hearts memories of the boundless desert did not care about space? The fact is that in these wide-open streets, you shall be burned by the noon sun, whereas all the southern cities of the Middle Ages evaded that with great prudence by means of balconies which, hanging from houses, would create some manner of cover above the streets. The Arabs were fond of spaces; they were fond of spacious houses, painted, decorated with arabesques, and gilded; they liked spacious courtyards, laid out in mosaics, twined with thick, green vines and fig-tree branches, with a cooling fountain that would never dry out. There might have been no comforts of the kind that we have, yet there was luxury, languor, food for fancy in the time of domestic troubles. Be that as it may, the fact is that the only monument of purely Arabic architecture that has remained fully intact hitherto shall soon disappear, and our offspring shall be obliged to study it in pictures and in legends.

I looked round with intent curiosity; it seemed to me that this city, so different from others, must also live a different life, that the spirit of the caliphs, sad and desolate though it might be yet still keeping its favorite city under its patronage, must be hovering above: the surroundings were variegated but not lively, with poverty and hardship showing their sharp angles from beneath an old, gold-embroidered *burnous* . . .

Lost in observation, I nearly collided with a strange pair, one of them, ragged and ugly, beating a tambourine with all his might, the other, all but naked, roaring at the top of his voice.

"What is this?" I asked my guide the dragoman.

"Fancy."

"But what is it?"

"Fancy," he repeated in a disdainful tone, throwing a couple of *para* coins[9] upon the tambourine spread before us. *Fancy: so be it*, thought I, following his example.

Meanwhile, wild sounds of some other music rushed right at us, approaching, and once again, we hastened to step aside so as to give way to a procession. First there marched an entire orchestra, playing deafening Turkish music; in its wake, under a heavy baldachin supported by several stalwart porters, something was moving, slowly, very slowly, something that was being led or, more precisely, dragged, quite closed, quite invisible, resembling a coat-hanger laden with various rich fabrics, all piled up in a haphazard fashion. Behind them walked a crowd of people, some shouters among them; finally, there was a boy of about six years of age, elaborately dressed in gold-cloth, riding a horse, its harness richly decorated; and behind him, another crowd thronged, making more noise.

"What is it?" I asked.

"Fancy," the dragoman said smugly as he continued to look upon the procession with curiosity.

On hearing the word *fancy* I reached for money again, in the manner of someone who understands what is going on, but the dragoman shook his head in negation.

"So what is it then, this *fancy* of yours?"

"Why, it is but fancy!" he said in a deeply confident tone. Nothing to be done—I had to wait for another occasion or another person who might be able to explain that Cairo *fancy* to me.

"They shall take her across the entire city," the dragoman said, proceeding on his way and without turning to me.

---

9 One-fortieth of an Egyptian piastre. One hundred piastres constituted an Egyptian pound.

"Fancy?"

"The bride."

"But where is the bride?"

"Can you not see? She is under the baldachin."

Oh, so that moving coat-stand is a bride! Could she be fancy, too, by any chance? However, there certainly was no bride amongst the ugly figures we met earlier—one naked, the other ragged—and yet there was some fancy.

We were on our way to see the Russian Consul. To cut the journey, the dragoman took me through some courtyard and then through a little garden, full of oleanders and roses in blossom. I halted despite myself to admire them.

"It is not worth looking at," the dragoman said to me, "the garden in Shubra[10] is really something, whereas this—this is just fancy."

What, fancy again!? *Truly this is the most fanciful city of all*, thought I, this time without enquiring about the meaning of the word. We proceeded on our way in silence and soon reached Azbakiya,[11] where the Consul lived.

Another scene awaited us in the square: a sad, painful scene that disturbed my heart, despite my having seen it ere this. There was a woman standing there like a convict, in full view of everyone, barely covered with rags. It was easy to conclude from her features and complexion that she was Abyssinian, and from her expression, that she was a slave. Nearby stood her seller, carefree and indifferent to her fate. I hastened to shelter myself in the Consul's house.

Soon after my arrival, an Egyptian official came to the Consul and announced that there were lodgings ready for me at the house of Kamil Pasha,[12] the son-in-law of Mohammed Ali, whereto we presently went.

The house of Kamil Pasha was similar in its layout to the palace where we had stayed in Alexandria, as well as most houses of wealthy Turks: a cross-shaped hall with a room, or sometimes two, in each of

---

10   Also Shoubra, a quarter of Cairo.
11   A neighborhood in Cairo.
12   Yusuf Kamil (1808–76), head of the civil affairs department of the Khedive government.

выраженію — что это невольница; не далеко отъ нея, стоялъ равнодушный къ ея участи, безпечный продавецъ ея. Я поспѣшилъ укрыться въ домѣ нашего консула.

Вслѣдъ за мною, пришелъ къ консулу египетскій чиновникъ и объявилъ, что мнѣ приготовили квартиру у Камиль-паши, зятя Мегемета-Али, куда мы и отправились.

Домъ Камиль-паши расположенъ какъ и дворецъ, въ которомъ мы жили въ Александріи, какъ почти всѣ домы

Abyssinian female slave

Jellab, a slave trader

its corners. The only difference was the luxury of the rooms and indeed their tasteful furnishings. I was met by the host.

He is one of those pure-bred Turks, if I may so express myself, who unfortunately are dying out everywhere. His manners, full of nobility and dignity, make you instinctively respect him: his face has a meek and paternal expression; his talk, although florid and polite, is devoid of flattery. Kamil Pasha has had an Oriental-style education—that is, in addition to Turkish, he speaks an excellent Arabic and Persian, as well as a decent French, even though he has not been learning it for a year yet. He is currently writing a history of Mohammed Ali's rule, at the behest of his father-in-law. The speech the latter gave at the assembly of his officials—which surprised everyone by the novelty of its ideas and made quite a stir, a speech imbued with many noble feelings—had been written (needless to say, under Mohammed Ali's influence) by Kamil Pasha rather than Semil, as many have claimed.

Chapter III

Mohammed Ali and the Pyramids

On the same day, we were invited to dinner at the residence of Mohammed Ali—an honor he rarely bestows on anyone. He frequently invites people to breakfast, at times even ladies, especially the wife of the French Ambassador, Barrot,[1] but it is only his close associates—all of them Turks, mainly his relatives, six or seven people at most—that dine with him.

When we entered the dining-room, Mohammed Ali was already seated, and after greeting us cordially, he bade us sit down. His face spoke of a severe illness, it being the beginning of a disease that was to strike him later, so suddenly and so horribly. His hands were shaking, he could scarcely hold a spoon and ate almost nothing, and yet his voice was firm, and overcoming his affliction, the old Pasha remained a welcoming host.

I studied with curiosity the face of a man who had been the subject of Europe's attention for so long. He has been variously portrayed as a genius and as a villain, but whatever kind of man he might be, the story of his life, beautiful and mysterious at any rate, must have often made the hearts of those reading it beat faster. The story is widely known,

---

1 Théodore-Adolphe Barrot (1801–70), consul general of France in Cairo.

and I shall forego a detailed account of it, relating instead only its most momentous events.

Mohammed Ali was born in Rumelia,[2] in the small seaside town of Kavala,[3] in 1769, as he himself says, although Kavala's elders claim that he is now all of 90 years old. Orphaned as a child, he was taken in by a kind *aga*,[4] who grew fond of the boy and distinguished him among his household, later choosing quite a rich bride for him. Thus helped, the young Mohammed Ali started off in tobacco trade, made a little fortune for himself and was planning to extend his business, when suddenly an order came to Kavala to recruit 300 men and send them, along with others, to Egypt, where the Turks had been fighting Napoleon's army. Mohammed Ali happened to be chosen among those 300. He was brave, which everyone gives him due credit for, and so it is little wonder that he soon became prominent among half-savage Albanians. After the battle of Abukir,[5] he was promoted to *sareshesme* (commander of 1,000),[6] and when the French left Egypt he was sent to fight the Mamluks[7] as a detachment commander.

Henceforth, a new path begins for Mohammed Ali, a treacherous, thorny, and at the same time slippery path that power-seekers take to attain their aim—an abyss at their feet, one wrong step leading inevitably to their ruin. It must be said, however, that not all of these pirates of happiness take this path deliberately, oh no! Sometimes it is chance that pushes them onto it; at other times it is fate that leads them on. Through a series of victories, intrigue, and the might of his invincible will and supple mind, Mohammed Ali reached a point where the sheikhs of Cairo, having expelled Koshrud[8] from the *Pashalik*,[9] offered Egypt to

---

2 A region of the Ottoman Empire in Europe, mostly in the Balkans, that included the territory of today's Bulgaria, Greece, and Turkey.
3 A port city in today's northern Greece.
4 An honorific title for an Ottoman civilian or military functionary.
5 In the Battle of Abukir (1799), the French under Napoleon defeated the Ottoman forces' attempt to invade Egypt from the sea.
6 Kovalevsky is mistaken; the Ottoman title for the commander of 1,000 was *bimbashi*. Possibly he heard that Mohammed Ali was promoted by his cousin in Kavala, Sarechesme Halil Aga.
7 A military class in Egypt historically formed from slaves.
8 Kovalevsky is mistaken. The predecessor of Mohammed Ali as the *wali* (governor) of Egypt under the Ottomans was Hurshid Ahmet Pasha (d. 1822).
9 A territory governed by a Pasha—in this case, Egypt.

the brave Albanian. Mohammed Ali played rather a peculiar trick that is common to people in his circumstances: he feigned refusal awhile before finally agreeing to do the people and the sheikhs of Cairo a favor and accept Egypt. The Porte, in spite of all its resistance, was forced to approve his appointment as Viceroy, followed by a *firman*[10] on the 9th of July 1805.

I shall omit a number of Mohammed Ali's subsequent victories and the conquest of Arabia, Syria, Sennaar,[11] and Kordofan.[12] The liberation of the holy cities of Mecca and Medina from the hands of Mohammedan heretics, the Wahhabis[13] who the Sultan's army had been helpless against, brought him great fame and respect in the Mohammedan world. But soon afterward, a chain of misfortunes of every kind awaited Mohammed Ali: the death of his favorite sons, Toussum and Ismail; the terrible defeat in Greece; the frequent occurrences of the plague in Egypt; and finally, the loss of Syria and Arabia—and after that, the destruction of the many monopolies that had brought him immense profits, a measure he had to take against his will. Yet the old Pasha, without losing heart, carried on as before with the task of transforming Egypt, or what he had left of it, including Sennaar and Kordofan. In the course of our journey, we are going to see how he did this; and now let us return to our dinner.

The dinner was very good and served in the European style. Everyone was in a hurry to eat or missed courses so as not to tire the ailing man out by sitting at the table for too long. A French butler, who knew everyone's wishes, was working briskly, the servants moving in complete silence, like shadows, and the only thing you could hear was the measured, clear, cadenced speech of an interpreter who, together with the Grand Dragoman (an extremely important figure in the ruling of Egypt), stood by the Pasha's chair and passed his words, barely audible, unto us in French.

---

10 A decree of the Ottoman sultan.
11 Also Sennar, a sultanate in what is now Sudan, Eritrea, and Ethiopia.
12 A region in Sudan conquered by Mohammed Ali.
13 Followers of Ibn Abd al-Wahhab, a religious movement in the Arabian Peninsula allied with the House of Saud and, in the early 19th century, opposed to the Ottoman and Egyptian power.

Mohammed Ali is not tall; shriveled by age and illness, he seemed diminutive, his tiny hands and head matching his entire figure; his thin white beard and small mustache did not conceal his face, once handsome but now pale and wrinkled, although not in the least unpleasant, as it can often be said of old men—on the contrary, it made you respect and trust him, whilst his light-brown, deep-set eyes, quick and alive, still glinting, illuminated his figure in a peculiar way, evidence that he was still sparkling with vitality and possessed of a rebellious spirit, just as active today as he had been 20 years ago. Only from time to time could we hear some terrible exclamation that seemed to erupt from the ailing man's deepest soul, all of a sudden, through no effort of his own. It frightened us, but the others were accustomed to it, for Viceroy's illnesses had always been accompanied by similar cries, which neither his strong will nor the efforts of doctors could eliminate. They say it occurred in consequence of the extreme moral stress that he had suffered during the war with the Wahhabis. Surrounded by the strong enemy on all sides and threatened by his own men, many of whom were no longer willing to obey him, he resolved to do an audacious deed: storm a fortress that was, one might say, hanging over his head, decimating his camp. That was the only opportunity for him to revive the sunken spirits of the men he still had left, to open a way into the country, and to instill fear in the enemy. He had but a handful of men, and it was them whom he led to storm the fortress in the middle of the night. Their sudden success brought the matter to an end, and the war with the Wahhabis took a different turn, but upon his return from the battlefield, Mohammed Ali felt for the first time those nervous, fitful cries that would at first plunge him into complete desperation.

The dinner talk circled round my expedition. Mohammed Ali wanted me to sit out the rainy season in Cairo and then set off for Sennaar. He said that the first rains in the Sudan were due to start in the following month (February). I was alarmed by the thought of sojourning in Cairo with nothing to do; also, even though Mohammed Ali had once crossed into the belt of seasonal rains and could therefore judge from experience, nevertheless, people who had visited those parts in every season had told me that the *kharif*,[14] heavy rains that people and beasts flee, would not start in the mountains until the month of May. I was so bold as to explain that to Mohammed Ali—needless to say, in the lightest way possible. He shook his head in doubt and addressed the question to the others. Many of the present company had been to the Sudan, yet only one man, one of the servants, plucked up the courage to reply that, although Effendi[15] was quite right and it could rain in February, still the rainy season mainly occurred in May. Mohammed Ali gave him a look that made him involuntarily step back to the wall behind him. The old Pasha, however, immediately announced that he would be quite happy to let me go whenever I liked and that he would give orders to equip the expedition without delay. It was only for the sake of my health that he wished me to remain here for longer. Indeed, as I was to find out later, Mohammed Ali, on the advice of the good Clot Bey, wanted us to acclimatize in Cairo, and it was for that reason, as much as for the skirmishes with Abyssinia that had recently broke out on the Sennaar side, that he wished to keep us near him awhile, even though he himself could not wait to see the results of our expedition, which he had great expectations for.

"I have ordered the Governor-General to send 10,000 men to Fazoglu,[16] to work in gold-mines," the Pasha said, "and I will send as many more if need be."

I listened to him in surprise. *What were we to do with 10,000 men*, thought I, *when there were no mines yet, let alone mining people who could manage that horde?* However, I had been warned in advance and could see from experience how much the old Pasha disliked any contradictions, spoiled by his own people and by Europeans, who tended to agree with him in all matters out of respect for his age and achievements, or perhaps out of fear; so I decided, rather than contradicting him this time, to have a more substantial interview at our next audience, to show him where things stood. "Inshallah," I said, "God willing, we shall find some gold!"

---

14 A strong southwesterly wind, usually accompanied by heavy rains, in Sudan and parts of East Africa.
15 An honorific title or form of polite address.
16 Also Fazogli, a region in what is today Sudan and Ethiopia.

"Oh yes, you shall certainly find gold and silver and copper; there is plenty of everything there."

I was about to speak, but everyone's eyes turning to me imploringly forced me to remain silent.

After dinner we adjourned to another room, luxuriously furnished, painted in the Oriental taste with flowers and arabesques, with enormous mirrors on partitions and two soft *divans* along two of the walls. Mohammed Ali sat cross-legged in the corner of one of the *divans*, now completely immersed in his fur coat, while we sat nearby in comfortable armchairs. Out of the entire company present in the dining-room, only the Grand Dragoman had followed us. Having partaken of coffee and taken a few drags on large diamond-encrusted amber pipes, we were about to bid our farewell so as not to tire the ailing man out.

"I am bored. Please do stay, let us have a little talk about something," he said amiably.

So we set to talking. Aware of the Pasha's weakness, the Consul commenced a conversation about trade, and Mohammed Ali grew more lively and engaged. We stayed with him for about an hour after dinner.

I shall never forget the words he uttered with a special expression, speaking like a prophet. "We are three peers," he said, "Louis Philippe, the King of France; Metternich; and myself. If one of us falls down, then the others shall follow at once." Those words were to come true too soon.

Preparations for the expedition were going fast—Mohammed Ali knew how to make his men work briskly.

There were about seven of us Russians in Cairo at the time, an extremely seldom occasion, and most of us had long known each other. In the mornings we would ride outside the city to see either the petrified forest, or the pyramids, or mosques; the evenings were mostly spent at the Consul's house. Every Russian must remember with gratitude the unfailing attention and the cordial hospitality shown to him by our consuls in the East.

In the evenings we would be visited by the respectable Dr. Prus[17]—a member of the Paris Academy of Medicine, in Cairo on a mission to

---

17 René-Clovis Prus (1793–1850), French physician; wrote on plague in the Middle East.

study the plague, who had been treating Mohammed Ali—and by Clot Bey. They said they came to the Russian colony, as they referred to our company, to repose after a day of hard work spent with the patient, of whom they told us news, which was not always comforting. It was not we alone but the entire Cairo that was waiting with some trepidation for this illness to end.

It is time I said a few words about the pyramids; all possible arguments, exclamations, and superlatives appearing to have been exhausted on their subject, there remains little for me to add.

The pyramids, when you behold them from afar—for instance, from Mohammed Ali's palace—truly astonish you with their magnificence, especially considering that your imagination has already been primed for all things miraculous. But as you approach them, they shrink, become smaller, and assume an ordinary appearance, until finally you are presented with an immense, cone-shaped mass of hewn stones placed atop one another in steps and raised into a single point at the top. The pyramids were once plated with slabs. The space inside them is all made of the same stone, except for two or three rooms—you can only reach them with difficulty if you huddle up and crawl along dark and low corridors—and perhaps also a few yet unexplored vaults.

A rock that has been cut down and flattened serves as a base for the pyramids; a giant Sphinx with a pensive face guards the entrance: a creature battered by time, seemingly lamenting the fate that, rather than completely eliminating it, allowed it to witness a new, miserable epoch and new events that a Sphinx living in the time of the pharaohs would have found incredible.

Until now, the pyramids were wrongly considered to be the highest structures in the world; the bell tower in Revel[18] is, in fact, higher by a couple of feet. It has been calculated that if you take down one pyramid, you can build a small wall around the entire France with its stones. So much labor has gone into it, so much human sweat and blood has been spilt—oh Lord!—and with such little use. The most justified view today is that these pyramids were used as tombs for the pharaohs; so that was the vain object that thousands of people were sacrificed for!

---

18 Tallinn, now the capital of Estonia.

But let us listen to Herodotus, the one who admired—nay, loved—the wisdom of priests, the truthful Herodotus who occasionally deviated from the path of truth, seduced by his own impartiality and enthusiasm for the subject. This is how the pyramids were built:

> Cheops [. . .] shut up all the temples, and having first kept them from sacrificing there, he then bade all the Egyptians work for him. So some were appointed to draw stones from the stone-quarries in the Arabian mountains to the Nile, and others he ordered to receive the stones after they had been carried over the river in boats, and to draw them to those which are called the Libyan mountains; and they worked by a hundred thousand men at a time, for each three months continually. Of this oppression there passed ten years while the causeway was made by which they drew the stones [. . .] For the making of the pyramid itself there passed a period of twenty years.[19]

"Cheops moreover came, they said, to such a pitch of wickedness, that being in want of money he caused his own daughter to sit in the stews, and ordered her to obtain from those who came a certain amount of money (how much it was they did not tell me)," Herodotus continues. "She requested each man who came in to her to give her one stone upon her building: and of these stones, they told me, the pyramid was built."[20]

One has to add that in the time of the pharaohs, whatever might be said about Egyptian wisdom, they knew no mechanical tools. The drawings on the walls of ancient temples have accurately preserved for us the method used for transporting stones in those days: a thousand men, harnessed with ropes, draw a sledge carrying a pillar or a stone.

I must admit that it was not delight, which I had been prepared for by all the descriptions of travels in Egypt, but rather involuntary horror that I felt as I beheld that colossus, witness to 5,000 years of the

---

19 Herodotus quoted throughout from *The History of Herodotus*, trans. G. C. Macaulay (London: Macmillan, 1890), http://wps.pearsoncustom.com/wps/media/objects/2426/2484749/chap_assets/bookshelf/herodotus.pdf.
20 Author's note: Herodotus, book II, 124, 126.

pharaohs and their tyranny. If its gracious forms and art enthralled you, making the memory fade, that would be a different matter. Perhaps I, too, should later get rid of the initial surprise, but not until I have expressed myself; or it could be that I am too old-fashioned to admire the beauty of the pyramids! Still, my eyes linger on an element broken off a Greek statue, a severed arm or leg, and I use it to reconstruct the whole in my imagination, lovingly, like a zoologist reconstructs a long extinct animal from a single bone.

I climbed all the way to the top of the pyramid, I descended into the depths of its secret recesses, searching everywhere for the miracle admired by travelers, and, unable to find it, returned home in a fatigued state. I shall omit the dimensions of the stones, the number of steps, and the divers entrances and exits in the pyramids. If you are interested in them, reader, you shall find them all in any account of a *journey in Egypt*. I shall also leave the other Cairo monuments till my return, giving my immediate attention to the present instead.

The Viceroy felt somewhat better, and I went to bid farewell to him. Anyone who has already been introduced can visit him freely, this being an ancient Oriental tradition. Mohammed Ali was still weak, yet in good spirits, as a man recovering from an illness. He was allowed to go out into a reception room, where he was surrounded by visitors. Having sat me down by his side, he asked me about Russia, about Siberia, while also making jokes, eager to present the journey awaiting me in a pleasant light.

Here, he said incidentally, you have to constantly change your underwear for perspiration, but in the Sudan, no sooner has it got wet than it dries and begins crackling like paper: crack, crack!

I told him that a similar thing could happen in Siberia too: no sooner has your underwear got wet than it freezes, and then it also begins crackling like paper: crack, crack! He was much amused by my remark.

Then I realized that everyone wanted, in their turn, to cheer the old Pasha, as if he were a spoilt child. I must say, however, that Mohammed Ali did not abuse the readiness with which people would sacrifice themselves to mockery; he was very meek in his teasing and only flickered his eyes cunningly this way and that, as if watching the impression it made upon others.

I spent about two hours with him. His unassuming manner of talking; his concern about my trip, which embraced the most minute things, things I myself had forgotten; finally, his remarks, at times childishly naïve, at times imbued with deep thoughts, and his very appearance, exhausted and meek, filling you with love and compassion—all that, especially set against the vivid background of his past life, produced a great impression upon me . . .

What I have written here suggests praise, but if it be praise, let it be: Mohammed Ali, curious about everything that is written about him, shall never know that—alas, the light of comprehension has been taken away from him! . . . Also, I write what I feel, and it is with the same impartiality that I shall describe any bad things, which I shall undoubtedly see any number of in the course of my journey.

Pleasant though my sojourn in Cairo was, the expedition was a burden on my shoulders: I had to hasten my departure. The respectable Clot Bey, Khosroff Bey,[21] and some others were active in helping me to prepare for it, and 10 days later everything was ready.

Non ut, [. . .] claram delatus ad urbem
Delicas videam, Nile iocose, tuas.

Nor am I sailing to Alexander's famous city
To see thy pleasures, merry Nile.[22]

—Ovid

I must note, however, that the *merry Nile* has changed a lot since the time of Ovid, and when matters take their ordinary course, a traveler risks dying of boredom on its banks. My only regret was that I could not be present at a celebration that was due to commence a few days henceforth, when caravans with Mohammed's worshippers returned

---

21 Most likely Mohammed Bey Khusraw, Mohammed Ali's son-in-law and finance minister (*Defterdar*).
22 Ovid, *Tristia. Ex Ponto*, trans. Arthur Leslie Wheeler (Harvard: Harvard University Press, 1924), 16–17.

from Mecca. The celebration ends in extraordinary festivities that one can only see in Cairo—I am talking of *doseh*![23]

Early in the morning, a crowd of Dervishes carrying banners flock to al-Azbekiyah. An old sheikh comes out, the head of the Saadi[24] order, powerful and important in the Mohammedan world. Then a hundred or so people of the order prostrate themselves on the ground, and the Dervishes of other congregations arrange them closely next to one another, thus making a live bridge of human bodies. Several people run over them, as if to test the construction, crying and beating a tambourine, while the crowd watches the miracle in awe. Finally, the sheikh, riding a grey horse (which has long been seen at these ceremonies) and dressed in a light-blue fur coat and a green turban (the latter indicating his high birth), treads over the bodies on the ground. Two people lead the horse—whose hooves, it should be noted, are shod—one walking over the heads of the Dervishes, the other over their feet. Anyone whom the horse has already trodden over jumps up and follows the sheikh, crying "Allah! Allah!" and proceeding thus all the way to his house. They say that no serious misfortunes ever occur at these ceremonies. Lane[25] notes, however, that the horse once balked on this human path and was about to gallop over the men's heads; but even then he saw but one Dervish who, upon getting up, huddled up and winced hard.

---

23 A dervish religious ceremony.
24 It is likely Kovalevsky mistook the name of Saadi Shirazi, a mystical poet who was himself a dervish, to mean a dervish order.
25 Author's note: Edward Williams Lane, *An Account of the Manners and Customs of the Modern Egyptians*, London: Knight, 1846.

Chapter IV

Our Departure from Cairo and Voyage down the Nile to Minya[1]

On the 8th (20th) of January 1848,[2] several people gathered at my place, most of them Russians and close to me in many regards. We sat down and stayed quiet awhile, and then we crossed ourselves and . . . bid farewell to each other! But we did not part yet—I was accompanied to the steamboat. Two Russians and a Frenchman sailed with us to Aswan,[3] the first cataract, which steamboats dare not pass through: that would have been about 1,000 versts[4] from Cairo.

The steamboat was smoking; there was hustle and bustle on board. Arabs always fuss around whenever there is something out of the ordinary, let alone on such an occasion: we had to take all the essential supplies to last us for a long time, for there was nothing to be found along the way. Many people looked upon these preparations with certain sadness—and Europeans with certain surprise. Bidding me farewell, Mohammed Ali gave me some fatherly advice to ensure I look

---

1 A governorate and city in the upper Nile region.
2 Kovalevsky gives the dates according to the Julian and Gregorian calendar. The Julian (old-style) calendar was used in the Russian Empire until 1917.
3 A city in southern Egypt.
4 Approximately 660 miles.

after my health, bearing in mind my quick transition from Siberia to the eighth parallel.

The bell sounded, accompanied by a shrill noise of steam being let out. Farewell, farewell! God knows when and where we shall see each other again. Farewell, Cairo! God knows how many of us shall return! . . . And so the steamboat, true to the Egyptian custom, went full steam ahead, paying little heed to sandbars on the Nile or to barques sailing toward it and across, whence the cries of fear and futile requests could be heard. Fortunately, the boat had a shallow draft and was a great runner, like most Egyptian steamboats. Made in England, she had just arrived at Cairo, this being her maiden voyage on the Nile.

The materials and men required for the expedition had already been dispatched to Fazoglu. The following people traveled with me: T.,[5] a young Russian naturalist; a doctor of Slavonic descent assigned to me by the Pasha; a dragoman, an Arab brought up in France; a Frenchman employed as a painter and architect; and in place of a *firman*—indeed, much more powerful than any *firman*—Lieutenant-Colonel Yousuf Effendi, a Circassian by birth. The importance of such an embodied authority in Egypt is well known: one Turk is able to disperse an entire village of Arabs. Apart from the above-mentioned people, I also had with me Russian mine foremen; servants of every nationality and color, white, black, yellow, and brown; and finally, the Pasha's maître-d'hôtel. That was our company, small yet motley, which was for many months to share the travails of the journey—traveling by water in a steamboat and in a barque, across the Nubian Desert on camelback, then on horseback and on a donkey, and finally, in the Sudan, on foot—enduring all the vagaries of the expedition.

As I have already noted, our company was enlarged for five days or so, and in a most pleasant way for us.

On one side we could see the gardens of Boulac[6] and Rhoda[7] flashing past, some of the best gardens in the world; the city rising in an uneven, grey mass, launching its minarets—those harbingers of prayer

---

5 Lev Semenovich Tsenkovskii (1822–87), Russian botanist and microbiologist; a corresponding member of the Imperial Russian Academy of Sciences from 1881.
6 Boulaq (also Bulaq), a quarter in Cairo.
7 Roda (also Rawdah), an island on the Nile in Cairo.

and repentance—into the sky; the citadel; and finally, the Mokattam Hills.[8] All that soon merged into an almost lifeless desert. On the other side, the desert emerges immediately opposite to Cairo, or even earlier, and the Libyan sands are brightly prominent. The desert accompanies you far along the way, and in its midst, following the Nile, rise those age-old tombs—the pyramids, first in Giza, then in the Sahara—all the more colossal and dead for that! . . . Occasionally a copse of palm-trees flashes past: so there is a village there, but you cannot see it as the banks are low, or if you do, it is but some heaps more akin in aspect to molehills, animal shelters rather than human dwellings.

Finally, here is a *bender*, a town, the dragoman says proudly, pointing to some ruins. A great town indeed! Here is another, and another—we go right past them. But at last, here is Benisuef,[9] one of the most prominent trade and industrial Egyptian cities, situated by the Bahr Yussef Canal,[10] which brings the waters of the Nile, its fertility, and trade to the Fayyum Oasis.[11]

The Bahr Yussef Canal—or as everyone, including the wise Clot Bey, refers to it, the Joseph Canal[12]—emerges opposite to St. Anthony's Monastery.[13] Why is it called a canal? Ask not, reader, for this is one of those wisdoms consecrated with age that no-one can even begin to doubt.

I may be seeing the monuments of ancient Egypt from a different perspective, but I do not impose my opinion on anyone; indeed, I do my best to avoid any scientific conflict with others, knowing from experience that arguments never prove anything, and God only knows how much they bore the readers, whose noses are rubbed in all manner of Egyptian, Greek, and Latin wisdoms, the intention being not to teach them, oh no, but rather to show off the author's own erudition. As for the subject of the arguments, it remains obscured in the fog of uncertainty.

---

8   Also Muqattam Hills, a range of hills and a quarter in Cairo.
9   Beni Suef, a city in central Egypt.
10 Bahr Yousef Canal.
11 Faiyum, a city and oasis in central Egypt.
12 Author's note: A. B. Clot Bey, *Aperçu général sur l'Egypte*, Paris: Fortin Masson, 1840, vol. II, p. 360.
13 A Coptic Orthodox monastery in Egypt.

Were it concerned with the Joseph Canal alone, I would stay silent, but there is another question related to it, one of great importance to ancient Egypt: the question of Lake Moeris.[14]

Firstly, consider the Joseph Canal. Without going deep into any historical studies, I shall only point out the natural side of things to you, such as the thousands of meanders that Bahr Yussef uses to lay its course, as if taking into consideration the willfulness of the Nile, whose bed it runs parallel to—meanders that would amount to twice the length of the canal, compared to the length it would have were it dug in a straight line (which would be, I should like to note, a more convenient route). So let me ask you, reader, what kind of people would be unable to comprehend that, even while still in their infancy (and you know what great wisdom is attributed to the Egyptians), and would dig a canal in such a fashion? Let us presently turn our attention to its bottom: everywhere you can see the exposed quartz limestone that constitutes the surrounding formation, which, as if following the capricious flow of the current, goes alternately up and down, representing every feature of a natural river-bed. The incongruous and varying width of Bahr Yussef, unusual for a canal, is another matter, but that can at least be explained by collapsed banks and deposits of silt.

All that should suffice to confirm the view that the Joseph Canal is but a branch of the Nile: there are many similar branches emerging as the river, constricted by natural obstacles, rids itself of any surplus waters, which lay their own course until they encounter a convenient slope whereby to return to the lap of the mother river.

Why then, the reader will ask, is this branch named after Joseph? We cannot fail to see, even now, that cities erected and lands discovered bear the names of people who have nothing to do with either the construction of the former or the discovery of the latter. Withal, there really is a small canal here, dug from this branch into Fayyum; supposing that this canal, whose ancient age is beyond any doubt, was dug on Joseph's orders, that would have sufficed for the entire branch to be named after him.

---

14 An ancient freshwater lake, now Birket Qarun (also Birqet Qarun), a saltwater lake in the Fayyum Oasis.

We shall presently consider the location of Lake Moeris, which the Joseph Canal, it has been suggested, once filled with the waters of the Nile.

Until recently, a lake situated in Fayyum (the ancient Arsinoites), known as Birqet Qarun, was believed to have once been Lake Moeris. The geological structure of the lake's shores is in itself proof that it owes its existence to natural causes rather than to human efforts. However, such a refutation of the established view, for all its clarity, would be too simple. To refute views based on ancient evidence, one has to rely on historical studies, which the wise Linant de Bellefonds understood well, dedicating a substantial part of his work[15] to the refutation of the above hypothesis. Quoting the very same ancient writers, he managed to show the incongruity of the hypothesis, undermining its every point, destroying its foundations and then scattering the very dust of it, so that no-one believes in it any more. I refer the curious readers to the learned work. They will read it with even more pleasure than they will the scholarly studies of a certain Jomard, published in an immense volume on the explorations of Napoleon's French expedition in Egypt.[16]

You would think that the respectable Linant Bey might leave it at that—but no! Having been carried away by the studies of the ancients, having started on a path that is tempting and slippery for many scholars, he could no longer resist the temptation to rush down it headlong. He thought it absolutely necessary to find Lake Moeris, his timid imagination frightened of losing this monument of Egyptian wisdom; he was terrified of depriving the world of one of its wonders: a wonder one is accustomed to since one's early days, just as one is accustomed to such things as the Colossus of Rhodes, the legendary Gardens of Semiramis, or the Tower of Babel. And so Linant set forth to search everywhere for a surrogate for Lake Moeris. Naturally, his principal concern was to situate it at a place where you would also have the maze

---

15 Author's note: Linant de Bellefonds, *Mémoire sur le lac Moeris*, Alexandrie: La Société Egyptienne, 1843.

16 Edme-François Jomard (1777–1862), French scholar and engineer, editor of *Description de L'Égypte*. This multivolume series with contributions by numerous specialists, published between 1809 and 1829, was commissioned by Napoleon.

and the pyramids, the road from Memphis and Crocodilopolis[17]—in a word, as many as possible of the various pieces of evidence that could be found in the ancient writings. He had searched for such a point for a long time until finally—oh joy—he found it! . . . Indeed, is there anything an intelligent man possessed of good-will would not succeed in doing!? When I say that he found Lake Moeris, reader, you must not think that it was a *lake* that would accord with your old conceptions of one—not in the least! Firstly, it has not a drop of water in it; secondly, it forms a plain; but I hope that you are able to make some small concessions for the sake of such an important discovery. So what natural signs of a lake are there?

M. Linant found in several places heaps of stone and brick, which he ascribed to an ancient structure designed, in his opinion, as the lake's shorings. The entire Egypt contains more ruins than places of habitation, and yet the author, having discovered the desired evidence, draws a line through it, using his imagination to fill in the territories[18] where the line has to break off, thus outlining an area that includes, most aptly, the locations mentioned by the ancients. I deliberately quote the page number in Linant's treatise so that you can verify my words; as for the names of those villages and landmarks through which Linant draws his line, I forego them, for no-one is obliged to be acquainted with the geographical features of Fayyum in all their detail.

Following Linant's tactics, and to confirm our opinion, we shall cite the very same ancient writers that he mentions to justify himself. Herodotus believes the circumference of the lake to be 3,600 stadia.[19]

As it is indeed an immense space, we readily agree with those who suggest that what is meant here is the short stadium, equivalent to 99.75 meters, which still amounts to an area of 359,100 meters.[20]

In converting ancient measurements into contemporary units, we shall always follow Jomard as the best-known scholar, therefore keeping the French measure so that anyone can verify it.

---

17 Krokodilópolis, the Greek name for Fayyum.
18 Author's note: Bellefonds, op. cit., p. 19.
19 Author's note: Herodotus, book II, 149.
20 The figure refers to the lake's perimeter.

Diodorus repeats Herodotus's words,[21] whilst Pliny's evidence[22] may, with a slight exaggeration, be interpreted in the same fashion. Pomponius Mela,[23] however, ascribes quite another measure to the lake.

Certainly we accept the statement made by Herodotus as the most widely recognized true fact.

Thus we have established that, according to Herodotus, the area of Lake Moeris occupies 359,100 meters. Its depth is 50 *orgyas*,[24] which constitutes nearly 92 meters.

The above should allow you to readily calculate the amount of soil that needs to be taken out in order to produce a basin of the aforementioned size, and the figure thus obtained, amounting to 1,000 billion cubic meters, is bound to horrify you.

Ignoring the fact that labor of such proportions is nearly beyond human capabilities, especially within a single reign, I shall ask one question only: where has it gone, the huge mass of soil taken out, which would be impossible to obliterate in 400 centuries, let alone in 40, in a country where it almost never rains? . . . There is not a trace of it, and yet there are hillocks still visible along the banks of small canals built in the time of the pharaohs.

Moreover, Lake Moeris was designed to drain any surplus water during the inundation of the Nile and to replenish it when necessary at low water. Herodotus says that for six months the waters of the Nile flowed into the lake, and for another six months the waters of the lake flowed into the Nile—all the while, let us note, through the same canal. The fable told, I should like to consider his statement in earnest. One look at the country should suffice to convince you of the impossibility of such a condition ever being met. Yet there is more. Having calculated the amount of water carried per minute during the river's greatest influx, and having taken into account the area and the depth of the lake, you shall see that the entire Nile would have to drain into it for some time, thus leaving Lower Egypt without water. Linant Bey is too knowledgeable an engineer not to be able to readily verify my

---

21 Author's note: Diodorus Siculus, book I.
22 Author's note: Pliny the Elder, *Natural History*, book V, 9.
23 Author's note: Pomponius Mela, *De situ Orbis*, book I, 9.
24 Author's note: Herodotus, book II, 149.

words. But the learned author of the treatise would say—indeed does say—that Herodotus made an error in his calculation of the circumference and another, even more egregious error in his estimation of the depth. Aha! So he is mistaken exactly where you want him to be so. Why, then, do you not think yourself mistaken, or indeed, why do you not say also that the father of history is mistaken in his idea of an artificial lake and that his story is a fable told him by priests, especially if we recall that, as M. Linant has quite rightly noted, the ancient Egyptians were as boastful as their successors are today? They misled Herodotus, and not merely once—Herodotus, he whose geographical details sometimes strike you as being precise and correct to this day. It is quite possible that Moeris did dig a canal which, by means of Bahr Yussef, used to take away any surplus water from the Nile to Birqet Qarun. The wholesome influence of that measure on the inhabitants of provinces situated upstream filled them with surprise and awe for the Pharaoh; they could not believe that a single canal could do them so much good, and so thought his deed a miracle; the rumors of him gradually turned into a fable, which was facilitated by the priests, and finally the fable was told as fact to Herodotus, who related it to the world, to everyone's surprise. Other historians repeated it after Herodotus—those who, unable to find any other lake but Birqet Qarun, took it for artificial, as Herodotus himself must have done.

But what are we to do, reader? Are we to concede Lake Moeris altogether?

You may disagree with me, but I myself do not for one moment believe in it! Indeed, where would the Egyptians—with all due respect for their wisdom—find such a considerable knowledge of hydraulic works as would allow them to accomplish such a giant project? For we know that entire deserts situated, as it were, in the center of Egypt were left uncultivated, for the simple reason that that would have required a somewhat complicated canal system.

We shall presently return to Benisuef.

With regard to factories, Benisuef is famous for its carpets and its cotton fabrics—of the simplest kind, needless to say: *milayas*, or striped cotton fabrics used for outdoor clothes, mainly women's. It is also famous for its name, seeing that Benisuef means "sons of sabers"; however, it does not owe its name, as you might conclude, to the courage of its own sons, for it was others who once fought here with their sabers and thus decided the matter. Also, Benisuef stands where ancient Ptolemydon[25] once did. This important fact is complemented by another, that sheep are very cheap in the city, which attraction, more than any other, made our quartermaster ask permission to remain here for an hour. Given so many reasons, one could not but accede. Yousuf Effendi immediately went to the local ruler for provisions, whilst we went into town.

It was about 11 P.M. The light of the full moon and a host of stars was at its brightest, albeit I could not say whom it was meant for, considering that there was not a soul in the streets: the town appeared dead, despite having as many as 8,000 inhabitants—it was similar to Pompeii as it is now. An unaccustomed observer would be struck by the peculiar sight of houses with no roofs, oftentimes half-ruined and windowless, houses where you have to look hard for some creep-hole that serves as a door, if indeed there is one; that labyrinth of stores, dwellings, and mosques constitute a whole of sorts, something with no separations or shutters, and yet you cannot see or hear anything inside. Finally, our presence in the streets—here were human beings and Europeans to boot, the kind of people that could be sniffed out from afar by dogs—awoke and disturbed the most restless of the dogs; the first made much noise barking, thereupon others followed its example, and soon there were dogs everywhere, coming at us from above and from below and scattering about our feet to chase us all the way back to the boat. Yet still we saw no people. We did see several houses, in the proper sense of the word, and good houses at that; they all belonged either to Turks or to traders, confidants of Mohammed Ali and Ibrahim Pasha.

Even prior to reaching Benisuef, the surroundings liven up somewhat. You can see more villages, and animals can be glimpsed on the banks, now camels, now oxen or sheep. There are *sakhiehs*[26] everywhere,

---

25 Kovalevsky appears to be mistaken. There is an ancient Polemon, part of the Fayyum Oasis.
26 Sakieh (also sakia), a water-lifting machine (a wheel with bowls attached).

all of them working; the crops of sugar cane are visible, yellow, not quite ripe yet, telling you that you are not far from a large sugar factory owned by Ibrahim Pasha, Kamil Pasha, and other people close to Mohammed Ali, whom he is not ashamed of doing trade business with. Here palm-trees no longer grow in groves, but make up entire forests. A palm-tree is beautiful when it stands on its own amidst these lifeless sands, or when there are three or four of them making a copse together; but an entire forest of them lacks variety, having neither shade nor bright leafage in the absence of any other trees. There are occasional sycamores, always standing alone, near a *sakhieh* or, more often, near a holy tomb. These tombs are as wholesome for the faithful as they are for the infidel; there is always shade near them and at times even water, put there by someone pious. It is not difficult to be recognized as a holy man by the Mohammedans; we have met divers kinds of them. This man never once desecrated the waters of the Nile, never spat or threw any rubbish into them, nor even seemed to ever wash himself with the Nile's water—and there you go, his much-respected tomb rises in Minya now. Another never spilled a drop of blood, not even a chicken's, nor hurt a fly—and now he is a holy man. There is another tomb in Minya, the tomb of a holy man who prevents crocodiles from going down the Nile; not a single crocodile has ever gone beyond his tomb: it is only up to Girga[27] that the monster can be sighted by all, and the higher upstream, the more often. I have not seen a crocodile yet, even though we have long left Minya behind.

A range of low hills, having approached the right bank of the Nile at el-Aft, no longer deviates from it, serving as a frontier for inundation and a defense against the sands for the fertile strip. This is known as the Arabian range. Another, named the Libyan range, runs along the Nile on your left as you look downstream, situated beyond the Bahr Yussef Canal and hence scarcely visible.

I have forgotten to mention St. Anthony's Monastery, a little further down from Benisuef, on the opposite side to it. This is a Greek Coptic monastery, although you cannot guess that unless you have been warned. Only the cross, that symbol of salvation, which is incessantly

---

27 A city on the Nile in central Egypt.

Mosque in Cairo

being carried outside from the altar during mass, indicates the significance of the place. Their dress; the mixture of languages, Arabic and Coptic; the church itself—everything strikes you in a peculiar way: it is not poverty, it is desolation! St. Anthony's Monastery occupies a picturesque situation on a steep scarp.

Of Minya, one can say the same thing as of every Egyptian town, with the exception of Alexandria and Cairo—namely, that it is worse than the one preceding it. As you travel up the Nile, you notice that more and more until you finally reach the Sudan, where men and beasts live and work together, as taught by mother nature.

Chapter V

From Minya to Esneh[1]

How beautiful are the nights, how warm and abundant with stars! New stars appear, shining as they never do in the North. It is hot during the day: 20 degrees[2] at noon is quite ordinary. Sometimes there are clouds strolling across the sky; but you must not forget, reader, that it is winter now, the month of January being only half-gone. Our steamboat is flying fast, stumbling over sandbars, threatening any moment to stick its nose into the silted bank of the Nile, whence it would take much time and effort to pull it free. The boat's captain is an Arab, his knowledge limited; withal, the Arab is careless; he observes everything that unfolds before him with indifference, as if in a daze, and keeps saying, "*Allah kerim!*[3] What is it these Muscovites fuss about, whither are they hastening? Whatever is written in the stars, so be it. Inshallah! . . ." So many times have I mentally thanked Mohammed Ali for providing me with a steamboat. Firstly, we can now cover a daily distance that would ordinarily take five or six day in a barque; secondly, he afforded me the opportunity to enlarge our company by several Russians for another five days or so.

---

1   Esna, a city in central Egypt, 55 miles south of Luxor.
2   25°C.
3   Arabic for "Allah is generous."

Of course the banks of the Nile had heard Russian speech and seen Russian men ere, albeit seldom, but this must have been the first time they heard a Russian choir song. Time passed quickly and imperceptibly. Objects gave way to more objects. Villages and towns fled us, as if able to guess that we were coming with a special order from the Pasha. The worst thing about these towns and villages is that they bear a strong resemblance to dried mud, and for quite a natural reason too: they are built of mud or of brick made from silt, with some straw added, dried in the sun. The only thing that brings some variety to them are dove-cotes, which rise like pepper-castors, white-washed—nay, smoothed-out. There are numerous dove-cotes everywhere; pigeons are eaten here, they are sold here, whereas in Constantinople or in Mecca, killing a pigeon is regarded a crime. On the left bank of the Nile, there is a village called Burach, which we passed not long ago; there they have a rule that no-one should be allowed to marry until he sets up his own dove-cote. This is what happened once with regard to this rule.

One Mohammed Ali, or Ali Mohammed (there are more Mohammed Alis and Ali Mohammeds here than there are Ivan Ivanovichs in Russia) wanted to marry, but he had no dove-cote. So off he goes, first to the father of the bride and then to the *mullah*. "Where is your dove-cote?" the latter asks.

"I have none, but I will have one anon."

"Then shall be the time for you to marry."

"The father will not let his daughter wait."

"You shall choose another."

"No-one else will give his daughter away to me, for I am poor."

The *mullah* contemplates that, but lets him go without permission.

After a while, Ali Mohammed comes to him again and is asked the same question. The young man answers in the affirmative. The *mullah* goes over to assure himself and sees that the groom's dwelling has been made into a dove-cote.

"But where will you live yourself?"

"The law says nothing about that," says Mohammed Ali, and soon afterward he marries, having set his marital bed in some hole he has dug the previous day.

In the houses of most peasants, you shall find nothing, except perhaps a pot, as well as a great many children; a piece broken off a palm-tree serves as furniture, a rag made of palm leaves as a bed; almost everyone has a rag, its thickness depending on the owner's wealth. Then again, were he to have anything else, it would be taken by the Turk or swept away by the Nile during its inundation. I must say, however, that it is not so much the taxes levied on the population that cause poverty—the taxes, as we shall see, being not very substantial—as it is the carelessness of the Arabs.

We were much amused by rafts laden with clay pottery, which were never out of our view, being floated from the upper parts of the Nile; that is a pretty clever idea. Thousands of pots and jugs, *goullehs*,[4] are tied together three-fold, the bottom ones placed neck-down, all floating in the shape of an immense raft, about 15 sazhens[5] long and almost as wide; at its top are four half-naked rowers propelling the raft, each using instead of a paddle a bundle of palm branches, entangled together in a haphazard fashion and tied at the end. They travel in this manner for some 1,000 versts[6] down the Nile. When a steamboat approaches, they try to steer aside, as far as possible, for waves buckle the rafts as if they were leaves. I can imagine what happens to them when a strong wind blows—and there can be rather strong winds on the Nile.

Every day we would halt for a few hours for the purpose of stocking up on coal. That would, of course, occur at the larger cities. Siut[7] is one of Egypt's most prominent cities, with 20,000 inhabitants. This is where the insurgent Mamluks once found shelter, giving the place an aspect of independence which until recently distinguished its people. But Mohammed Ali knew how to bring them to the same level: rather than giving people more influence, so as to ensure they had equal rights with the aristocracy that had established itself here on its own will, he shoved closer together the aristocracy and those who had been sticking out their heads high from behind them and thus provided

---

4 A bottle used to filter water and keep it fresh.
5 An obsolete Russian measure of length, about seven feet. Fifteen sazhens is approximately 100 feet.
6 Approximately 660 miles.
7 Assiut (also Asyut).

them all with a common denominator—they now enjoy an equality of sorts. I once asked a Greek priest whether his parish was oppressed by the Mohammedans.

"We no longer distinguish between confessions of faith in Egypt," he said. "Everyone is equal under Mohammed Ali."

"So everyone is content?" I asked further. The cautious Greek said nothing.

Siut is orderly and clean. One building is easily noticeable amidst the rest: the palace where Ibrahim Pasha lived when he ruled over Upper Egypt. The city stands on the site of ancient Lykopolis.

Girga used to be rather a prominent city too, but the Nile has gradually eaten away nearly a third of her. Situated not far from ancient Ptolemais,[8] she was once the capital of the Sayyids.[9] There are merely 9,000 people here today, including those belonging to a paper-mill owned by Mohammed Ali.

I visited the mill and inspected it in all its detail. Up to 700 people work here daily; their wages are calculated per output of yarn and per piece of paper fabric, which amounts to about 50 kopeks in paper money; a substantial daily pay for the natives. The interior is spacious and clean, the men neatly dressed, cheerful and healthy-looking, working so deftly as you would never expect from Arabs! How can it be related to the omnipresent poverty and other things you see and hear around yourself? Thus as you describe only those phenomena that present themselves before you, without forcing your views to conform to any previously formed opinions, you are occasionally bound to contradict yourself or waver in your definition of things, until finally a chain of experience learned over a long—alas, too long—time allows you to draw a positive conclusion.

We went to a Catholic monastery and were met by a man in a turban and half-Turkish, half-Arab dress, rather dandy: he was a priest, a Franciscan monk from Tuscany. The church is good, but their mass is too aberrant, although less so than what we had seen at St. Anthony's Monastery.

---

8 Ptolemais Euergetis (also Fuyyum).
9 It is not clear what Kovalevsky has in mind here. Possibly the reference is to the fact that the city was a seat of Persian governor during the Sassanian period.

There are black spots in the sheer cliffs of sandstone that accompany the flow of the Nile, and sometimes one can see pillars there: these are ancient necropolises or caves where the Christians once hid themselves from persecution; a great many of these caves have witnessed the martyrs suffer painful deaths. It is sad to think that in the era of horrible disasters, at its very birth, Christianity was spreading wider and faster than today, in the time of complete religious tolerance.

Our Consul General has an agent in Keneh for the patronage of Russian Mohammedan *hajjis*, the pilgrims who usually travel from thence to Mecca via Cosseir.[10] The agent is a Coptic merchant who acts as an agent for most nations. Keneh is situated half an hour away from the Nile, on the bank of a dirty canal, and there is nothing good to be said about it.

At last the dull groves of the date-palm, *Phoenix dactylifera*, have been livened up by the emergence of a new variety of the palm-tree, *Cucifera thebaica*, known in these parts as *doum*. This is the only palm-tree that is twiggy; it produces quite a rich shade and has bright, green-yellowish foliage; its leaves, wide and pointed, stick up in bunches; its fruit, large and with a core in the middle, is filled with pleasant liquid while itself having an astringent taste.

We visited the ancient city of Thebes, as well as Luxor and Karnak,[11] and the tired soul awoke once again . . . I no longer thought that anything would be able to astonish me to such a degree. Wilkinson[12] is almost right in saying that these are the largest and the most glorious ruins of the ancient and modern times. Champollion Jr.,[13] in awe of the marvelous sight of these ruins, exclaims, "I shall refrain from describing anything here; my images would either fail to achieve even one-thousandth of what they should be or indeed, were I to present a mere light sketch devoid of colors, I would be thought a zealot or possibly a madman."

---

10 El Qoseir, a port city on the Red Sea in eastern Egypt.
11 Thebes is the Greek name for the ancient Egyptian city of Waset; Luxor is a major city in Upper Egypt; and Karnak is an ancient Egyptian temple complex in Luxor.
12 Sir John Gardner Wilkinson (1797–1875), British traveler and writer.
13 Jean-François Champollion (1790–1832), French scholar and founder of modern Egyptology, best known for his work on deciphering Egyptian hieroglyphs.

In this chapter I shall forego a detailed description of ancient Thebes: the city requires thorough study, and on the way back, I shall dedicate a few days to its exploration and possibly a few pages to its description. Presently, let me give you a sketch of the pharaohs' holy city.

A series of Sphinxes runs along the road from Luxor to the ruins of the temple and the palace in Karnak: an entire street of Sphinxes, all enormous in size, capable of dwarfing any of their European replicas if one were to put them next to each other; yet it is all corrupt, disfigured, half-buried in sand. One enters Karnak amidst pylons, quite preserved and covered with hieroglyphs from top to bottom. Thereupon on one's right there emerges an entire row of pillars, the size of which no-one would ever dare attempt to achieve today; the bright strip of the Nile shines through them, spangled with the rays of the setting sun, and further beyond is Thebes, the City of a Hundred Gates, so battered and scattered that one can hardly make out its remains. Only the so-called statue of Memnon[14] and another one stand by the necropolis, the field of death.

All that is situated under a marvelous, transparent sky, against whose horizon copses of palm-trees are vividly outlined; it is here, near these majestic ruins, near these magnificently pensive faces of the Sphinxes, under the breeze of omnipresent mystery, that these palm-trees truly belong.

Let us turn to Karnak. From the walls that have been preserved in many places; from the hundreds of pillars that are still standing, supporting enormous capitals; from the obelisks of which but one has retained its primaeval beauty, the rest having been reduced to mere rubble and plinths—from all that you can readily imagine the whole: one room is nearly equal in size to St. Peter's Church in Rome! Also present are heaped stones, striking in their immensity and clearly showing how the room used to be furnished. There are no Arab huts here (except those clinging to the place on the left side, in the manner of swallow nests), which affords you the opportunity to embrace the entire site of the ruins in one go. Not so in Luxor. You have to search for the walls of the temple over an entire Arab village where they have been placed:

---

14 The Colossi of Memnon, the twin statues depicting Pharaoh Amenhotep III.

прильнувшихъ съ лѣвой стороны, въ видѣ ласточкиныхъ гнѣздъ, и это дастъ возможность обнять все мѣсто развалинъ съ одного раза. Не то въ Луксорѣ. Вы должны отыскивать стѣны храма по всей арабской деревнѣ на

которую ставятъ ихъ тамъ примкнута изба, тамъ высится голубятня; комната древней гробницы служитъ жилищемъ цѣлой семьи; подъ портикомъ помѣщается хлѣбный магазинъ паши.

В Луксорѣ поражаетъ васъ обелискъ: это лучшій какой мнѣ случалось видѣть; другой, соотвѣтствующій ему, находится въ Парижѣ; примѣчателенъ также ги-

here is a hut adjoined to it, there rises a dove-cote; the chamber of an ancient tomb serves as a dwelling for a whole family; a bread store owned by the Pasha sits under a portico.

In Luxor you are amazed by an obelisk—the best of all I have ever seen; another, similar to it, is in Paris; also of note is a giant Sphinx. Like Karnak, Luxor consists of a number of monuments, the earliest of which belong to the time of Amenhotep III, the latest to that of Ramses. More rows of pillars, scattered here and there, oppress with their mass the poor village whose site they occupy; many are half-buried under drifts of sand and rubbish, some overgrown with prickly shrubs and scanty grass. There is no trace of a bridge to be seen, however—one that would link this part of the city to that on the right and to the necropolis; if a bridge did exist then it was probably a pontoon one, although it seems more likely that they used to cross the Nile in boats.

Chapter VI

Almehs[1] in Esneh and, Generally, Women in the East

We seem to have already happened to note that in the reign of Mohammed Ali, the people of Egypt are given quite an insubstantial role to play in the general government system of the country; on the other hand, the Arabs have always suffered the same fate under any conquerors; it is written in the stars, they say with remarkable self-sacrifice. All posts, even secondary ones, are taken over either by Turks; or by former Circassian slaves; or by Mamluks, a name applied to any white slaves; or indeed, by Greeks or Armenians. Egyptians of all colors and various tribes serve in the army as soldiers or as low-rank officers, their village-dwelling folk being *fellahs*,[2] poor *fellahs* . . . Meanwhile, many of them are educated at schools, oftentimes even abroad, and yet they are never appointed to any administrative posts. Then again, they are hardly capable of anything else. The Egyptians have no self-confidence whatsoever, neither will-power nor character, not a shade of personal dignity or self-respect. Could that be a consequence of the never-ending deprecation and slavery they have long been subjected to? Upon completing

---

1 Female entertainers, dancers, and singers in Islamic Egypt.
2 An agricultural worker or farmer in Egypt.

a course of studies, Arabs, Berbers, Copts, and other natives are sometimes hired as teachers at schools; or more frequently, as translators and interpreters to serve Mohammed Ali and his Pashas; and finally, as manufactory foremen. At the very most, they can be entrusted with the running of a manufactory, a steamboat, or another small vessel.

If such are the circumstances in which the male part of the Egyptian population lives, then its female part—seen as a lower species in the East in general and, especially, in the Mohammedan East, often excepted, or at least exempt, even from prayer and other religious rites as undeserving and deprived of God's attention—the females are diminished in Egypt more than anywhere else. The aristocracy (that is, the Turks) take wives from their own circle or, more often, marry slaves from the mountains of the Caucasus, from Greece, or from Abyssinia. The whiteness of the body is a necessary attribute of beauty for a Turk; native women, with no exception or differentiation, all belong to the lowest class of the population. However, many among them are pretty: they are tall, slender, well-built, and brown, ash, or swarthy in color, depending on the tribe they belong to, with excellent white teeth, their features smoothed-out rather than harsh, and so very different from Nubian and Sennaar faces, as we shall see later. They age early: many are married at 10 years of age, or at 8 in Sennaar. Women cover their faces in towns but rarely do so in villages. Apathy and laziness are characteristics common among them, as well as among men.

Some French writers have spread the opinion that lack of education, fanaticism, and intolerance in the East depend primarily upon the absence of women in society, upon their confinement and slavery. I shall attempt to refute such an opinion. Firstly, a woman in the East is not a slave—a fact that those who take it upon themselves to write about these matters should have learned by now, unless they ascribe too wide a meaning to the word *slave*. Women leave their houses whenever they like; they go out or ride out, depending on their circumstances; they go to bath-houses and bazaars; they visit their female friends without asking their husbands' permission and certainly without being accompanied by them. To go out unaccompanied by a man is as improper for them as it is for our women to go out alone: it is a prejudice, a superstition, which, like any other, is of no significance or consequence. Moreover, a husband, upon seeing *babouches*[3] left by his wife's visitors at the entrance to her room, will never take the liberty of coming in or asking the names of the guests. A woman follows her heart when choosing her acquaintances, quite without taking into account her husband's *interests*, and no husband has ever dared use her as a device for the achievement of his aims, even though it would be one of the most efficient means in the East; and it is only by force or by too cleverly conducted intrigue that one can take a woman out of someone else's *harem*. In a *harem*, a woman is surrounded by all manner of pleasures, even by luxury if her husband be wealthy. The husband himself, always modest in his desires, lives in rooms sparsely furnished with a bare *divan*; he dresses simply, spends no money on himself, and sacrifices everything for the decoration of the *harem*: it is his heaven on earth, where he spends most of his spare time. It is only Europe-obsessed Turks that seek entertainment in company. Add to this life at least some color, some emotional energy rather than pure sensuality, and you shall see what meaning the domestic, internal life of the Oriental woman *could* take on, centered as it is round a single subject—for here, just like in our land, it is no more than a conventional division of tasks between husband and wife. The husband is burdened with public responsibilities when his station in life is on the same level with them, or he is busy providing for the family when this work suffices to fully occupy him; whereas the wife is given the best but also the hardest part: she looks after the family and takes care of the husband, ensuring that domestic bliss rewards him for his labors, sufferings, and all manner of hardship, for the never-ending struggle that he conducts in this whirlwind of the world, whilst she, the Oriental woman, enjoys peace within her family.

The accusers, those who speak of the imaginary slavery that the Oriental woman is being subjected to, should also bear in mind what sufferings, what excruciating passions she evades! Ask many of our women who have devoted their lives to society: What have they gained from it, and what have they relinquished there? The sincere answer would be as follows: they have gained early signs of aging and nervous

---

3 Slippers, North African and Middle Eastern footwear.

ailments, having relinquished some part of their rent hearts and their often tarnished names . . . How happy they would be to have never known their society. Listen to the words of one of the most intelligent women, a French author: "The burden of conventions, hypocrisy, and coercion that a woman has to carry is capable of killing the most fervent soul: she is a slave to society, a slave to her husband, a slave to her duties, and for all that, she has no rights but the right to men's feigned worshipping, which should insult any intelligent woman, having at its core either concession for her weakness or an attempt against her honest name. I repeat: she is a slave, just as she was a thousand years ago, the only exception being that she is now aware of her slavery," &c. Here is another voice, a quieter and simpler one, yet none the less convincing for that, belonging to a Russian author, a maiden: "No creature is as tied and enslaved by conventions as a maiden, the retributive power of society lying the heaviest upon her. It behoves her to live with a carefree smile on her lips, whilst her life is no use to herself or to others, having neither purpose nor occupation." These are not empty phrases but a voice that has burst from the depths of the heart in a moment of sincerity. It is a fact inscribed in blood by the heart, written into the record of the woman's sentence, and hence I quote it here as evidence of my words.

I do not in the least wish to proselytize that the woman should be banished from society, and yet, firstly, I believe that she already has other duties, too great, important, and sacred, and that in dedicating herself to society, she makes a sacrifice that it cannot give her due credit for. Secondly, some might say that it is this sacrifice that purifies society, and that it is therefore necessary. I shall refer them to one of the most enlightened nations, which knew how to achieve its high aims without participation of women—and what is more, at a time when the entire world was more or less benighted. I am talking of Mohammedan Spain in the times when it was ruled by the Arabs, upon whose exile the clergy publicly burned 1,200,000 books in Córdoba alone! There are scarcely so many books in Spain today—in Spain, whose caliphs demanded books for peace and fought for enlightenment! . . . In those days the woman played among them almost the same role as she does in the East today, whilst elsewhere in Europe she was already praised and idolized.

Consider the above question from another, more material point of view: the participation of women in society engendered thousands of crimes in France alone. In 1847, 20 women were tried and convicted in Turkey, and 18 in Egypt. Do you still believe that women soften mores? All or nearly all of them were tried for *harem* crimes, for adultery, which is not even an indictable crime in our society, or for poisonings that had been caused by jealousy. True, those *harem* crimes can at times be horrible, but have stories like that of Lafarge[4] and similar others not unfolded before our eyes?

I repeat: I am not a persecutor wishing to rid society of women—far from it; yet I am quite convinced that it is not their absence that causes ignorance in the East: when all is done, the Turks used to possess, and some still do, high virtues even without them. I am also convinced that the Oriental woman is neither a slave nor an eternal sufferer; often she is even capable of influencing public matters, which can be observed in present-day Constantinople, at the very palace of the Sultan . . . In some cases she is diminished, especially if one assumes the European point of view, yet the idea of her immunity is at the heart of the Mohammedan mores. Thus a criminal who has reached the threshold of the *harem* of his Sultan, or of any of his judges, is pardoned by law: he is under female patronage . . .

Should the discussion turn to the importance of education for Oriental women, however, we should completely agree with the idea, firstly, for the entirely natural reason that education is good for all nations and for both sexes, and secondly, because children, living as they do in a *harem*, remain under female influence for longer here than in the West. Some might say, "Oh, but the Quran is against female education"; that is one of the common-place facts Europeans are quite wrong to accept as true. No law-book is more agreeable than the Quran—it permits everything as long as you interpret it properly. Excellent proof of that is the present rule of Mohammed Ali: What has the Quran

---

4 Marie-Fortunée Lafarge (1816–52), a French woman convicted of poisoning her husband in 1840.

not permitted him to do, what has it not forgiven him for!? The Viceroy, as if wishing to show his triumph over the holy book, the Book of Books, decided, prompted by the indefatigable Clot Bey, to establish a school for the education of midwives, and now it is one of the best schools. Mohammedan women study medicine and anatomy; young girls, who until recently would never be so bold as to appear before a man without a veil, now keep their faces open as they listen to the most strange talk of the French; they also—oh triumph of triumphs—cut with their own hands the human body: the body, a sacred, untouchable thing, under a Mohammedan woman's knife! . . . Given all that, you cannot but agree that the Quran will permit anything; you only have to know how to deal with it, which skill Mohammed Ali has mastered to perfection. The Pasha was able to convince his clergy—the same clergy that, once strong, bestowed power upon him and won him the people's trust—that he would be much better at managing the valuable property of the mosques, and so he took it away from them, handing out to *mullahs* what he saw fit, as a charitable act, and thus gaining full control over them. In consequence, he left the mosques to destruction on the pretext that to touch a holy shrine with the unclean hands of workmen is a sin.

After all I have said, how strange it is to find *almehs* and *ghawazis*[5] in Egypt, two professions that have now merged into one, both in mores and in dress. The common level of convention, which applies to everyone except the Pasha, constitutes the condition and the law of life, being perhaps even more important than the Quran itself. There was a time when *almehs* and *ghawazis* paid the same taxes as all women of dubious virtue, which field of industry brought great amounts of money to the Viceroy. Depravity, especially in Cairo and Alexandria, exceeded any description. *Mullahs*, people quite set in their moral ways, and European consuls, indignant at the sight of temptation that would constantly present itself in full view in al-Azbekiyah Square, tried to persuade the Viceroy to stop this new kind of lease but to no avail. At last some Dervish resolved to do a brave deed. Hand in hand with an *almeh*, he went out on a road which the Pasha was due to pass; as soon as

---

5   Female dancers in Egypt.

the latter appeared, the Dervish took up a most alluring position with his companion. Mohammed Ali stopped for a moment; the Dervish went on with his business, paying him no heed ... Finally, the Pasha told someone to cover the couple with a *burnous* and proceeded on his way. Rarely one to allow the first feeling of anger to carry him away, he realized upon contemplation that he had no right to punish the Dervish, having himself encouraged depravity. Be that as it may, the Pasha, whether affected by the above occasion or prompted by the urgent demands of others, abolished the tax levied on the women, whereupon they were subjected to terrible persecution. Not only those who sold themselves but also those who had anything to do with the trade were driven out of Cairo; they were beaten and sent away to remote provinces; *almehs* and *ghawazis*, whom no religious celebration had previously excluded, were banished to Esneh. I know not why it was Esneh that was chosen as their abode, but it is here that they, being exiled convicts, are given a soldier's rations and even permitted to ply their former trade as dancers. Needless to say, they perform solely for curious travelers, for those who, striving with great avidity to learn everything in their long travels, reach Esneh with the sole object: to experience strong sensations which these women are capable of providing. Such is the nomadic tribe of travelers! They vanish at the second cataract, however, from whence they return home to proudly tell their stories of traversing the tropics, seeing the pyramids, crocodiles, Thebes, and *almehs*! ...

Nearly all the *almehs* and *ghawazis* of Esneh gathered in the house where we were staying. There were Syrian, Greek, Coptic women, and indeed, Sophia herself ... Sophia had once been a favorite of an *important person* and, despite her discovered infidelity, had been punished very lightly for it. Musicians were brought in; this kind of Oriental music is well known: creaking, buzzing, thundering, it includes divers drums, something akin to a one-stringed violin, and a pipe, sounding the better the more it makes one's flesh crawl. At first the *almehs* sang, and then two of them came forward and began dancing. They were dressed in short, rather rich gold-embroidered little jackets, merely fastened at the bottom and sleeveless; underneath, one could see transparent muslin shirts; their heads were decorated with gold and silver coins and threads, cascading through the locks of luxurious black hair; on their arms the dancers wore thick bracelets; their outfits were complemented by wide *salwars*,[6] flowing down like skirts. The dance of the *almehs* consisted for the most part in their poses, mimics, and the shaking of the bottom half of the body, and yet these movements were so lustful, so sinuous and full of bliss, trepidation, and emotion that it was indeed impossible not to wonder at them. Vivid and lustful though the dance of Gypsy women is, there is much wildness, much orgy in it, whilst *almehs* have more bliss, more calm. The difference is due to climatic reasons.

The *almehs* sang, drank, and smoked. Thus cheered, some of them were emboldened enough to perform the *Wasp* dance, or *nahle*.[7] The idea is that the dancer imagines being stung by a wasp and searches for it in her dress. An *almeh* came on stage; she dared not dance awhile, until at last, encouraged by songs, body movements, music, and hoots (which were growing ever louder and more frenzied), and warmed by wine, she burst into flames and, little by little, to the chants of *"nahle-egu, nahle-egu!"*—that is, "oh, wasp, oh, wasp!"—began searching for the fateful insect, shedding her dress . . .

It is not only the movements of the *almeh* that show her bliss and the luxury of her body. Her face is full of lust; her eyes languid, half-covered by the eye-lashes; her cheeks aflame; her lips half-opened. She is completely entranced by her own dance, enjoying its lust to the point of ecstasy.

There is another attraction in Esneh: a well-known temple with images of Zodiac.

The temple, which until recently was covered with rubble up to its very capitals, has now been cleared. Soil and rubbish have been taken out, not to show it in all its magnificence to the eyes of the traveler, of course, but rather to use the soil for the production of saltpeter. The portico of the temple has been marvelously preserved: it is supported

---

6 A type of trousers. In Russian, this garment is called "sharovary"; it was worn by different peoples within the Russian Empire.
7 Also *nahla* (Arabic), a bee.

by 24 pillars covered with hieroglyphs, all immense in size, which you can only see in the ancient buildings of Egypt. The present name of Esneh was read by Champollion in hieroglyphs. The Greeks called it Latopolis, apparently because there was plenty of fish called *lato* near it, in the Nile. The Copts call it Sna. Not far beyond Esneh, one can make out with difficulty the half-ruined pyramids of Kom-el-Ahmar.[8]

About two hours' journey from Aswan, steep, lifeless strata of sandstone cut into granite, which, upstream from Aswan, holds the Nile in, invades its bed, forming the first cataracts. Further upstream, the river often has to fight it in a manner much more energetic than that in which the Nile has hitherto fought against the sands of Libya.

Aswan is the last city in Egypt proper; it is situated in lat. 24°4′45″ N. and has always been of utmost importance to the country as a forepost separating it from savage tribes. The Romans had their garrison here; the Christians had their episcopate here in the early days of the spreading of the Christian faith; in the time of the caliphs, they had a famous academy here; today there is nothing but half-ruined houses with 5,000 inhabitants. What the plague and time had spared was destroyed by Nubian invasions. This is where the Egyptian army was first trained and formed, under the command of Suleiman Pasha (Sève),[9] who covered himself in glory with his many heroic deeds and audacious bravery during that reform.

It is not without reason that I refrain from talking about this man, whom I had known quite intimately. Let the enclosed portrait, a true likeness of him, speak for me, reader, if you accept that a man's appearance expresses his inner qualities.

This is where we abandoned the boat, and while the Governor arranged for our things to be transported on camels beyond the cataracts and for barques to be built for our subsequent voyage, we visited Elephantine and Philae,[10] glorious in the ancient times.

Elephantine consists entirely of Egyptian, Roman, and Arab monuments reduced to rubble; there is nothing here that one might use to

---

8 A village in Egypt on the site of the ancient city of Hebenu.
9 Joseph Anthelme Sève (Suleiman Pasha al-Faransawi, 1788–1860), French officer in the Ottoman service; recruited by Mohammed Ali; headed the military academy in Aswan.
10 Islands on the Nile, part of the city of Aswan, known for its archeological remains.

Элифантина вся состоитъ изъ обломковъ памятниковъ египетскихъ, римскихъ и арабскихъ; въ ней нѣтъ ничего, почему бы можно создать воображеніемъ цѣлое, какой-нибудь отдѣльный портикъ или даже колонну: тамъ кусокъ сфинкса, тамъ нога огромнаго размѣра, тамъ ба-

рельефъ; и все перемѣшано съ надгробными памятниками новаго кладбища, и можетъ быть рука Мемнона-Ра подпираетъ чалму на могилѣ правовѣрнаго!... Превратности всего свойственный востоку. Окрестная природа соотвѣтствуетъ этимъ развалинамъ. Горы изрыты, разметаны,

Portrait of Sève (Soliman Pasha)

re-create a whole from a part in one's imagination, not a single portico nor even a pillar: a piece of a Sphinx here, a giant foot or a bas-relief there, all mixed together with the tomb-stones of a new cemetery so that it is not unusual for Memnon-Rah's[11] arm to support a turban on a believer's grave! . . . Vicissitudes are the commonest thing in the East. Nature around the place is a good match for the ruins. Mountains are dug up, scattered, and eroded, yet you must not think that it was the flow of the Nile that, having broken through the cataracts, deformed the mountains—no, its bed had been prepared earlier, by another cataclysm.

We returned to Aswan. Aswan was previously known as Syena, a city famous for its stone quarries; the ancients believed it to lie on the Tropic of Cancer; they even said that there was a deep well here whose bottom reflected sun-rays at equinox.[12] But there is no trace of the well in Aswan, and it is in vain that one endeavors to find it here. It is difficult to imagine that the Greeks and the Romans (and even the Egyptians) could be so wrong in their location of the tropic; it would be more apt instead to position the city of Syena itself somewhat farther south. Magnificent ruins by the village of Kelyabshi, right below the tropic, justify such a supposition, especially considering that the famous stone quarry of Syena would still be situated nearby, except on the other side. Traveling from Aswan, one has to go round the cataracts by road; the distance is not great, about half an hour's journey; here, too, there are ruins and nothing but ruins! The barques were not ready yet, and the camels had not arrived. Taking advantage of spare time, we set off to visit the isle of Philae.

Philae is very beautiful. A small isle, it has a very well-preserved ancient temple dedicated to Isis.[13] There is a portico—not quite completed, as one can see—and an entire gallery of pillars! I shall describe it on my way back, when I shall deal solely with the description of antiquities. Pillars, temples, and pilasters vividly silhouetted themselves against a transparent sky. The Nile is quieter and calmer here, nature being more

---

11 A Greek mythical hero, an Ethiopian king. He was mistakenly associated with the Egyptian ruler Amenhotep III, and Kovalevsky repeats the mistake.
12 Here equinox is confused with summer solstice.
13 One of the central deities of the Egyptian pantheon.

luxurious than anywhere else hitherto. On the opposite side is the isle of Biche, covered also with ruins. This place was chosen as the setting for *One Thousand and One Nights*; indeed, there is enough room here for one's imagination to go wild. We spent the night in bivouacs, but on the following day, by means of threats, we brought all the authorities to a state of extreme activity. By about 8 A.M., everything was ready, and so sailing before a favorable light breeze, we proceeded forward.

CHAPTER VII

Nubia along the Nile

Nubia[1] is a land of "savage, strong people armed with enormous shields and swords," the ancients used to say. You shall not find such a country here, try as you might. All that is left of its ancient fame are the nakedness and black skin-color of its people. The Nubians are weak, lacking power, and rather humble. True, they are still armed with little spears which, moreover, are sometimes soaked in a vegetable poison; yet Mohammed Ali has subdued them to a great extent, and it is only very few villages that have succeeded in evading the taxes everyone has to pay, their inhabitants having removed themselves to distant mountains, out of reach of the soldiery.

The mountains come closer to the banks here. On either side of the Nile, strips of cultivated land stretch like two narrow ribbons, and a short distance past the Aswan cataracts, granite once again gives way to sandstone.

Towards the end of the day, the wind began to subside. How beautiful the evening was! The sun was setting down behind the Libyan mountains, which were engulfed in what appeared to be some kind of golden vapor; meanwhile, the peaks of the Arabian range opposite

---

1 A historical region stretching from Aswan in the south of Egypt to central Sudan.

were already darkening and frowning; the foot-hills were pale, of temper color, with palm-trees and shrubs of acacia—picturesque in their greenery, despite being rather unremarkable in daylight—standing out vividly against them. The sun having fully disappeared, there was only a bright-red stripe left after the sunset; against it, the Libyan mountains silhouetted themselves in sharp zigzag lines. The sky was a clean, lofty sapphire color, with not a single cloud on it; I even thought, *What a pity to see it so empty*; but then a star shone in the East, followed by another, and suddenly the sky was all a-sparkle. The night fell—it all happened quickly. Our four *dahabias*[2] easily glided along the smooth waters of the Nile, the sails barely filled with a light northerly wind. All round us was silence; the Arabs sat, their heads hung down, as if the night was bending them to the ground, causing them more anguish than the day. How different they are from the nomadic Kyrgyz[3] of Mongol tribes, or even from the negroes, who would be able to appreciate the beauties of such a night to the full, spending it under the star-shooting sky without sleeping a wink. Indeed, the night was beautiful; everything on the Earth was mysterious, half-dark, as if the Earth was saying: "This is better, I can see the sky better now."

Why, then, do I, like an Arab, wistfully gaze into the night, dissecting it as if in an anatomy lesson? Time was I used to know how to describe such nights, how to spend them, how to enjoy them! Yes, I can comprehend the exquisite artistic nature of the divine effect of this night, but my soul is silent! Truly, I know not why. Presently someone on one of the barques commenced murmuring a Russian song. Oh sadness! I believe the air is dry here; and although one cannot say that it is hot, one's lungs would not absorb the air willingly, not even after a sultry day, as they would absorb the coolness of Neapolitan nights. There now, is that so? It must be so . . . Everything is asleep. The lights have gone out on the barques, and we are sailing forth, quietly and invisibly, like the spirits in magic fairy-tales. Sleep will not come—what a pity. A bitter thought moves heavily inside my breast, wishing to express itself.

---

2 A river boat.
3 In the 19th century, the Russians referred to ethnic Kazakhs as "Kyrgyz," whereas contemporary Kyrgyz were called "mountain Kyrgyz" or "Kara-Kyrgyz."

What good is it!? Proceed with your story without delay and tell us some facts, says the reader. What do we care for your dreams? ... Yes, let us proceed. Be patient, my gentle reader. Tomorrow, tomorrow! The moon has now risen; it is about midnight now: time to go to sleep. You, too, should go to sleep if you are able to do so peacefully. Sleep is a good thing.

On the day following, we crossed the tropic line near the village of Kelyabshi, in lat. 23°37′44″ N. Balbi[4] is correct to note that the Tropic of Cancer is the hottest and the most difficult to inhabit. To our right, there were some ruins and, farther along, a magnificent entrance to caves.

It was the 15th (27th) of January. The sun was scorching. Past the tropic, there is no night dew any more, and it never rains beyond the belt of seasonal rains, which commences at about 20°. The only irrigation comes from the Nile, whence *sakhiehs* raise water day and night for the purpose of watering the fields; the air is very dry.

We climbed the Libyan mountains, which lock in the Nile extremely tight. Their peaks constitute a large stony plateau; there are no signs of life around: not a single blade of grass, not a single animal! We asked the native Nubians how far this stony desert stretched and whether it reached the sands. But who ever goes there, they answered, who knows? ... Meanwhile, the Bedouins[5] of the Libyan oases pass through these mountains in certain places, in search of water and coolness on the banks of the Nile. Indeed, some people, as I have already mentioned, use the mountains as their place of habitation: negroes, escaped slaves, whom anyone capable of overbearing them captures and sells back into slavery, and Nubians who hide themselves here temporarily from the payment of taxes and from Egyptian soldiers ... and yet it is true that animals themselves are afraid of these mountains!

Now and again you can hear a shrill screeching sound from the bank, produced by *sakhiehs* and *shadoofs*, this last being similar to the water-raising "crane" pump we have in the Ukraine. A long pole goes through a beam, with a water-skin or some other vessel on one of its ends and a

---

4 Adriano Balbi (1782–1848), Italian geographer.
5 Nomadic Arabs, the inhabitants of the deserts of North Africa and the Middle East.

stone, used as a counter-balance, on the other. The water is scooped by hand out of one basin and into another and thus to a raised bank where the crops are. A *sakhieh* is similar in its mechanism to that employed for the dredging of canals. A number of ropes hang off a vertically installed wheel, with two rows of pots attached to them. When one row, consisting of empty pots, is lowered, the other one rises, emptying its full pots into a special basin. Thereupon it stops. The mechanism is very simple and useful; it is operated by bulls or horses. Its object is the same: to bring water from the Nile up and onto the level of crops. Harvest comes soon: barley, for instance, takes less than two months after sowing to grow completely ripe. They reap two or three harvests a year, depending on their labor; all they need to do is water the field perpetually; the sun works hard.

Where the riverside mountains are low or narrow, the sands of the desert are transported over them to the fertile banks of the Nile, replacing any vegetation in some places, spreading devastation and death. A rare single palm-tree of a mimosa bush can survive; but still, it shall all soon be swallowed by the sweeping sands.

How vividly the ancients[6] expressed the struggle of the elements in the three-fold myth of Osiris, Isis, and Typhon. To Egyptian priests, Osiris was the Nile and Isis was the Earth. The horrible Typhon was the epitome of the desert, hurling masses of sand onto the banks of the Nile and thus burying the latter. Hence the eternal struggle between these gods. Osiris the ruler died by the hand of his brother, the monstrous Typhon. Isis, the spouse of Osiris, avenged his death by slaying Typhon and reigned as a sole queen.

Kiris is quite a jolly place on the right bank of the Nile. The valley is wide and covered with vegetation. Little houses or huts are scattered around in a motley fashion. We went inside many of them to find them as empty as those in Egypt. The wealthier ones have small courtyards paved with stone; to understand what a luxury it is, allow me to add that it is the yard itself that makes up the main dwelling. Leading off the yard is a blind alley taking you to the back wall of the house, which you must walk round before you can find the door. The owner apparently

---

6 Author's note: Heliodor, *Aethiop I*, IX.

wishes to conceal the door from the gaze of the curious, yet it is all so miniscule that even a child would not be lost in this imaginary maze. Inside the hut, there is a bed made of clay, a niche in the wall to keep pigeons in, also a knife and a jug—that is all they have in the way of household implements. A handful of straw serves as a roof while letting in light. Still, these cages are rather clean, unlike those in Egypt. Pariset[7] says that these dwellings are occupied by families together with bullocks and camels: in fact, were a camel to stick its head inside, the entire house would topple. Leaning against this cage is another, intended for the wife and children. In the courtyard, you shall find a large pot of barley or *dourra*:[8] this is the household stock from which to pay taxes. The Nubians themselves are modest in their needs, usually eating food straight from the field. There they have a little of everything, and at any time, there is something ripe, be it beans or barley, peas, lentils, or *dourra*. There is a large variety of grains and pulses, yet the quantities of it all are meagre, making one wonder how these people can survive while also paying their taxes. It is rare for someone to have five or six sheep and a camel. The reader will ask, "But where are their agricultural implements, such as harrows, spades, and axes?" They have almost none at all. What they do have is a kind of plough, although they would be better off without it. They usually make little holes in the soil with their hands, sowing a few seeds in each. The sun and the Nile—or, more precisely, the *sakhieh*, which, by contrast, works day and night—do the rest.

The Nubians have darker skin than the Egyptians, the latter being called—not quite justly—white, the former referred to as red. Both peoples—I mean *fellahs* here—go semi-naked; both differ little from each other except in their language. The Nubians, it must be said, are kinder, better than the Arabs. The Barbars, who inhabit Dongola,[9] are a loyal people, dedicated to their master, and therefore preferred to all others for employing as servants in Cairo and Alexandria.

---

7 Author's note: Étienne Pariset, *Mémoire sur les causes de la peste et sur les moyens de la détruire* (Paris: Baillière, 1847), 127.
8 Durra, a sorghum grain found in the dry regions of Africa and Asia.
9 A city in northern Sudan. The term *Barbars* most likely comes from contemporary Egyptian usage and denotes people of non-Arabic descent.

Christianity was originally brought to Nubia by St. Matthew the Evangelist, the Nubians remaining Christians until 1500. In Lower Egypt, the Christian faith was spread by St. Mark the Evangelist, whilst Abyssinia, which to this day remains more or less true to our church, was converted by St. Frumentius in the 4th century.

How deserted the Nile is. Sailing from Cairo to Aswan, we would see the occasional *dahabia*; upon leaving Aswan, all we have met in five days are three large barques with Sennaar slaves; note, however, that the water is low. Not a single fishing boat! People living on the banks, who often have nothing to eat, could be much helped by fish, but they have no fishing rods, let alone nets. Still, after each inundation of the Nile, they gather some small fish that remains there along with silt and scarcely even has a name: something full of bones and not good, similar to roach in our rivers.

At last, we saw a crocodile nearby. A giant animal, about three sazhens[10] long, it was basking on a sandy bank. A bird resembling a grey ibis, its constant companion on dry land, stood by on guard. The bird, frightened by our approach, must have awakened the reptile; the crocodile wagged its tail and plopped from the bank into the water. This bird is not the trochilus[11] described by the ancients, for the latter, if they are to be believed, provides the crocodile with special services, picking worms out of its tongue—which, as we know, sits very deep in its throat—and completing other similar tasks. Another bird, with a beautiful two-pronged tuft on its head and a curved beak, somewhat larger than a woodcock, is quite fit for this purpose.

Humboldt[12] notes that some crocodiles eat people, while others do not; that is true. The natives, aware of the habitation of cannibal crocodiles, take precautions there; but as far as other places are concerned, their carelessness is amazing, and they often pay for it. Children, animals of small size, calves, and donkeys fall prey to crocodiles the most frequently. Oftentimes a crocodile can overbear a bull. Wrapping its tail round the bull, the reptile drags it down to the bottom of the river to devour it there.

---

10   Approximately 20 feet.
11   Also the Egyptian plover; believed to have a symbiotic relationship with the crocodile.
12   Friedrich Wilhelm Heinrich Alexander von Humboldt (1769–1859), German scholar and traveler.

The inhabitants of ancient Ombis[13] domesticated small crocodiles. Their males fight a terrible war with their females. These last pay dearly for their love: firstly, it is accompanied by frightening tokens of crocodile tenderness, and secondly, the females know that the fruit of this love can fall victim to the males' insatiable voracity. Hence they lay their eggs in places that are most hard to reach, such as high banks, burying them in the sand and eliminating any traces round them. Another creature to prey on the eggs is the ichneumon. The ancients worshipped the ichneumon, and not without reason: it fights an irreconcilable war with the entire crocodile species. The Nubians eat crocodile meat after cutting out of it, immediately upon killing the animal, the mucus bags, and yet the pungent smell of mucus is strongly felt.

About three hours' journey from Korosko,[14] the Nile becomes locked in by the mountains and the sands so tight that any cultivated land is reduced to a mere slope of the bank—that is, a space of about two or three sazhens[15]—and beyond it, there is nothing but the desert, death, the Kingdom of Typhon! ... The Nile continues mostly thus. When you think of the population of Egypt and Nubia, all of them crowding its narrow banks with the exception of a few oases and the Delta, you are bound to ask yourself, What would become of this population, up to five million people in number, were the Nile buried under the sands of the desert ambushing it from all sides?—which would be quite likely were it not for the annual flood tides that clear the river-bed.

Right at Korosko, the Nile turns abruptly to the west, describing an arc, which is the reason why, even when the water is high and there is no danger of cataracts, travelers often leave the river and cut across the desert. Thus they gain about 10 days while also avoiding the second and largest cataract on the Nile, impossible to pass when the water is low, as well as several lesser ones.

The Great Nubian Desert used to be impassable in consequence of attacks launched by the Arabs, and therefore caravans would usually choose a route through the Dongola Desert (which we shall also learn

---

13 Ombos, contemporary Naqada.
14 A settlement on the Nile, about 200 miles south of Aswan.
15 Between 15 and 20 feet.

about on our way back), but these days, Mohammed Ali has an agreement with the Ababde[16] tribes which obliges them to guide and protect the caravans, thus making the route completely safe in this regard.

The above-mentioned circumstances allowed Korosko, a recently established settlement, to gain certain importance. This is a place for caravans carrying ivory, *senneh*,[17] and slaves (these last being nothing more than goods) to stop and load their cargo onto barques; a place whence they send camels laden with divers supplies for an army detachment stationed in the Sudan, as well as with merchants' goods—in a word, with everything that is brought to Korosko by water, the reason being, as I have already noted, the double necessity to cross the desert, how terrible soever it might be. Korosko is situated in a beautiful location and immersed in the greenery of its pastures, palm-trees, and *doums*, its little houses only coming into view when you approach them. There is much activity and life about the place but no pleasure at all! Where is it, then, if one cannot find it even here?

---

16 A subgroup of Beja; a nomadic people living between the upper Nile and the Red Sea.
17 Senna (*S. alexandrina*), a plant used for medicinal purposes and to make tea.

Chapter VIII

The Great Nubian Desert

An unearthly boom was echoing in my ears; I scarcely knew whether I was asleep or awake. A boundless steppe covered with snow stretched before me; a long chain of camels slowly moved along, one after another; there were snow drifts on the sides: a camel would fall and be thrown down into the snow chasm, then another, and another. But lo! The boom has subsided; now savage cries are heard from everywhere... Aha! I am in the mountains. Spuž is nearby; the Turks have made a sortie. With God's name on our lips, we launch ourselves at them; banging and shouting ensue; I shudder despite myself and wrap my head tighter. Then it all seems to quieten down. An attractive scene unfolds before me. A small village; a dappled, pretty little house seen through an overgrown thicket; a meadow nearby with a playful river running across it; I walk over a bridge, through the thicket and the meadow, approaching the pretty house, already able to hear jolly talk coming from it; someone is waiting for me there, someone is beckoning to me from thence, and here I am, about to step over the familiar threshold; when suddenly, a savage, penetrating roar shakes me to the very core... the jolly little house, the silence, the happiness—all gone; it was all but a dream! The only thing that would not subside upon my awakening was the roar . . . I came out of the tent. A hundred camels, on their knees, roared so horribly they could rouse the dead. They were being loaded.

What a roar, how the camel-drivers cry! It is worse than in the Kyrgyz steppe, those events having perhaps been forgotten by now, while this noise can be heard here in all its ominous savagery.

"*Geh, sheikh Abdel-Kader! Geh, sheikh Abdel-Kader! Ahmet! Bas-Boch! Bas-Boch! Yah, yahwolet! Sheikh Abdel-Kader!*" they cried all round. Abdel-Kader[1] is the name of the patron of caravans in these deserts, whom they never cease to summon for help.

The frenzy went on awhile. The Arabs argued amongst themselves about whose camel was more heavily-laden; some men from our party searched for the best dromedary, others did not know which one to mount, yet others did not know how to mount and looked in horror at that tower, which would kneel before a mere child, obsequiously offering its hump. Poor camel! The things people do to it all over the world, wherever it can be found!

"*Geh, sheikh Abdel-Kader!*" heard for the last time, the caravan commenced to move! It was the 20th of January (the 1st of February new style), 8 A.M., and yet the sun was scorching as it would never be in St. Petersburg, not even at the height of summer, when it is in its zenith—which, as we know, is a rare occasion for Petersburg.

The mountains would crowd together and then part again. Our caravan weaved between them like a ship maneuvering between underwater rocks, not touching a single one of them. As for the strange formations of sandstone in these mountains, which in many places reveal their volcanic origins, I have described that in a separate article.[2]

As we proceeded on our way, at first there were some signs of life: the occasional acacia-tree (but Lord, what a tree! Nothing but half-withered branches and spikes); a raven hovering over the caravan, although even that did not last as the bird turned back toward the evening; a cave with the tracks of a hyena still visible in it, although the hyena did not live in these waterless parts for long. On the morrow,

---

1 Likely a local Sufi saint.
2 See also addendum.

the desert presented itself in all the horror of destruction and death. Every 10 paces or fewer, we encountered carcasses of camels and bulls. Not a single worm, not a fly, not a blade of grass: it was as if there had never been any life here. The mountains, low, solitary, scattered, half-buried in the sand, bore a complete, astonishing resemblance to tombs. Situated on a vast sandy plain, they gave it the aspect of a cemetery. Never in my life have I seen anything more terrible! The sky was as empty as the earth—nay, emptier still, owing to the horizon being wider. The sun was scorching, the heat attaining 34 degrees Reaumur,[3] and during a 10 days' journey, we encountered only one watering-place, the water tasting bitter and salty at that, so much so that one drank it entirely out of necessity.

The caravan, which had been noisy and lively just yesterday, proceeded in silence, in depressed spirits, and in bodily exhaustion. Mirages were still only in the minds of those who had not seen them, but on the third day, when we came on to the so-called River of Sand, Bahr-el-Khattab, mirages stood before our eyes constantly, causing us more torture. There were lakes spreading all the way to the edge of the horizon; there were rivers flowing before us, with all the luxury of vegetation reflected in them, which made our thirst even more unbearable; our eyes were fatigued from straining and hurt by the brightness of the sands under the rays of the sun. The Arabs call the mirage a devilish apparition. Once, in a valley, as if in the sea, we saw some peculiar figures quivering in the shape of giants; at first we thought them a mirage, but they would not vanish or disperse at our approach, instead becoming smaller and taking on certain forms. After an hour's journey, we drew level with them; it was a caravan carrying the *harem* of the Pasha of the Sudan: wives and children sat on beds attached to the humps of camels, each with a little canopy, swinging as if sitting in a ship's bunks. A long camel ride is difficult at any time, but now it seemed unbearable. The camels, including dromedaries, are all one-humped here, and the position of a rider is akin to that of an Indian *fakeer*[4] spinning on the end of a sharp-pointed pole. In the course of my caravan journeys, I had never

---

3 42.5°C.
4 Fakir (also faqir), a Sufi ascetic.

ridden a camel, always having had a horse, and it was not until now that I was able to fully understand the words of general M., who had been with us on our expedition to Khiva:[5] were he to see a camel in a picture, he said, he would gouge its eyes. After a while, I was fortunate to find a donkey in the caravan and proceeded partly on its back and partly on foot, for how strong soever the Egyptian ass being might be, the animal, who was only given water every other day, would grow exhausted carrying me.

I understood the sufferings of Alexander the Great, who had traveled through the Libyan desert to worship Amon-Ra;[6] on the third day of his journey, however, the heavens sent him rain; heaven protected Alexander and, later, rewarded him by telling him that he descended from Jupiter; as for myself, all I was promised were the bitter consequences of a similar journey. Now I can see how the army of Cambyses[7]—on its way to destroy the temples that Hercules, Perseus, and Alexander the Great had worshipped—was buried under the scorching sands of Libya; I can see why caravans and travelers constantly perish in this so-called Great Nubian Desert, one of the most terrible deserts in Africa.

The *simoom*—or, as the Arabs call it, *khamasin*, which means "50"— blows for a period of 50 days in the months of April and May (not incessantly, of course, otherwise it would devastate the entire Egypt in 50 days). The *khamasin*, which can also suddenly swoop down at other times of the year, is almost always accompanied by deaths of travelers in the desert.

It is difficult to foresee the approach of the *simoom*. True, the air thickens in anticipation of it, assuming a purple color; blood rushes to the traveler's face; his eyes seem to be about to pop out of his head, and he feels dizzy; yet it all happens so quickly that men and animals, even though they know the signs perfectly well, scarcely have the time to fling themselves prone upon the ground and bury their heads in the sand, as deep as possible. Now the *simoom* seems to have passed safely, having covered the caravan with but a thin layer of sand. The

---

5 A campaign by Russian troops in Central Asia in 1839–40, led by V. A. Perovskii.
6 Amon (also Amun), an Egyptian deity, later merged with the sun god Ra.
7 Cambyses II (r. 530–522 BCE), known for his invasion of the Kingdom of Kush in what is today Sudan.

men and the animals rise to their feet; their parched lips are thirsty; everyone rushes to their *gherbe*—the water-holding skins—and . . . oh horror! There is not a drop of water left. The *simoom* dries out skins full of water in the blink of an eye unless they have been put away and covered with rugs or hidden in the ground; but we have already noted how difficult it is to foresee the approach of the *simoom*. Then the caravan, if it be a long way away from the nearest watering-place, finds itself in most miserable circumstances. Usually, here is what happens to it: the slaves, entire crowds of whom are being led across the desert, sit down on the ground in a circle and silently wait for death to come; the Arab guides calculate very precisely, often from experience, whether or not they can reach a watering-place with their supply of camel blood and thereupon act accordingly: if they can, then each kills his camel and sets forth without delay; otherwise, no-one is going to make a vain effort, and each of them, in a manner that is obedient and fatalistic, dooms himself to death. Thereupon the mysterious desert rings with the kind of songs that are usually sung to mourn the dead and with the kind of cries that accompany those departing for the other world: a scene more frightening than the silence of the negroes. The Turks, however, never die without fighting death—desperately, to the last moment of their lives. Being, for the most part, the owners of the caravan, they find somewhere between the bales a little water or wine while stocking up on camel blood also, then they choose the best dromedary in the caravan and ride toward the Nile; no-one resists them, for the Arab guides, even in their utmost desperation, never lose their respect for the master. During their ride, they mostly perish in great sufferings.

It is not the *simoom* alone that can cause deaths amongst travelers. Every year, there are several accidents in this desert that have nothing to do with the *simoom*. Most mountains and other places are named after their victims. Here is where the commander of the Sudan cavalry perished: his guide mistook one mountain for another and lost his way in the desert. And here is where 12 of Mohammed Ali's *kawasses*[8] perished: the guide set forth to search for a camel that had fallen behind; the *kawasses* waited for a long time; the Nile was already near, and anyone

---

8   Officers in the Ottoman army.

who has ever crossed a desert knows how avidly men and animals thirst for fresh water. The men had already traveled that route, and so they proceeded by themselves. Meanwhile, the guide returned; having found no-one there, he followed their fresh footprints; however, neither the *kawasses* nor the guide ever came back. They were later found at short distances from each other, the last one four hours' journey from the Nile. Such accidents are too numerous to recall.

Bodies stay uncorrupt for a very long time. There are, as we have noted, no beasts around, neither predators nor any other kind, nor any insects, so there is nothing to devour them. The bodies, desiccated by the sun, lie there as if alive, and one is often mistaken when seeing them from afar.

Here is a mountain called Habesha, or Abyssinian. Once, after a *simoom*, an Abyssinian slave woman was stranded here, amongst others. Other slaves patiently waited for death, but she, who was young and beautiful and used to enjoy, no doubt, a better life than the rest, was sorry to part with it. She waited for death in great pain and suffering. And then two *kawasses*, a Turk and a Circassian, happened to ride up on her. Together with their caravan, they, too, had been caught in the *simoom* but were prompt enough to save one *samsamieh*, a small water-skin, which they hid from the others, and then fled on their dromedaries. The Abyssinian rushed to them and wept, begging them, imploring them to take her with them. The Turk wavered.

"Listen," he said to his comrade, "if we carry her to Cairo we can sell her for 10,000 piasters."

"True," the Circassian said, "but if we share our water with her, all three of us might die."

"The Nile is not far," the Turk went on, "and we are accustomed to hardship . . ."

Upon realizing that the Turk had taken her side, the Abyssinian begged ever more passionately, addressing him alone. Desperation gave her more strength, eloquence, and perhaps, beauty. The Turk was touched and positively insisted on taking her with them.

"Very well," his companion said, apparently also wavering, "but you shall put her on your dromedary."

That might have been just what the Turk wanted. So forth they set. The Circassian, who rode behind, took out his pistols, shot the Abyssinian and then the Turk, who was not quick enough to whip out his own, and then, having taken the *samsamieh*, he safely reached Berber. They say that he himself used to tell the story to his people, adding that, even if he had to share the water only with the Turk, still it would not have sufficed and one of them would have had to kill the other; thereupon the mad Turk took on another drinker, one who was not used to hardship at all; and at any rate, he did a kind deed by killing both: he shortened the suffering of the Abyssinian whilst also departing the Turk to the other world not alone but in the company of a woman with whom he had fallen so in love that he was willing to die for her.

We traveled for 12 or 13 hours a-day without halting anywhere. The camels remained true to their monotonous, measured pace from daybreak to dawn and from the first halt to the last. As for forage and water, they could only see it from afar and only during mirages at that. They were given a couple of handfuls of *dourra*—a variety of millet—in the evening, and among the Arabs, only those who minded the camels had a handful of *dourra* a-day, even less, and nothing else. During the entire journey, they kept the same monotonous pace as the camels, with the guides walking ahead, never sitting down, never stopping. The heat did not seem to affect them—it was not even hot for them.

"Can it indeed be hotter?" one of our men asked an Arab.

The Bedouin laughed.

"Why, is it hot?" he said. "It is winter now, after all, although it is drawing to an end; it is different in summer."

"So how is it different?"

"So that we ourselves cannot walk in the desert in the daytime, but have to walk at night."

"It must be lovely here in summer, then; a pleasure still awaiting us."

It is during night passages that accidents beset caravans the most often. The Bedouin Arabs are not good at recognizing stars; they are guided by signs that have been placed on mountains, by the very position of some of the mountains, and finally, by the human and animal bones that protrude out of the sand or have not been buried in it yet.

In the darkness of the night, they cannot see their guideposts and oftentimes mistake one place for another, especially amidst the boundless sands. Mistakes are all the easier to make considering that sand hillocks are perpetually being transported from one spot to another, and it is not hard to see what consequences the slightest of errors can have.

I seem to have already happened to note that it is mostly the Arabs of the Ababde tribe who serve as guides. They say that if an Ababde crosses the desert once and drops a pin, then on the way back he will find it; otherwise he is not an Ababde. The Ababde are liars; like all Arabs, they like to boast a little, especially when talking of themselves. The thing is that, employed as caravan guides, they are inferior to the Kyrgyz. To a Kyrgyz, everything in the steppe is a sign: the stars, which he knows well; the incline of grass; the direction of wind; tombs that no-one else can tell apart amongst thousands of similar others, scattered across the steppe; and birds, migrating or stray. Day or night, he will lead you from one end of the steppe to the other, as if following a straight line. But what the Arabs cannot be excelled in is their ability to bear the labors of a journey. Approaching a halting-place, after a 13 hours' journey, after several such daily passages, the Arabs run ahead, dance, grimace, and play the clown. A Kyrgyz would never do that, even though anyone who has traveled in the steppe knows what hardship, what labor he is capable of enduring.

The Ababde were perpetually at war with other Arab tribes, especially with the Bishari.[9] Such is a fate shared by all nomadic peoples (Mohammed Ali having recently subdued them); yet the Arabs of these parts have less courage than some—although, of course, not many—Kyrgyz tribes. There are quite a few similarities between the two, however, as there always are between any nomads. Although both peoples are Mohammedans, they are very weak in their faith, the Arabs, living closer to Mecca, being somewhat more pious. Cattle is their only property. Settlement and agriculture are their horror, their scourge. Wild independence is their idol. Hospitality is conventional for both. Avenging an insult is a matter passed from one generation to another. The Kyrgyz are armed with bows, arrows, and long lances;

---

9 An ethnic subgroup of the Beja people.

the Arabs have small spears and swords, similar to those possessed by knights in the old days; both rarely have guns, and if they do, their guns mostly have fuses but no matchlocks.

The Bedouin Arabs are rather tall, well-built, and handsome. They differ from the *fellah* Arabs in all respects. The former are free. Although subjects of Mohammed Ali, they have negligible duties, and even those they easily find ways of evading. Mohammed Ali himself pays a certain sum to some of the Arab tribes for the safety of his frontiers and of Mecca pilgrims, while the Sheikh of the Ababde has the right to levy a tax on any cattle driven through the Great Nubian Desert, whether it be owned by Mohammed Ali or by merchants: three piasters per camel, one and a half per ass. The sheikhs of other tribes do the same in their own deserts. Meanwhile, the fate of the *fellahs* is such that I have hitherto been reluctant to talk about them in much detail. Upon studying the subject sufficiently closely, I might be likely to see it in a less grim light than at first glance. Travelers who have run across Egypt where it is easily passable have judged the matter and made their conclusions under the first impression or, more often, under someone else's influence, and therefore their opinions are so contradictory, so exaggerated and superficial as to make one, despite oneself, deal with the matter carefully.

Our guide, Ahmet, was a superior guide. A wealthy and noble Ababde, he was employed only on important occasions; nevertheless, he was half-naked; and come summer, it is but a small piece of fabric, hung where it belongs, that makes up his entire costume. His *ferdeh*,[10] on the other hand, was draped excellently, like the toga of some statue of Nero or Cicero, the Bedouins generally wearing it in a very picturesque fashion. Ahmet was well-built, his hair meticulously waved and besmeared with grease (that being an important part of the toilette of the entire half-naked Arab tribe, men and women without exception), and his body had enough fat on its bones. His features, the glint of his eyes, the liveliness of his speech, his gesticulation, and indeed, his

---

10 A garment Kovalevsky describes below as worn by men, draped around the body. Another account mentions *ferde*, a scarf worn by a woman. See John Petherick, *Egypt, the Soudan, and Central Africa* (Edinburg: William Blackwood, 1861), 109.

passion for money—all were strongly reminiscent of a descendant of the Jews. I have no space here to describe all the facts, references, and evidence that I gathered in those parts; but I shall find another occasion to state them separately, in order to confirm my theory that the Bedouin Arabs of the Ababde tribe and of the inner part of Africa descend from the Jews, those who stayed behind, fled Palestine, and settled in Egypt.

The guide walked ahead, wistfully humming a song, impromptu, true to the custom of all nomads. The song told, as always, of a woman, a camel, a night—it usually is night—and was, like most of them, very unharmonious.

"Ahmet, what mountain is this?"

"Mount Devil."

"Why is it called that?"

"One can hear the Devil play music here at night."

"Have you heard it?"

"Many times!"

"Is it good?"

"It is only pipes, and sometimes drums: a true Sabbath. Let it rot!"

"So why is there music here?"

"Long story."

"You have enough time to tell it, even if you were to start from Adam."

It is true that Arabs, whatever they are talking about, always commence from such a distant point that one hardly ever has enough patience to listen to the end, but in the desert you are ever so happy for time—if merely an hour—to pass without your noticing it. Usually you have to live that hour consciously, till the last second, and suffer till the last drop of patience. Every minute that remains ere the next halting-place will let you feel itself, as if wishing to say: you claimed once that you cherished me, you were willing to stop the sun in order to keep me, so there you are, the sun standing still right above your head, you are free to live your life and enjoy me, here I am in my entirety, long as well as dull . . .

And so Ahmet began, but he did so and continued in a much more protracted way than I shall now speak.

Once upon a time, there was a Devil who lived in the Sudan, and his life had been full of jaunty escapades—until he married! Then it took a bad turn. It is said that Mohammedans treat their women as if they were nothing, an object, a piece of rubbish; that is only how things appear to be, whereas in reality a woman is always a woman, and if she wanted to take a man in hand, she could do so with anyone, be he a Turk or Satan. There are numerous examples of that in history; this one has not entered its annals yet. So bad it was for the Devil that one night he left the blessed land of the Sudan and fled, rushing headlong for a place to which his better part would never be able to follow him, the Great Nubian Desert, which in those days had the same name and was just as frightening as it is now. It was not until he got here, to this mountain, that he stopped for a moment to catch his breath and, glad to be far from his wife now, threw a party for himself, which could be heard at the other end of the desert. A scholar from Cairo was passing by just then. He had been walking for a long time and so, out of fatigue and hunger, he resolved to join the noisy party, how suspicious soever it might have seemed to him in the middle of the desert, for hunger gives courage even to scholars. The Devil was glad to have a visitor; he was, you see, a sociable Devil, and loneliness bored him. They began asking one another questions: how, why, and whence?

"I come from Cairo," the *effendi* said.

"And I am going to Cairo," said the Devil. "How is life there?"

"Bad! My wife never gives me a moment of peace. I have left her!"

"There you are! And I have fled the Sudan to leave mine."

Misfortunes are known to bring people close to one another, although it used to be less known that they could bring the Devil close to man. At a jolly supper, the evil one offered the *effendi* a deal.

"Let us go to Cairo," said the Devil, "and make our acquaintance with women. I shall possess one after another, choosing the most noble and wealthy ones, depend upon it, so that you could exorcise me with your incantations. I shall obey and leave my dwelling-place, only to move to another, even more exquisite place, and you shall earn money for your art. It shall be a truly gay adventure."

The scholar was a clever fellow. He hesitated, making as if the deal was not to his liking; he cited complications due to arise from his conscience, his wife, &c.; he went on about all sorts of things that one always says when making a deal with the Devil; and in the end he agreed. The Devil did not even demand the *effendi*'s soul for himself, either being a kind Devil or not caring for such an acquisition. Indeed, what the Devil would he need an *effendi*'s soul for? You can buy one for a few pennies in Egypt.

Aided by Satanic powers, our travelers promptly transported themselves to Cairo. The Devil began his debauch. First of all he possessed a vizier's daughter. The maiden went berserk; the entire household was in turmoil. They went in search of a healer and found our *effendi*, who cured her completely, as if by magic. The Devil leapt out of her pretty little body—only to transport himself into another, an even better one—more developed, luxurious, full of languor and fire—in which he then lived as if in his element. I forget whose body that was; however, the *effendi* drove him out of it too without batting an eyelid. In a word, they were making remarkable progress. The *effendi* was showered in money and lived without a worry in the world.

Finally the Devil, how stupid soever he might have been, realized that he was working for someone else, dutifully and selflessly. He went to the *effendi* to reason with him, to persuade him that the money earned should be shared fairly. But the learned scholar—who was, true to the Turkish habit, in a hurry to take his pleasures from life, knowing that the morrow would not be his to enjoy and seeing that his partner was of no more use to him, having already visited all the wealthiest families—the learned scholar refused him bluntly.

"Very well," said the Devil, "I shall be able to destroy you. None of your riches shall help you."

And so he possessed the Sultan's favorite wife.

The *effendi* could see what he was up to and, guessing that this time the Devil would never agree to leave his dwelling-place, fled. But the poor man was caught and told that he would be beaten until he drove the evil spirit out of the Sultan's wife—or until he died.

The scholar humbly appeared before the Devil, he begged him and implored him, he promised him not half of his riches but all of them, yet he pleaded in vain: the Devil resolved to take his revenge.

"Very well," said the scholar, "I shall perish, that is true, but you, too, shall be in no less trouble."

"How so?"

"Upon fleeing Cairo, I encountered your wife, who was seeking you and asked me to tell her your whereabouts. I told her everything; she is not far."

The Devil jumped out of the Sultan's wife body and fled, rushing headlong, while the *effendi* began enjoying life once again, having hired his own wife out to some poor man at a substantial gain in money.

"But why the music on the mountain? And why Mount Devil?" I asked, having already forgotten the beginning of the story.

"Why," said Ahmet, "the Devil had a bivouac here and feasted with the *effendi*—and ever since, the music has been echoing around the mountain."

"Right, right!"

Lord, how hot it is! How thirsty we are! And what we are obliged to drink! Half-way to our destination, at the bitter-salty wells of el-Murat[11] we filled our *gherbe* with water; but on the third day this water (which was barely drinkable to begin with), having been churned in the skins together with salt (which had melted under sun-rays), took on a disgusting smell, taste, and color. Take a glass of clean water, mix in a couple of teaspoons of mud, add salt and one part of a rotten egg, infuse it all with wormwood, and you shall obtain the kind of water similar in all respects to the kind that we had recently been drinking in the desert.

This drink and the heat, to which we had not yet become accustomed, made the skin of our faces and bodies go blotchy with red spots.

I have not told you the names of our bivouacs: for what use would they be to you, those names you would forget immediately! Besides, you can find them on the map. The route through the desert was determined by me geographically, the elevations measured by means of a barometer, as much as the heat and thirst permitted.

---

11 An important source of water on the trade route across the Nubian Desert.

Of course there is scarcely—if I may so express myself without sounding indelicate—in a word, there is scarcely a *human being* who would conceive the idea of visiting the Great Nubian Desert; yet a traveler might find himself in a situation similar to mine in a different part of the world, and it is to him that I offer the following advice: never use any strong remedies at the beginning, but instead save them for the future; how poorly soever you might feel, bear in mind that it shall be even worse toward the end. For instance, if you feel dizzy with heat, simply raise your hat; the slightest wind, the quivering of the air, inevitable in the desert, should suffice to cool you down to begin with. Later, when it no longer helps, you can use eau-de-cologne for a while, but when that, too, fails, as it is certain to do, then you can sniff spirits, and finally, as a last resort, should you have protracted fainting fits, use blood-letting. Otherwise you shall become accustomed to strong remedies, subsequently rendering them ineffective. You never feel hungry in the desert, for fatigue and thirst kill any appetite, but you would pay any money for an orange, a pomegranate, or a lemon; therefore, lay in a stock of all that in Cairo. A month's journey shall not spoil it, as the extreme dryness of the air seals the peel tight and dries it out like parchment. Tea, the most reliable thing to quench thirst, constitutes the only food and the best drink, how bad soever the water may be. Who has not experienced its wholesome effect! When a traveler, frozen to the bone on a winter journey, enters the room of a station master, the sight of a boiling samovar alone suffices to revive him, its gay burbling awakening pleasant thoughts, and the poor wanderer feels life return as the healthy liquid flows into his blood to warm it up!

My skin was so dry in the Great Nubian Desert that it seemed to come off the body; my head was burning; I had a high fever; yet after a few cups of hot tea I would revive. He who first introduced the consumption of tea was a truly kind-hearted man, and what a pity that his name is not known to grateful posterity. As early as in the 3rd century, the Chinese were drinking tea to their heart's content. One cannot recall without horror that we were all but deprived of this wholesome drink for a long time: in the 18th century, the Chinese, despite all the signs of displeasure shown by the Russian Embassy in Beijing, forced a few boxes of tea on them; the Russians were about to throw it away, but some shrewd Muscovites, having tasted the brew properly, were able to give it its due. It was not that long ago, and now Russia receives about 10 million pounds of tea, while another 50 million pounds is sent to Europe, where tea was introduced by the Dutch at approximately the same time, and to America.

So great were our thirst and disgust caused by the liquid kept in the *gherbe* that, upon our arrival at the last bivouac, we sent a courier to the Nile for water, so that the time when we could drink as much as we wanted would come sooner, if only by a few hours. Just after 9 A.M., as the heat was becoming unbearable, we met the courier carrying water, followed by a vulture. That was the first creature we saw after a 10 days' journey: birds of prey are always the first to meet man, be it on land or sea, and the last to abandon him, accompanying him to his grave and staying there long after his friends and family are gone. Avarice is always more patient than affection.

Reader, you can imagine our joy when we made it to the water. No, you cannot imagine it unless you have experienced circumstances similar to ours. On the 29th of January (10th of February), at about 2 P.M., we saw a vague blue stripe on the horizon . . . that was the Nile. Soon some little grey houses appeared, as well as copses of palm-trees (*Phoenix dactyilifera*) and *doums* (*Cucifera thebaica*), those inseparable companions of the Nile's banks in Nubia: it was the village of Abu Hammet . . .[12] That was not, however, quite the end of our sufferings. True, we were not to leave the wholesome Nile again for long, nor to have any shortage of water; but we still had to travel to Berber—a four day's journey—on camels or donkeys. In different circumstances, such a journey would be no trouble, but the weak condition in which we all were and the heat, 30 degrees Reaumur,[13] did little to facilitate it.

Let us halt for a moment and once again cast our eyes back, how frightening soever what is behind us may be. Now we can observe in a calmer manner that which previously evoked nothing but a painful feeling.

---

12 A settlement on the Nile at the end of the Nubian Desert trade route.
13 37.5°C.

The Arabs still have a custom that they follow eagerly, for it brings them a few piasters. At the exit from the mountains into the desert, by the so-called Waterless River, they erect tombs for every traveler, mourning his imminent death with howls and chants. The traveler, as if asking for their protection and patronage, throws them a few coins, thereupon they scatter the stones of the tomb and then proceed forward, singing and dancing gaily.

The Nubian Desert is a tomb, a dead tomb, in a manner of speaking, devoid as it is of the slightest elements of life that any other tomb possesses. But has there ever been any life here, and can there ever be any? Those are the questions that inevitably occur to anyone crossing the desert, anyone whose mind is able to produce any question at all.

The ancient Egyptians, who bequeathed us the giant monuments that cause the most fervent of imaginations freeze, brought no life hither. Indeed, had life happened to arise here in some random fashion, they would have destroyed it. They needed the desert, which was a safer stronghold against the incursions of the ancient Ethiopians than the first cataracts at Syena. There are no signs of antiquity anywhere to be seen, and according to everyone I have spoken to, there are indeed none. The only thing that exists, a day's journey from el-Murat, on the right, toward the Nile, is a cavity hewn from granite, but that belongs to a later epoch, perhaps that of the caliphs' rule; it was probably made by some pious Mohammedan rather than by the government. Wherever there is water in the desert, one can even now find wells dug out by private persons, either to honor a promise or out of zeal. There are also a few wells, extremely deep, and a few tanks, built at a great expense, which belong to the reign of Mohammed Ali; but alas, all the expense was in vain, for there is not a drop of water in any of them. The seasonal rains come here sometimes, but only once in 10 years or so; there having been none in the last six years. But when they do come, nature advances in all its beauty. Quick-sands, mountains with not a foot of alluvial soil to be seen on them, and plains—everything is covered with vegetation; meadows, tanks, and caves are filled with water to last two or three years. Arabs flock hither in their numbers, bringing their cattle with them, jostling, fighting for land—the same land that they had previously evaded—beasts and birds arriving even sooner. A new world is created quickly, but it does not last long! . . . The red-hot sun destroys it in two or three months, especially considering that dew is unheard of here; it is only caravans that take advantage of the rainy season for a long time afterward, finding water in hollows and tanks situated in certain places.

So this desert is not doomed to eternal death! If nature is capable of extracting it from the hands of death in such a short time, then man, too, is able to achieve the same by virtue of labor and time.

The reader will remember that the route across the desert, which shortens the distance and goes round the cataracts, is very important to the Sudan, since recently a rich province of the Viceroy. A canal joining one stretch of the Nile with the other, from Korosko to Abu Hammet, would make a safe route for uninterrupted communication by water, as well as opening up the space for the population and enabling agriculture. It is a colossal enterprise, albeit not an impossible one, as my barometric measurements have shown. I will not try the reader's patience with any detailed considerations of this project. The canal must be more than 300 versts[14] in length, but in many places, there is a bed ready for it (for instance, the dried bed of the Korosko). Finally, the effort it would require could hardly be greater than what has gone into the building of the famous dam designed to raise the Nile, which has already been continuing for several years, costing so many millions, and God only knows if it can ever be achieved on the anticipated scale. The canal would join the provinces of Egypt that are presently separated by the waterless Nubian Desert, so much so that a bull that costs 60 rubles in Cairo is sold in the Sudan for 10 rubles in paper money.

Upon leaving the naked sandstone mountains, we found crystalline rocks, developed in a large formation. Three or four hours' journey from el-Murat, nearly half-way across the desert, we took some alluvial deposits from a ravine and, having washed them at the wells, obtained traces of gold; further, we found separate pieces of rock, broken off from their deposits, which were tinted with copper-green. There seems to be no reason to doubt that mining would soon facilitate the enrichment

---

14 Approximately 200 miles.

of this country, which would be joined to the Nile and therefore to Egypt much more closely than are the numerous separate oases scattered across the Libyan desert. When all is done, the latter do hold out against every effort—the advance of the moving sands and the ignorance of the Arabs.

On our left, to the east of our route, there is another one that crosses the desert directly from Aswan; it is five or so days longer; nevertheless, in the past, when the tax on slave caravans used to be collected at Korosko, many would evade it; but now that Mohammed Ali has established a toll in Aswan, that route has been all but abandoned. Farther east, mountains become significantly higher, and one can often encounter water there; there may not be grass everywhere, but at least bush is omnipresent, serving as forage for cattle. The nomadic Arabs travel across the area all the way to the Sea of Reeds, where the lack of rain gives way to abundant dew.

Chapter IX

From the Great Nubian Desert to the Confluence of the White Nile and the Blue Nile

Abu Hammet is a small village, very much enlivened by the arrival and departure of caravans. It appeared especially picturesque to us, although perhaps in consequence of our having come out of the desert. Traveling in Egypt and Nubia, one is struck by rich vegetation: one can see, at one and the same time, bright greenery, flowers, and fruits all year round.

In the month of January, they sow pulses here: beans, peas, &c. Oranges, lemons, and pomegranates are in blossom; the fields are green with wheat; in some places they cut sugar cane and *senneh*, as well as clover, which they sometimes let cattle graze on. In February most of the fields are covered with vegetation; watermelons, melons, and cucumbers ripening; rice sown and barley reaped. In the month of March, thick-trunked trees and shrubs are in blossom; they harvest a crop of wheat sown in December. April is the time for picking rose flowers; again they sow wheat; clover is cut for a second time. In May a crop of winter-sown wheat is harvested; acacias and *henna*-trees[1] blossoming; fruits such as early season grapes, figs and annona ripening. In the month of June, they sow *dourra* and, in some places, cut sugar cane. In the Sudan they pick grapes, of which, however, there is little. Come July they sow rice and maize, pick cotton and flax; in Cairo, this verily is the time of grapes. In August sown grass is cut again for a third time; water lilies and jasmine blossom everywhere; date-trees bear rich fruit. September is the season for picking oranges, lemons, tamarind, plums, and once again, rice. By October grasses have grown to the full; fragrant acacias and thorny shrubs blossom. They hasten to harvest every crop. The Nile is inundated. In November, once the waters of the Nile have subsided, wheat is sown; the fields are full of violets and daffodils; figs are picked. In the month of December some trees shed or, more precisely, renew their leaves, but there are a variety of grains and flowers springing up from the earth; this is the true spring.

I have described for you a full year of vegetation, blossoming and ripening in Egypt. Although I did on this occasion enquire of local people as well as resort to Champollion Sr., having also seen much with my own eyes, nevertheless I must have missed something. Even as I write, things keep coming to my mind, such as lupines, turnips, and corn (this last, however, not being cultivated in large quantities).

Our camels had to admire that rich vegetation from afar, being only allowed to come close to mimosa bushes covered with nothing but thorns—and even those were so big that you could not bring your hand close to them without fear—yet the hungry camels devoured them voraciously. How their mouths were not torn by that harsh food, I know not; palm leaves, somewhat less thorny, were offered to them as a delicacy.

A scholar named Ritter[2] has recently written an entire treatise arguing that the camel lives only in those lands where there is the palm-tree, while the latter cannot exist without the former, and that the two are life-long companions; a touching yet completely wrong argument. Mongolia, the Kyrgyz steppe, and the Crimea have no palm-trees

---

1 Also Hina tree (*Lawsonia inermis*), a plant native to semiarid and tropical zones; a source of dye henna used to color hair, fabrics, and so on.
2 Carl Ritter (1779–1859), German geographer.

whatsoever, and yet the camel is no less widespread there than in Africa. Carried away by his idea, Ritter has forgotten about them. It would be fairer to say that wherever there are nomads, there are also camels or deer to serve them; without them there would be no nomadic life; and if the camel is called, with such expression and eloquence, the ship of the sands, then the deer can be called the frigate of the forest.

In the course of my life I have become quite familiar with the camel; having acquainted myself with it well in Africa and Asia, I can say truthfully enough that the northern camel is stronger and more resilient than its southern relative. The Kyrgyz camel can carry 16 poods,[3] 14 being its ordinary burden, while in these parts, camels cannot be loaded with more than 12 poods. There now, I notice that I frequently get carried away from my narrative when I talk of camels, but what can I possibly do if the subject is so close to my heart! You have already seen that from my previous travels if you are cognizant with them. So close the subject is to me that I shall, it seems, even end my days on camelback.

How exhausted and ill soever we might have been, nevertheless, on the morrow we set forth from Abu Hammet. The haste with which we proceeded very much surprised the Turks and Egyptians around us, especially those who had to equip us and see us off on our onward journey. When I said to the ruler of Korosko, upon our arrival at the place, that we set forth the day following and therefore the camels and skins must be ready by the morning, he could not see, try as he might, how it would be possible to prepare as many as 100 camels for an arduous passage like ours in less than a day. However, we also had important levers given to us by the Viceroy and intended to spur the activity of the Egyptian authorities, and so the ruler of Korosko, having worked all night together with all his men, equipped us by the evening of the day following. He later said that he had never in his life been in such a desperate situation, and after our departure, he spent a month in revelries. We had our reasons to hasten. At the end of May, the rainy season commences in Fazoglu, from which even Arabs flee, and we wished to spare as much time as we could for our work. Therefore, upon our

---

3 An obsolete Russian measure of weight, about 36 pounds. Sixteen poods is approximately 580 pounds.

departure from Abu Hammet, we covered the same daily distances as we had in the desert, even though we were no longer worried about the lack of water.

At 5 A.M. the caravan would leave its bivouac, halting for the night at 5 or 6 P.M. The Nile would appear before us in all its majestic silence, and then it would be concealed again behind copses of palm-trees and mimosas. Vegetation is more varied here, the cultivated strip of land wider. One can notice the approach of the belt of tropical rains, which occasionally, if rarely, touch these parts.

The huts of the poorest in these parts sometimes have furniture of the kind previously unseen; a wooden bed—albeit, of course, with no sheets—being not a luxury but a bare necessity. One cannot sleep on the ground for numerous crawling insects, amongst which scorpions, serpents, tarantulas, and other venomous creatures are entirely common and frightening even for the careless natives. The bite of a serpent or a scorpion usually leads to death, although it rarely occurs here, as the natives know many remedies. A traveler must always have ammoniac with him, which he must immediately apply to the sore spot and in addition take 10 drops a couple of times. The bite of a scorpion or a serpent is much more dangerous to a foreigner than to a native.

On the morrow we halted for the night in Bagher, a very picturesque village. We never stayed in houses, not even in cities, but rather put up our traveling-tents in a field, and when sailing on the Nile, we spent nights on the barque.

Thence Wadi Khamar begins, the largest and most dangerous cataract after Wadi Halfa.[4] The Nile is full of islands, sedge-bushes (which seem to grow out of the water), and rows of granite boulders. The noise of water, crashing against them and churning, can be heard from afar, and yet it does not deafen an approaching traveler, as the ancients wrote of the first cataract at Aswan, which is much weaker than this one. The falling of water at any rapid is insignificant, the real danger being the rocks.

What bliss it is to be drinking sweet water whenever you like, and the Nile's water at that!

---

4 The cataracts (shallow, rocky parts) of the Nile.

Having walked 180 versts[5] in four days, overcome with fatigue, exhausted, still not quite recovered from the weary passage through the desert, we barely shuffled into Berber,[6] and there our journey on camelback ended—alas, only temporarily!

Berber is a town similar to those of which we have encountered so many in Egypt and of which there is so little good to be said. It has its own characteristic feature, however: *tukkels*, or round wicker huts, welcoming in outward appearance and, most importantly, roofed. Conical roofs commence thence, heralding the rainy season. They present a lovely picture amongst grey clay houses. Another distinguishing feature of Berber: there is depravity in full view of everyone. We have not encountered that hitherto. In Egypt it is persecuted, and even in Esneh it is veiled by a certain mystery. In Nubia we only visited villages whose inhabitants, for the most part, would flee at our approach, as well as the desert. Berber is the first town in the Sudan!

The Sheikh of the Ababde Arabs and the *Mamur*,[7] who in his turn obeys the *Mudir*[8] of Dongola, live here. To explain all these titles, I shall presently tell you about the government of the East Sudan.

The Sudan is ruled by a governor-general (*Hakumdar*), whose power is substantial. The material wealth of the province and its location, far from Mohammed Ali and beyond the reach of his soldiery, gave Ahmet Pasha Aboudan[9] (the Father of Ears, the Long-Eared One) a bold idea: to separate the province from the Viceroy and, assisted by the patronage of the Turkish Sultan, to gain independence. The example of Mohammed Ali is tempting. Ahmet Pasha acted rather cautiously and indirectly; using money and endearment, he charmed the army troops stationed in the Sudan, strengthened them with slaves, and entered into a secret liaison with the Pasha who ruled Arabia, with whom he could easily communicate via Souakim.[10] Yet one unlucky day, a messenger from Cairo came to the disobedient Pasha and, in

---

5 Approximately 120 miles.
6 A town in Sudan at the confluence of the Atbara River and the Nile.
7 An administrative officer or local governor in Sudan.
8 A provincial governor.
9 Aḥmad Pasha Abu Widan (d. 1843?), governor of Sudan in 1838–43.
10 Suakin, a port city in Eastern Sudan on the Red Sea; at the time, the main communication hub for the Arabian Peninsula.

the name of the Viceroy, summoned him to Cairo. Ahmet Pasha declined, pleading preparations for the taking of Darfour, which was one of Mohammed Ali's favorite ideas. The Viceroy promised to send an army detachment on the pretext of the planned campaign, but his real intention was, needless to say, to surround the Pasha with his own men and to watch him closely. However, it was not easy to deceive Aboudan, who replied that he did not need any soldiers, that one could recruit up to 14,000 slaves in the Sudan, and therefore he asked the Viceroy to send him only experienced officers, mentioning some men who were loyal to him. Further, he enticed the Viceroy with high hopes for the discovery of gold; in a word, he tried to remain in the ruler's confidence for as long as possible until such a time when he would receive the affirmative answer from the Porte. The Viceroy did send him some officers, albeit not the ones he requested, and then, having received new evidence about his criminal designs, he positively demanded that the Pasha come. Ahmet Pasha did not go for a long time, feigning illness, until finally he girded himself for departure. Forty of the best dromedaries were ready for a journey, but it was not Cairo that the Pasha wanted to travel to; realizing that his plans had been discovered before time, he resolved to flee Berber and go to Souakim and thence to Arabia, the Turkish realm. On the eve of the agreed departure, he was visited by one Omar Aga, who brought him a letter with but a few words in it: Mohammed Ali demanded an immediate reply as to whether or not he was coming to Cairo. The Pasha told Omar Aga that he was ready for departure and together they went to the barque, on which all his things had already been loaded. On his approach to the shore, however, he saw 400 Arnaut[11] soldiers on the opposite bank of the Nile. Escape was impossible. Pretending to have been struck by a bout of illness, the Pasha postponed his departure till the day following and returned home. There he ordered his eunuch to bring the medicine box, took out some powder, dissolved it in a cup of water with some sugar, drank it, and an hour later died with truly Turkish composure. The Turks know not how to live, but they are good at dying.

---

11 Also Arnavut (pl. Arnavutlar), the Ottoman term for Albanians.

After that accident, the Viceroy did not appoint a governor-general in the Sudan for two years or so. Mohammed Pasha Melikhli[12] governed the province as a controller, a plenipotentiary of Mohammed Ali. Finally, about three years ago, Khalid Pasha[13] was appointed Governor-General, and he continues to rule the Sudan to this day. Schœlcher[14] is mistaken when he claims that Ahmet Pasha was shot in the presence of many (namely, Mohammed Ali's men sent by Omar Aga) merely for provoking a suspicion—not quite justified—in the mind of the Viceroy. It is difficult to conclude to what extent Ahmet Pasha was guilty; we all judge by the rumors that we believe to be the most plausible of all. Yet his death is too public an affair, and I did hear the story from Omar Aga himself in the Sudan rather than in Cairo, 2,000 versts[15] from Khartoum, where Schœlcher heard it.

The Sudan consists of six *mudirlyks*, or provinces. Here they are, beginning from the North: Dongola, Khartoum, Kordofan, Sennaar, Fazoglu, and Taka, which stretches to the Sea of Reeds. The provinces are governed by *mudirs*, who, following the accident with Ahmet Pasha, were at first given much power by the Viceroy and thus set against the Governor-General, which only led to interminable arguments amongst them, and so in the end, the Pasha of the Sudan remained the sole ruler. The provinces are divided into boroughs that are governed by *mamurs*; which are further divided into districts, governed by *nazars*; and finally, into villages, which are in the charge of their own sheikhs: the administrative system is almost the same as in Egypt.

The *Mudir* came to me accompanied by a Copt, who was his secretary; that small engine propelling all things great and thus all things evil. The Copt, like all his kin, strutted ceremoniously in his long dress; his elongated lips, his head, inclined to one side, a copper ink-well under his belt, a turban on the head, and a quill behind one ear all made him appear significant in the eyes of *fellahs*. Usual greetings exchanged, Yousuf Effendi told the *Mudir* to prepare barques for us, the *Mudir*

---

12 Ahmad Pasha Manikli (also Manlikli, c. 1795–1862), governor of Sudan in 1843–45.
13 Khalid Pasha Khusraw, governor of Sudan in 1845–50.
14 Victor Schoelcher (1804–93), French writer, traveler, and abolitionist. Kovalevsky refers to his book *L'Égypte en 1845* (Paris: Pagnerre, 1846).
15 Approximately 1,325 miles.

addressed the same demand to his secretary, and the secretary replied that at present there were no spare barques in Berber, according to the papers. Thereupon Yousuf flew at the Copt with all the might of his power and wrath: he called him disobedient and rebellious, he cursed him, he threatened him with the gallows and the *kibosh*;[16] the *Mudir* repeated Yousuf's words. The Copt's face soon lost its significant aspect and assumed utmost humility. He assured us that he himself was willing to turn into a barque so as to carry us, and should that prove impossible, he would still carry us all on his own shoulders. The implacable Yousuf demanded a barque, advising him to spare his shoulders for the rods that awaited him.

In consequence of these energetic measures, the barque of the Governor-General, the best in the Sudan, appeared by the pier, followed by another, intended for our men. In this country you should never despair upon hearing an initial refusal; on the contrary, you should be prepared for it and still pursue your demand.

Whether it has been said ere or not, everyone must have noticed that in Egypt one either beats or gets beaten. In your dealings with the natives, and especially with the authorities, you should always appear cold and imperious, not demanding the impossible from them yet always insisting on your demands. A familiar tone shall be fatal for their opinion of you, for they do not think of themselves highly, so anyone who condescends to them is bound to be shown even less appreciation.

On the following day, the 3rd (15th) of February, we set off from Berber.

Once again, the Nile with its crocodiles and hippopotamuses; once again, the Nile hemmed by the narrow ribbons of its green banks, with its mysterious silence! . . . Soon we passed the mouth of the Atbarah. On the way back, I determined its location and found a slight difference between my measurements and the maps, perhaps due to some changes the bed of the river had undergone some time ago.

The Nile is the only river in the world that lets in precisely one other river, the Atbarah, over a space of more than 2,000 versts[17]—that is,

---

16 A long whip.
17 Approximately 1,325 miles.

between the confluence of the Blue Nile and the White Nile, that being the point where the Nile proper begins, and the Mediterranean Sea.[18] From its very origin to the separation into the branches that create the Delta, it is almost the same in width throughout its course. It is somewhat deeper by the Atbarah and generally more abundant with water in its upper reaches than in the middle or near its mouths, its waters being lost in the sands and in evaporation, as well as taken away into fields and canals, the only influx coming from the rains that occur in its upper reaches.

The surroundings of the Nile, as noted, changed somewhat; palm-trees were becoming rare, giving way to acacias that thickly covered the banks and picturesque islands, the latter occurring frequently and hindering our progress, for the Nile, shallow as it is, at this time grew even more shallow, divided into several branches by the islands. The cultivated strip went deeper into the country, albeit still timidly and indecisively; the inhabitants were even more fearful here than elsewhere, being Berbers and, partly, nomadic Arabs who came here with their herds.

We progressed slowly, towed in the absence of any wind by three or four dozen men: naked mankind of divers colors, a *chaush*[19] with a *kibosh* following them. Someone like Schœlcher is bound to say, "Lord Almighty! How can you possibly speak of it so calmly as you look upon such a heart-rending scene?" Enough of your momentous words and florid phrases, M. Schœlcher! I shall in due course write what I think of this mankind, but it is still too early to do so now: my imaginary fellow travelers must acquaint themselves with it properly to be able to make their own judgement.

On the third day, a favorable wind picked up and soon brought us in our three-masted *dahabia* to Shendi.[20]

Upon learning that the *Mudir* of Khartoum was here, we went ashore. Soliman Pasha, like most Egyptian governors, was a Turk; he, too, had the inevitable figure of a Copt at his side. Leaving the Copt to

---

18 Author's note: Like everyone else, I used to think so, but as we shall see below, I have found in the Great Nubian Desert another river, which flows into the Nile from the left.
19 Also chaus, a low military rank in the Ottoman army—in this case, an overseer.
20 A town in Sudan on the eastern bank of the Nile.

write all the necessary instructions for our arrival at Khartoum, we set to smoking pipes, drinking coffee, and talking. The Pasha asked our doctor, who had until recently worked in Khartoum and was his family doctor, about the health of his son, who remained in Cairo with his mother. The doctor regaled him with propitious news.

"What about your wife? Would you not like to hear about her?" he said in jest.

"What is a wife! It is but soil that can always be replaced, whereas my son is my seed, flower, and fruit. Should he perish, God knows if I am ever to have another."

The woman in the East only assumes significance once she has borne a child; consequently, children are always the subject of perpetual arguments in a *harem*, at times paying with their lives for other wives' jealousy toward their mother. Just recently, in one of the noblest *harems*, one wife stabbed another, who was pregnant, with a knife solely to ensure the woman would not gain any advantage over her. Such examples are common.

The town of Shendi was once great, but upon suffering a horrible catastrophe in 1822, it has not recovered still. At present it has as many as 4,000 inhabitants. We visited the spot where the favorite son of Mohammed Ali—Ismail Pasha, the brave conqueror of Sennaar—was burnt alive; a sad story in itself and terrible in its consequences. I shall recount it later.

Having spent three or four hours in Shendi, we obtained the necessary papers and bid farewell to Soliman Pasha. Our *dahabias* speedily sailed toward Khartoum before a favorable wind.

We still had about three hours to travel to the confluence of Bahr-el-Abiad and Bahr-el-Azrak, the White Nile and the Blue Nile, when we noticed that the waters were divided into two streams, which grew more defined, little by little, until finally they took on clear outlines: the waters flowing along the right bank were white, whilst those on the left were light-blue-green. The two rivers still hesitated to merge into one. People living nearby much prefer the water of the Blue Nile to the silty water of the White Nile; those living on the left bank bring water from the other one. I was vividly reminded of two Siberian rivers, the

Biya and the Katun, which upon joining together into the Ob River, flow separately for a long distance, one turbid and white, the other light and transparent.

Having passed the town of Halfay,[21] the headquarters of the Viceroy's cavalry, on the 8th (20th) of February, we arrived at Khartoum, the capital of Sennaar and the entire East Sudan.

---

21 Wadi Halfa, a city in northern Sudan.

Chapter X

Khartoum and Sennaar

The Arabs usually give people and things nicknames in addition to their proper, given names to account for their distinguishing features: Ahmet Pasha has long ears and is therefore Abou-dan, the Father of Ears, which name causes him no offense. The Nile near Khartoum bends in the manner of an elephant's trunk, and therefore the city is named Elephant's Trunk, or Khartoum.

In Khartoum, like in the rest of the Sudan, they used to build houses with roofs (made of straw, of course); but a few years ago, it was prohibited in towns to prevent endless fires. Now that there is nothing in the clay city to catch fire, the fires have stopped of their own accord; on the other hand, during the rainy season, the city spreads every which way, so that its inhabitants cannot find the ruins of their own dwellings without difficulty. The houses are scattered in a rather picturesque fashion and surrounded by gardens, which require little care: they grow and grow thanks to the wholesome climate and the rains. The streets are clean and the only square is spacious, the Blue Nile running by the very walls, the White Nile in full view. In a word, Khartoum is perhaps, with the exception of Cairo and Alexandria, the best city in Egypt. It is believed to have 18,000 inhabitants and innumerable pigeons . . .

No sooner had we moored than the Turkish authorities paid us a visit, true to their custom; they invited us to move from the barque to the city for repose. We were indeed in need of repose: during the entire month of our journey we had not stayed anywhere; also, a house was likely to have, if not comfort, then at least space, whereas life on the barque had proven harsh for us, making us shrink like dry sponges; and besides, some matters in hand required our closest attention. We had to replenish our expedition here and take on what had been forgotten by the Governor-General, who was waiting for our arrival in the land of the negroes. We also had to send him a message to agree on a meeting point beforehand, even though it was not easily done, for we were separated by a month's journey or so and by numerous obstacles of all kinds.

We were given the best lodgings in the city. There were passages and walk-ways, both in and out of doors, making up a single spacious courtyard, and in amongst them several houses stood, entangled in their maze; we chose the one that had the most isolated situation and overlooked the garden, which turned out to be the *harem* of the former owner. Clay walls, clay *divans*, clay floors—that was all the house could offer in the way of luxury. Soon, however, they brought in some furniture, dusted the place, sprinkled the walls and the floors so much that they became muddy, and the house turned into a cool and spacious home, to our complete satisfaction; especially once the crowd of various authorities and servants had finally left us alone.

Earlier, while still on our *dahabia*, we had a visit from missionaries of the Pope's Propaganda, who had arrived here several weeks earlier. A bishop named Cozzolani, who was in charge of them, himself served under a Jesuit by the name of Rillo, a man too well-known in the Catholic world, not so much for being the rector of the Propaganda[1] school as for his religious and political influence...

He was a man of about 50 years of age, thin and pale, the climate of the Sudan having already made its pernicious effect on him. Yet still Rillo's eyes were a-flame, revealing all the fervor of his inner life. Clever

---

1 The Sacred Congregation for the Propagation of the Faith (Sacra Congregatio de Propaganda Fide), an institution in Rome responsible for missionary work.

and eloquent though he was, I very much wanted to say to him that his talent would easily allow him to enthrall and seduce any woman—but alas . . . The presence of such a person created a certain atmosphere of awkwardness and heaviness; it would have been better to see no-one at all . . . Rillo was seeking a place for a colony; he wished to settle on the frontier between Abyssinia and the Sudan, rather than in the midst of negroes, and was considering whether he should send some of his missionaries with me to Fazoglu. I was curious to learn what this enterprise, more political and commercial than religious, would lead to. I could not help but remember Archimandrite Makarii,[2] whom I had met at Lake Teletskoye in the deepest Siberia, in the wilderness of a forest, surrounded by his converted flock. He was imbued with a lofty desire to convert idolaters to Christianity and had nothing else in mind; Rillo, in his turn, has many other designs which, even assuming they include any religious idea, do so obliquely, seeing in it a means rather than the end. That one prayed and persuaded, pointing to the heavens; this one enthralls, pointing to the Pope. Rillo is likely to read these notes, for he knows the Russian language and literature very well . . .

Sennaar and Kordofan were first conquered by Ismail Pasha, the eldest son of Mohammed Ali, in 1820; after the tragic death of the conqueror, the entire East Sudan rebelled; but the Viceroy's son-in-law, the notorious *Defterdar*, took his revenge on it by fire and sword, and so Sennaar and Kordofan, devastated and wasted, were adjoined to Egypt once again.

According to a legend, which I hasten to record in the history of the Sudan, and as suggested by a few vague facts mentioned by the ancients, Sennaar was known as Macrobia in the time of Cambyses. After him, 10 queens and 12 kings reigned in the Sudan. Then the Hejaz Arabs came. Finally, there came the Fung[3] people from the banks of the White Nile—that was in the year 890 of Hegira, or in A.D. 1484. Following a

---

2 Archimandrite Makarii (Glukharev, 1792–1847), Russian Orthodox priest and missionary in southern Siberia.
3 Funj, an ethnic group in Sudan linked to the rise of the Funj Sultanate in the 16th–18th centuries. Some scholars believe that the term *Fung* denoted not so much an ethnic origin as a social status (a view that Kovalevsky shares below).

decisive victory at Arbaha,[4] they took over the entire peninsula between the White Nile and the Blue Nile to establish a new, immense kingdom. The Fung, judging by their features and language, must belong to the tribe of Shillook[5] negroes living along the White Nile. *Fung* means conqueror, and they must have assumed this name upon conquering the Sudan—or some part of the Kingdom of Burum, into which they had found their way earlier. Their territory used to extend all the way up to Wadi Halfa in the north; as for the south, the frontiers of the East Sudan disappear in the lands of the negroes, more or less subdued. The first ruler of the Fung tribe was Amara Dunkas,[6] who reigned for 42 years; he was followed by 29 others, mostly known for the battles they fought with various tribes, and nothing else. The last of them was Badi,[7] the son of Tabli; it was during his reign that Ismail Pasha conquered Sennaar.

At first the government of Mohammed Ali used to move from town to town, depending on the taste of the Governor-General. It had stayed in Sennaar, the capital of the Fung Kingdom; in Wad Medina,[8] established by Ismail Pasha; and in Kordofan; until finally, 15 years ago or so, Khusraw Pasha completed the construction of Khartoum and transferred the headquarters there.

We left Khartoum on the 10th (22nd) of February. When circumventing an island opposite to it, we saw a few dozen crocodiles there, lying in the sun with their mouths open, enjoying their *kayf*.[9] Thence up the Nile, there are extremely many of them, but those that devour people are few and far between. For instance, one appeared this year very near Khartoum; another crocodile, who carries away several people in the course of every summer, lives by Wad Medina. There are some more near Kamlin[10] and elsewhere. Although certain precautions are taken against

---

4 Kovalevsky refers to the Battle of Arbaji (1504), in which the Fung defeated the Arab-speaking dynasty of Abdallabi.
5 Shilluk, an ethnic group in Sudan.
6 Amara Dunqas (r. 1504–33), the ruler of Fung, or Sennaar.
7 Badi VII (r. 1805–21), the last sultan of Fung, or Sennaar; abdicated as a result of the conquest of Sennaar by the forces of Mohammed Ali.
8 Wad Madani, a city in Sudan; at the time an Ottoman-Egyptian outpost.
9 Also *keyif* (Arabic and Turkish), a state of pleasant relaxation. The word entered Russian and other European languages in the 18th century.
10 Al Kamlin, a settlement on the Blue Nile in Sudan.

them there, the inhabitants of other places pay no heed whatsoever to crocodiles, bathing and swimming across the Nile in full view of them.

Here is one of the most characteristic crocodile tricks: after the tender caresses of love, of a most ecstatic kind, a male leaves his beloved on the sand, as if absent-mindedly; exhausted, she cannot get up by herself, beating and writhing about, while the crocodile, they say, enjoys her sufferings from afar, until the natives see her and kill her.

Here and there on the banks of the Nile, one can see herds of camels and sheep—a thing unheard of in Egypt, where the mere possession of a single buffalo or camel makes a *fellah* rich. Those herds belong to the Bedouin Arabs, who drive them to the Nile, their watering-hole, every two or three days; the sheep, too, have been inured to bear thirst.

The banks—overgrown with the tamarix, the willow, *Acacia gummifera*, and a large variety of creeping plants—become ever wilder. We saw herds of chamois and wild donkeys coming to the water to drink. Wild donkeys are more beautiful than their domesticated relations: they are supple and tall with long legs, the only thing making them ugly being their ears.

Bahr-el-Azrak, the Blue Nile, is faster than the Nile proper: it flows at a rate of three or even 3¼ versts per hour[11] now that the water is low; while the Nile, which I measured a month ago, was higher and its current was 2¾ versts per hour. The Blue Nile is pure and light-colored, and there is no need to let its water settle or purify it as one does with the water of the Nile, for it is naturally transparent.

The Nile's water is known to be the lightest in the world; it contains almost no extraneous substances and, once the inevitable silt has settled, apothecaries can use it instead of distilled water. They say that at the Sultan's palace, in Constantinople, no other water is used except that of the Nile.

Late at night we halted by the village of Saba. About half an hour's journey from the shore, the ruins of Saba[12] are situated; they are wrongly ascribed by many to a Christian town. A statue of Aries[13] with hiero-

---

11 Approximately two miles per hour.
12 The original name of the city of Meroë in Sudan.
13 A constellation of the Zodiac, representing a ram.

glyphs on its plinth (discovered last year by accident) and the capitals of the pillars disprove that hypothesis; it is a pity that the scholar Lepsius[14] has not seen the latest discoveries.

A favorable wind speedily carried our small flotilla along the Blue Nile, the Russian colors flying over its waters for the first time ever. On the morrow, we passed Kamlin, the location of the only factory in the Sudan.[15] They manufacture soap, rum, and sugar here; the factory is in a poor condition now that its former owner, Ahmet Pasha, and the foreman, a German named Bauer, are both dead: the former, as we have already said, from poison; the latter from a local fever. This is what all local enterprises come to, when all is done: there is no-one to continue. There are a few pigs left after Bauer, which, despite the Mohammedan law being intolerant to these poor animals, are flourishing and getting fat, for the Barbars do not care about any law.

The Ragat River was waterless when we saw it.

We reached Wad Medina after three and a half days, despite having run aground an innumerable number of times. Wad Medina is a town with 4,000 or so inhabitants, including 1,200 soldiers. About four days prior to our arrival, the negroes conspired to kill all the whites—that is, people of divers colors—and to retreat to their mountains; yet despite there being up to 1,000 blacks in the garrison and only 200 Arabs, Turks, &c., the conspiracy failed. That was not the first attempt at a slave rebellion, but so far all their designs have merely led to a few escapes and murders. However, when one thinks that Egyptians, Turks and Circassians amount to a mere one-fifth of the entire army of the Sudan, and even those are dropping like flies under the influence of the climate, one cannot but reflect on the humiliation of the natives by the foreigners, which equally manifests itself everywhere: in India, in Africa, in America . . . It is as though the state of slavery in itself completely destroys the spirit of the slaves.

Early in the morning, we set forth from Wad Medina ("Wad Modeyna," according to the maps). The sandbars of the Nile are full of game: there are myriads of cranes migrating north, fleeing the seasonal rains and

---

14 Karl Richard Lepsius (1810–84), German Egyptologist and archaeologist.
15 Possibly an indigo-producing factory.

summer heat in the south. One could not sleep at night for noise and cries whenever we happened to moor at a place chosen by them for a roost. On the shore, in the bushes, there are numerous pintados (or guinea-fowls, as we call them), their meat tasting very good. Tribes of monkeys amused everyone with their grimaces and absurd jumps, as if teasing us. They have a curious method for catching monkeys here: a large jug of beer, with some honey added to it, is placed under a tree; monkeys voraciously fall on the delicacy, get drunk, fight, and run riot until finally, half-asleep, they fall off the tree and on the ground, where they are taken with bare hands. You can choose any monkey for a piaster (six silver kopeks). When they later awake in captivity, their surprise, chagrin, and wrath are indescribable; yet they are tamed very soon.

In the evening of the same day, we passed the Dindir ("Dender," according to the maps), a rather substantial river.

There are many lions between Wad Medina and Sennaar. Three years ago or so, by the village of Sabila,[16] they attacked a small caravan, which consisted of six or seven donkeys and five men, and mauled both the men and the donkeys.

Another halt. We went ashore opposite the village of Saba Douleb. What nature! What a striking contrast with Egypt. Everything is wild here; one cannot find any wild grass in Egypt, whereas here the grass resembles rushes; and if everything is faded and dried out, it is only waiting for the rainy season to come. Wild apple-trees; bushes of ne-back, or *Ziziphus spina-christi*; acacias of divers varieties; and tamarix at the edge of the forest are covered with lianas, wild vines, and various creeping plants, so much so that one sits under them as if under a roof. Indeed, people who live here have no other roof over their head, the only exception being occasional tufts of grass which, lashed together, serve as a wall on the windward side. What people! What lives they live! In the midst of numerous monkeys, which inhabit forests and crowd around these dwellings, you cannot tell them apart from afar. How beautiful it is here, especially in comparison with the deserts of Nubia and the dull lands of Egypt, stripped and deprived of everything that could be taken from them, just as the people would later be deprived of everything; the

---

16 Sabil, a village to the southwest of Wad Medina.

lands where nature revolts against man—against the poor *fellah*, unable to decide what he should be defending himself against, whether it be the advance of the sands, the scorching sun, or the raids of the *Mamur* and bailiffs. Whereas here people are not pushed toward the Nile by the Libyan or Arabian mountains nor by the Libyan or Arabian sands: they are free to live anywhere, there being as much space as you like; nature is sprawled widely, in a manner reminiscent of Russia; there is sufficient room for both man and wild beasts, and myriads of birds, and various reptile creatures inhabiting these forests—indeed, man takes up the least space of all. What a variety of plants, what an extraordinary abundance of birds, what collections we will bring back for cabinets of curiosities! We have seen new humming-birds here; there are numerous parrots.

Not all the natives, however, live as nomads in the forests. The government takes care to gather the Barbars into villages; otherwise one cannot find them in order to collect taxes, and some might well evade paying them. Truly there is nothing in this thicket to herald a human dwelling-place, and if one does encounter it, it is a sudden discovery.

Some grow tobacco and cotton; yet they do not water their fields. Past Khartoum, *sakhiehs* are rarely seen, vanishing completely by Sennaar. Their weeping howls, their heavy movement no longer torture you. The natives sow during the rainy season and reap after it. The rest of the time they do nothing.

Yes, one can breathe easily and freely here. The high-noon heat is not felt so much in this overgrown thicket. While our men busied themselves near the barque, we sat in the shade of apple-trees, the only thing to occasionally frighten us being serpents and scorpions. The night, which fell quickly, the howl of a hyena nearby, and the roar of a lion made us return to the *dahabia*. Apropos the hyena, we had seen a special variety of it here, quite a rare one, with white stripes across its back.

On the 18th of February (the 1st of March) our progress was once again slowed down as the barque ran aground. Toward the evening, we attempted to moor; suddenly, the roar of a lion came from nearby; another responded to it, and then a third; hearing them approach closer and closer, we could even see the shadow of one of them flashing in the darkness. The crew wanted to sail off, but some of our men were on the shore, and we were extremely worried about them; at last some people appeared at the opposite end, walking together over sandbars: they were our men. They had heard the roar of the lions as close as we had and decided to go round the beasts by water, at the risk of encountering crocodiles on the way, the visible danger being more frightening.

On the morrow, I left the barque on the sandbar and walked to Sennaar, reaching it after a three hours' journey.

Sennaar, as I have already noted, was founded by the predecessors of the present rulers, the Fung kings; it used to be the seat of the kings, and their entire great land was named, after the city, Sennaar; to this day, the space between the White Nile and the Blue Nile is known among the natives as the Peninsula of Sennaar,[17] which, in our view, is much fairer. The name of the East Sudan, which embraces both this space and Kordofan and also some other lands ruled by Mohammed Ali—as well as, more generally, the Sudan, a name that is ascribed on our maps to most of Inner Africa—is accepted in too wide a sense and does not correspond to its meaning. The present division of the provinces, introduced by Mohammed Ali, has no significance here, relying completely upon chance, upon greater or lesser trust in the people who rule them, as well as upon many other arbitrary circumstances, whereas the most important things here are the character of the country, the ethnic provenance of the people, and natural divides.

The city of Sennaar was once great. In the time of the Fung, they say, she had as many as 25,000 inhabitants; even after she had been conquered by Ismail Pasha, 9,000 remained, as Caillaud[18] reports; yet since the Turks moved the government headquarters to Khartoum, Sennaar has emptied, there now being scarcely 5,000 inhabitants here, including soldiers; trade with Abyssinia has diminished, and the population has been impoverished.

According to Caillaud's calculation, Sennaar is situated in lat. 13°36′51″ N., and according to mine, in lat. 13°40′2″ N. and long. 30°24′34″ E., while the maps denominate its situation differently.

---

17 A misnomer. The region is delimited by the White Nile and the Blue Nile on the west and east sides and by the Abyssinian lands in the south.
18 Frédéric Cailliaud (1787–1869), French naturalist who accompanied Mohammed Ali's forces in the conquest of Sudan.

Chapter XI

Three Varieties of the Palm-Tree and the Baobab

Roseires[1]

Until now, at least as far as I am aware, there were two known varieties of the palm-tree in Egypt and the Sudan: the ordinary date-palm, *Phoenix dactylifera*, and the *doum*, *Cucifera thebaica*. The former grows all over the space between Alexandria and Khartoum, gradually becoming less wide-spread toward the south, while the latter, first appearing in Upper Egypt, overtakes it, spreading as far as Roseires and somewhat farther. Finally, there is a third variety of the palm-tree, which can first be seen between Sennaar and Walet Medina[2]—namely, at Saba Douleb—and henceforth all the way to Fazoglu.

This last variety is called *douleb* here. Its foliage is very similar to *doum* leaves, the only difference being in the way in which they are folded, almost imperceptibly, so that one has to look very carefully to notice that; its fruit is very different, resembling the so-called ananas melon in appearance, size, and especially smell; its flesh inside, filled

---
1 Er Roseires, a city in Sudan, near the border with present-day Ethiopia.
2 Perhaps Kovalevsky has in mind Wad Medina.

with fiber, has an astringent taste, which negroes and Arabs still find delicious; like the *doum* fruit, it has a stone in the middle. I do not find either very good to taste. Yet the principal difference between the *douleb* and the *doum* is in their trunks. As we have already noted, the *doum* divides itself into branches, which is why many exclude it from the palm species; as for the *douleb*, it is similar to any palm-tree in that it grows straight, having only one trunk, stock-like; but this is the only variety that widens in the middle, its top and bottom always being thinner than its middle.

The aspect of the date-palm amazed me at first, but those groves, continuously stretching along the monotonous banks of the Nile, cause fatigue, being so regular. I have already said that a palm-tree is better when it stands all alone, amidst the sands of the desert, its sprawling crown vividly outlined against the fading horizon in the evening. Then it is beautiful, and despite having admired it so many times, I can never get enough of this view.

Having grown bored of the uniform appearance of date-palms, one takes to *doums*, with their rich greenery and sprawling branches; yet soon they, too, reveal the regularity of shape characteristic of palm-trees. The *doum* always branches at a certain height, first into two halves, each of those branches, in their turn, also splitting into two identical parts, which grow in perfect accord with one another, like twins; each tree branches in this manner three, sometimes four times, with remarkable regularity. The *douleb* makes a pleasant difference to someone familiar with the *doum*! But then suddenly, one is struck by a giant of vegetation, whose size one's imagination has never been able to picture: the baobab!

The baobab-tree, *Adansonia digitata* (or *homr*), is one of the most ancient inhabitants of the Earth. Humboldt believes a certain baobab, growing on one of the islands of Cape Verde, to be much older than 5,000 years, the diameter of its trunk being about 30 feet. Having measured many trees, we found none exceeding 25 feet, while their age also proved quite venerable—namely, more than 5,000 years. The baobab is ugly owing to its thickness, being of incongruous height and having branches that are unwieldy and lack in richness and luxury, the proportions of their parts wrong: it is an enormous mass ending in thin branches; it is an elephant, a mammoth of vegetation. The color of its bark—metallic, steely—is beautiful; but what is especially striking about the baobab is that you can see budding leaves, flowers, and fruit on it all at the same time. The leaves are quite small and scarce; the flowers white and exquisite; each flower doubling in the middle, like the hollyhock; its petals bent back at the edges, like those of the lily; also, it has a fine almond smell; the fruit resembles the cocoa-nut with a thin shell, under which there is a farinaceous substance—pleasant, slightly acidulous, and very refreshing—as well as numerous stones, which Arabs sometimes roast and use instead of coffee.

The baobab's trunk is, for the most part, hollow, easily sheltering several people inside it from sun-rays and from the weather during the rainy season. There are always a number of other trees, creeping plants and parasites being especially common among them, that wrap their trunks round it or even grow into it altogether, thus increasing its shade.

In the Kordofan and Darfour deserts, nomadic Arabs look out for baobabs that are inhabited by bees so as to take out their honey and leave the hollow for the seasonal rains to work on it. In a short time the rains produce destruction in the tree, creating actual wells, in which water is kept in the driest of seasons. Such a tree constitutes the wealth of a nomadic family, which sells the water to travelers at a high price—and even if the traveler were dying of thirst, depend upon it, the Arab would not give him a handful of water without payment.

The first baobab can be found by Arbaji, three days' journey or so from Khartoum, but it really is indigenous to Roseires, there being a great many baobabs in the mountains.

Beyond Sennaar, nature remains unchanged: the same low banks overgrown with thickets; beyond that, in a distance, a small village or an encampment of nomadic Arabs, whom the drought has forced to move to the banks of the Nile. Why, then, do they never step out into God's world to come to the Nile itself, into the view of passers-by? The government is frightening, so much so that they flee their homes at the sight of a *tarboosh*; but there, beyond the thicket, are lions and hyenas! And yet it must be less frightening there.

The roar of these beasts, reaching us nearly every night, made our crew moor by sandy islands. The precaution also had another advantage for us: the packed mound of a sandbar made an excellent place for a walk. Those were the only hours in the day when we truly lived: breathing freely, voraciously imbibing the coolness of the night, surrounded by the night, with the sky always full of shooting stars, how cloudy soever the day might have been, complete silence engulfing us, disturbed only by the roar of a wild beast or the splash of a hippopotamus. Everything is wild and deserted; your heart tightens in involuntary anguish when you remember where you are and with whom. God only knows how many such nights we have spent on the deserted sandbars of the Nile, how many thoughts have gone through our minds. But on we go, past the deserted islands! Further on and on; yet everything is the same further on. Here, two days' journey from Sennaar, is Sero, a large place in comparison with others, but it is exactly the same as all the rest, the only exception being, perhaps, more *tukkels* and some government buildings made of clay.

As we proceeded on our way in a tranquil manner, behind us, on another barque, a horrible scene unfolded.

The weather was dead calm; the Arabs waded through the water that was up to their knees or higher, towing the barque with ropes. Suddenly, one of them disappeared and then came up to the surface again; a minute had not passed when he went down once again, as fast as a plummet. Everyone guessed what had happened; the men made a lot of noise, they began shooting, and then the Arab reappeared on the surface, his bloodied *ferdeh* dragging behind him; a rope was promptly thrown, and he was able to swim to the barque somehow or other, blood and water dripping from him. It turned out that the crocodile caught him above the knee at first, but then the beast must have got entangled in his *ferdeh*—a garment which the natives wrap round the lower parts of their bodies several times—and so it let go of its prey, leaving some traces of its teeth on his body; next, the crocodile caught him by the toes of the same foot, but then the shouts and noise must have frightened it; three toes were bitten off clean, as if with a knife. The man was offered medical remedies, but he refused them, saying that there was a witch-doctor at home; his first concern was his *ferdeh*, which he looked over, regretting the severe damage done by the crocodile; thereupon he asked to be taken home; three Arabs accompanied him, while the rest went into the water to tow the barque as if nothing had happened. What a lovely country! One cannot approach the banks for fear of lions and hyenas; nor can one remain in the water for fear of crocodiles. We were not, however, to remain cautious for very long! Instead, we would come ashore alone and bathe with a carelessness worthy of true Arabs—even at night.

Upon leaving Sero, on the third day we arrived at Roseires. A wild thicket of *doums*, *douleb*s, and baobab-trees, all growing together and covered with creeping lianas and parasites, separates the village from the Nile. One can imagine what the place is like during the rainy season! No beast would probably be able to pass through the wilderness. Equatorial nature is spread for everyone to see in all its mighty beauty. The village of Roseires is situated in a very picturesque place, upon hills, whence some blue mountains are already visible in the distance. Roseires is the headquarters of the *Mudir*, the Governor of the province of Fazoglu; there are about 3,000 people in the village, among them many negroes.

We left our *dahabia* there, unable to proceed by water, for a cataract stood in our way. We walked for two days along the Nile without losing sight of it, the ground rising somewhat; as we proceeded, we encountered plenty of ebony-trees, *Diospyros ebenum*; then on the third day, we came to Femaki, a small village, where we saw, situated on a picturesque spot on the bank of the Nile, the ruins of some building. It was called "the palace of the Viceroy" for the following reason: the Governor, unable to withstand insistent demands that he renounce his claims to Syria and other conquered lands (which were so dear to his heart) in favor of the Porte, announced that he would retire to the Sudan to be an independent ruler there rather than accede to such humiliating proposals, and he ordered that a palace be built in Femaki—which ended in a puff of smoke. The Pasha should have accepted the proposals made by the European governments, for the palace, built of raw brick, not unlike other official buildings and stores in these parts, had been ruined before it was completely finished.

A little further upstream from Femaki, where the Nile is not so deep, we waded across with our caravan; poor camels, with the water coming up to their breasts, were hardly able to resist the fast current; no accident happened on the above occasion, although that was rare luck.

From thence we traveled between the Blue Nile and the Toumat, keeping closer to the former. The Toumat flows into the Nile half an hour's journey or so downstream from Femaki. The terrain rises visibly, the foot-hills being the first outpost of the land of the negroes.

Part II

The Land of the Negroes

Visit to the *melek* of Uru Taor

Chapter I

New Vistas

Fazoglu is a name given by the Arabs to the mountain range, and it alone, that stretches from the Blue Nile to the Toumat; Turks, on the other hand, apply the name to a row of villages situated at the foothills. Their inhabitants are either negroes or of mixed negro and Arab descent; they are quite obedient to the government of the Pasha, like any valley people, whose land is open to the action of the soldiery advancing with their bullets and bayonets from any direction. This row of villages culminates spectacularly in Mohammed-Ali-polis.

Mohammed-Ali-polis owes its name to a journey Mohammed Ali made to these parts on his quest for the Golden Fleece. It was here and, particularly, at Khor-el-Adid that he had been promised mountains of gold—that is, rich deposits which, according to Russegger's[1] account, yield up to 251 lots of gold per 1,000 hundredweights!! (about 30 zolotniks[2] per 100 poods!!!). Boreani,[3] in his turn, had also promised miracles. An entire commission of Europeans gathered here in

---
1 Joseph Ritter von Russegger (1802–63), Austrian geologist; explored Sudan and Egypt at the request of Mohammed Ali.
2 An obsolete Russian measure of weight, about 0.15 ounces. The yield is approximately 1.25 ounces per 1,000 pounds.
3 Boreani, Italian mining engineer; served as Mohammed Ali's expert.

ГЛАВА I.

Новые виды.

Арабы дають имя Фазоглу собственно грядѣ горъ, идущей отъ Голубаго Нила къ Тумату; турки называютъ этимъ именемъ рядъ деревенекъ, который тянется у предгорій. Жители — негры, или происшедшіе изъ помѣси негровъ и арабовъ; они довольно покорны правительству паши, какъ вообще жители долинъ, отовсюду открытые для дѣйствій пуль и штыковъ солдатъ. Рядъ этихъ деревенекъ заключается блистательно Мегеметъ-Али-полисомъ.

order to discuss the matter; Mohammed Ali witnessed every sample being taken; no gold was found—there had never been any here! The only thing remaining from the Viceroy's visit and from all the wonderful hopes is the great name of Mohammed-Ali-polis, and even that exists solely on the map, for the natives still call the village by its former name, Kheri.

Kheri is currently the headquarters of the *Mudir* of Fazoglu, which does not, however, prevent the capital of the *mudirlyk* from being a village of the poorest kind! The sole difference between it and other villages is an enormous store where they keep the supplies for gold-mines brought here during the Viceroy's visit. And what an abundant store it is! Entire crucibles of platinum, theodolites, barometers, looking-glasses, an endless supply of mercury—in a word, everything a-plenty except that which is required for gold-mines. All these things, costing many thousands of rubles, are now in such a condition that none of them can ever be employed for any purpose whatsoever: everything is shattered, broken, stolen, or sold. One could not find a single undamaged thermometer!

Upon failing so triumphantly in the discovery of gold deposits, and in view of the miserable consequences that followed any attempts to persuade the Viceroy personally about the matter, the search was suspended for an entire decade, and the store of materials fell into disuse. Yet Mohammed Ali, firm in his intention, did not abandon his favorite idea for good.

It was at Kheri that we left the Blue Nile behind. Here nature no longer changes, nor does it become devastated upon parting with the wholesome river, being able to survive without it, nourished by the seasonal rains. As for the population, it is not the same any more: now they are pure negroes; none of them living on the plains, even though some traces of recent settlements are still visible here. They live entirely in the mountains, which are quite impregnable. There are a few mountains (such as the Tabi Hills, two days' journey west from Roseires) where, at an altitude of 1,000 feet, tanks have been built in which water never dries out during summer; those mountains have not been conquered, for they can withstand a siege and to storm them would not be an easy task for the Egyptian army in the Sudan, consisting as it does almost entirely of negroes.

About noon we were shown a little negro village on Mount Akharo, but despite being directly underneath, we could not see it properly. Huts with pointed roofs—covered with soot and grey, the color of the enormous rocks that they clung to, like bee cells—evaded the eye.

Some of the enslaved negroes have long enjoyed special rights, either since the time of the Fung rule in Sennaar or since it was conquered by Ismail Pasha. These days, of course, those who have no power to defend their rights are bound to lose them in Egypt. Akharo exercises its right to levy a tax on merchant caravans that pass through it; for the caravans it is nothing but a payment to evade robbery, the tax itself being negligible: four piasters per camel, two per donkey.

The tanks built at the foot of the mountain, between rocks, keep rather fresh water throughout the summer. Another distinguishing feature of Akharo is that they sow and reap *dourra* here. Other negroes live mostly off hunting, very few breeding cattle, the majority eating nothing but roots.

Lord, how hot it is! One can scarcely breathe!

By nightfall we reached the Toumat, which was to become the object of my researches in many regards; an object of joy and suffering!

In the months preceding the rainy season, the Toumat has no water on the surface; yet under the sand, a quarter down,[4] the fresh stream never dries out, flowing freely, and they say that it even has crocodiles in it. After the rains, the Toumat grows into a large river. It was here, near its banks, that we encountered for the first time the bamboo, *Bambusa arundinacea*. There is plenty of it further on, negroes employing it to make throwing-spears and various other things, especially *tukkels*.

We would usually get up before dawn. Once, our caravan lit by the sun, I noticed round me with surprise some well-dressed figures and shaven faces. I had seen nothing like this for a long time and could hardly recognize my habitual companions, Turks and Arabs. Yousuf Effendi's face shone especially bright, the folds of his dandy dress billowing around. Loud talk and frequent laughter could be heard in the

---

4 A quarter of a sazhen; about 1.75 feet.

caravan. The camels walked at a quickened pace. The donkeys brayed, and soon their braying was met with a similar response coming from afar. A while later, we heard a drum roll.

Yes, it was good, so good to hear that roll! Even though it did not herald anything in particular, it was still cheering to know that we were not alone in the desert, that there were other people who would stand on our side rather than against us, and that, finally, we would be given a hospitable reception.

Through a forest of trees, one could see tents and yurts flashing, and then at last human voices and the neighing of horses could be heard…

It was an Egyptian bivouac by the Khassan mountains.

The Governor-General had already been expecting us awhile. One could not proceed any further without a military reinforcement, this place itself having been reached by us not without worries.

"What do you think, Ivan, will they take us much further?" one of my Siberian men once asked another.

"They cannot take us any further than the good old sun," the other said nonchalantly, yawning and stretching himself in the bright sun-light.

And he was right: they did not take us any further than the sun but rather brought us right under the sun and left us to the mercy of its all-burning rays.

They had prepared yurts and *tukkels* for us in advance. Leaving the Turks who accompanied us to take care of them however they saw fit, we ourselves—tortured by the daemon of curiosity and by our desire to learn as soon as we could the solution to the problem that we had come to solve from such distant lands—set to work on the same day. Having built a gold-washer overnight, in the morning we commenced our search for gold deposits.

Time flew in constant labors and struggles with nature and with the ignorance of the Turks, who presented us, if not with obstacles, then with great hindrances. Finally, our labors were crowned with success to the surprise of many, which made us easy prey for those who were unable to comprehend that gold was to be found where we were searching.[5] There-

---

5 Author's note: See the geological description of the country printed in *The Mining Journal*.

upon, speak though they did (albeit in hushed tones) against our preparations for the construction of a factory, they obeyed us unreservedly.

The factory was progressing fast. We worked day and night. The Turks began saying again that nothing would come out of the enterprise: it was beyond their comprehension.

Lord, oh Lord! How human patience can be tried!

Meanwhile, the sun burned during the day as before, whilst at night the temperature would drop, as is its wont in these mountains, to 5 degrees Reaumur.[6]

At Khassan I received various visitors: *meleks*, as the rulers of the nearby mountains are known, guides, and *jellabs*, or small traders, some of whom had even been able to reach Fadasi from Benishangul.[7] Fadasi is a large market in Inner Africa where negroes are gathered from every land, including from beyond the equator. *Jellabs* are only able to reach it if they take certain risks; they walk from one mountain to another under the patronage of *meleks*, provided that the two neighboring mountains are not at war and with the assistance of gifts, of course; if, however, the mountains are at odds with each other, then they pass the place stealthily at night. Cupidity prompts the Arab, who is not famous for his courage in general, to engage himself in audacious enterprises. It was these people whom I gathered information from, having long planned a journey further down south—to the sources of the Toumat, which I now strove for with all my aspirations.

My researches of the Toumat soon convinced me that gold deposits were mainly situated in the basin of the river, along ravines and small rivers that flow into it from the left if one faces downstream; in these parts it is similar to Miass in the Zlatoust works or the Pyshma in the Ekaterinburg works.[8] To survey the river from the place where it enters the foot-hills all the way up to its upper reaches, and then to cross its western tributaries—which I was to do (and did do) later, on my

---

6 6°C.
7 A region in what is today Ethiopia.
8 Miass, a river in the Southern Urals; Zlatoust, a city with an important iron-producing works in the Ural Mountains; Pyshma, a river in the Urals; Ekaterinburg, the largest city in the Urals, a center of metal industry in Russia.

way to Jebel Doul[9]—was extremely important, for it would allow me to determine a locality where future searches for gold would be conducted, that being the principal aim of the prospective journey.

The other aim was of less importance to me.

A short while before my arrival at Cairo, French news-papers printed a letter to Arago,[10] which contained quite an affirmative announcement about the discovery of the sources of the White Nile—that is, of the Nile proper, made by the brothers D'Abbadie,[11] who put the location of the sources in lat. 7°49′48″ N. and long. 36°2′39″ E. (from Greenwich).

Following the Toumat all the way to its upper reaches, I was to attain nearly the same latitude while deviating only slightly from the designated longitude and, therefore, to run into the Nile, so to speak—or at least to approach it so closely that any native would easily be able to point the river worshipped by many—thus confirming the discovery made by the D'Abbadies.

Those who have never heard of an expedition up the White Nile undertaken on the orders of the Egyptian government by d'Arnaud[12] (who has hitherto not published any account of it) do not know that this traveler was the first to assume, having gathered some rumors from negroes, that the White Nile had its source not in the west, near Darfour, as they used to believe, but on quite the opposite side—that is, not far from the sources of the Blue Nile. It was not until later that the D'Abbadies, apparently speaking from factual evidence, confirmed the assumption made by d'Arnaud.

It can be seen from the above how important the journey to the sources of the Toumat was; in addition, I would be able to determine the course of this significant river, which, unknown hitherto, had been denominated on the maps by dots.

My enterprise required the government's assistance; I knew that it would appear too bold and meet with much resistance from the

---

9 Kovalevsky probably means Gebel Dair, a magmatic mountain in central Sudan.
10 Dominique François Jean Arago (1786–1853), French astronomer and mathematician.
11 Antoine-Thomson d'Abbadie (1810–97) and Arnaud-Michel d'Abbadie (1815–93), French explorers known for their travels in Ethiopia.
12 Théodore Louis Joseph-Pons d'Arnaud (Arnaud-Bey, 1811–84), French engineer and traveler.

Hakumdar, or Governor-General; but I had accustomed myself to the idea too much to renounce it without trying every means possible to attain the end.

Indeed, the first reply of Halil Pasha was in the negative. "But why?" I asked. "No-one has ever been there, you cannot even find a guide." "We do not need one. The Toumat is our best guide." "But you would approach the realm of the Galla;[13] moreover, you would enter it." Aha! So the sum of the matter was this: the Governor-General partly shared the opinion of the local inhabitants about the indestructible power of the Galla people. "More honor for your army," I said.

Knowing the Turks well, I did not abandon my idea. Time and the power of argument being on my side, I accustomed Halil Pasha to it and, little by little, began winning him over; all he demanded now was that I restrict my journey by some known point and, at the first news of the Galla and their incursions, return immediately.

At last, having agreed on all the matters of dispute, we commenced our preparations for the expedition.

I was assisted in all my preparations by Dashuri and Muhammet Ali. Yet I have said nothing of them hitherto: they were young Arabs who—having been brought up in Germany, in the Harz Mountains, where they had, of course, never seen any gold deposits whatsoever—had traveled with me all over the Urals. Little did I know then that our paths would cross again at Khassan! . . . It was these men that Mohammed Ali entrusted (needless to say, under the immediate guidance of the Governor-General) with the discovery of gold and the construction of the factory. Their search for gold was at least somewhat successful, conducted in accordance with the directions of the negroes and, most importantly, under the threat of wrath from the Viceroy, who, having already begun to lose patience, obtained from them, one might say by force, some propitious reports and then ordered them to proceed without delay with the construction of a factory designed for 2,000 workers *for the first run*. You can imagine the state the young men were in! With no sufficient information about the enterprise, hindered in everything by the Governor-General—who firmly believed that the best method of

---

13   The name used by the Ottoman Egyptians for the Oromo people of Ethiopia.

washing was the one used by the negroes, although, as you shall see, one cannot conceive of a worse method—and under constant prompting from Mohammed Ali, the young men were in despair, and my arrival, relieving them of their indescribable responsibility, made them truly happy. Moreover, they felt sincere loyalty to me.

Poor Dashuri, having already paid his due to the climate, had been ill ever since his arrival in the Sudan; as for Ali, nothing would affect him, the only thing troubling him being his pervasive fear of the supreme ruler's wrath. Dashuri was to stay with my men and oversee the factory works, while Ali was setting off with me.

On the 7th (19th) of March, we observed a total lunar eclipse at Khassan. The sky being clear and blueish, as it always is here at night, the eclipse began in calm weather, at 9:20 P.M. It moved slowly up from below, deviating slightly to the north, and fully covered the moon at 10:35 P.M. The moon had the appearance of a red spot slightly obscured by fog. At 12:15 A.M. it began to divest itself of its cover in the same direction and resumed its regular appearance at 1:15 A.M.

I shall forego any account of the fairy-tales that the negroes and the Turks exchanged on the occasion of the eclipse, despite everyone having been warned about it in advance.

Chapter II

Benishangul and Kamamil[1]

We set forth on the 13th (25th) of March. The black army marched in regularity, guns at the ready, drums rolling; the Governor-General accompanied us awhile, until finally he bid me farewell, entrusting me to the detachment, and the detachment to me, whereupon he took his leave of us. A command was given to stand at ease; the ranks began to waver and make noise.

The detachment appeared picturesque and motley. Sheikh Arbab rode in front of it, wrapped in his white *ferdeh*, his coal-black feet visible underneath and his face, blacker than the feet, above. He had been the husband of the famous Nasra,[2] who played an important part in the Sennaar state while it existed. Arbab had played the roles of her husband and one of her ministers, and he still retained a certain influence on the people, now as a subject of Mohammed Ali and in consequence of a *special* influence that Nasra had on the original conquerors of Sennaar, Ismail Pasha and the *Defterdar*. Sheikh Arbab rode in front as the principal, official guide, surrounded by several sheikhs and *meleks* of nearby mountains. Behind him rode some hundred men of the regular

---
1 A region in Ethiopia known for its gold deposits.
2 Nasra bit Adlan (1810–53), a member of the Fung ruling dynasty.

and national cavalry. The latter were black, the former white; the latter naked to their waists, the former wearing a variegated collection of dress. There were Albanians, Bosnians, Circassians, Epireans, Turks, and Montenegrins, all in their national costume, sometimes complemented by stray garments that happened to be to the owners' liking. That was the regular cavalry! In their wake walked rows of camels, donkeys, and mules, carrying either burden or riders; they were followed by the infantry, some thousand negroes of various tribes and mountains, amongst whom officers and two battalion commanders stood out for the whiteness of their skin. The soldiers were in rags, that was true, but their guns and ammunition were in good order; and as we shall see, these soldiers are no laughing matter, strange though a black army might seem marching in the manner of Europeans.

The march proceeded at a slashing pace, weaving through thickets of trees, now going down, now climbing mountains, now disappearing in hollows created by mountain streams. After an hour's journey, we proceeded to circumvent the Khassan mountains, covered with numerous *tukkels*, the mountains being very thickly peopled. Despite being under the protection of the government and very close to the principal encampment, some of the inhabitants watched the detachment approach with wild eyes, from afar, whilst others fled their dwellings altogether. The soldiers wanted very much to look inside the *tukkels*, to see whether there was anything left behind, a child or something else, anything that could be stolen and later sold, but a single word sufficed to stop them from any attempts at plunder.

Nature presented all the luxury of a mountainous country; yet these were neither Swiss mountains, reaching far into the clouds, nor those of Albania or Montenegro, craggy, naked, terrible, and impregnable—no, they were akin to the Southern Urals, or to the mountains of Serbia, with their splendid valleys (plateaux): picturesque and beautiful mountains! . . . The forest was not much changed; the baobab appeared again, and *Samadera* stood there in all its magnificence, its great fruit, reminiscent of giant pumpkins, swinging on long, thin stems.

The detachment marched without a halt for six or seven hours, and for all that, whenever a wild chamois appeared before them, several soldiers and Arabs would give chase, the Arab's spear reaching it more readily than the soldier's bullet. Those chamois and antelopes often amused us when, frightened by the crowd of people and deafened by the noise and the report of the gun, they almost invariably threw themselves under the soldiers' feet: poor creatures, did they really hope for mercy!? . . .

In the Ramleh stream, we found, to our surprise, an ample flow of water on the surface, while better rivers—proper, respectable rivers such as the Toumat—go under the sand owing to the heat, and it is only during the rains that they emerge into the world in all their abundance of waters, with all their crushing force of fast-flowing waves. Having quenched our thirst, we proceeded further and an hour later halted at the Disah. There was no water, but the soldiers knew where to find it; in a quarter of an hour, the entire dry bed of the Disah was peppered with small holes filled with water, dug with no other tools than the hands and finger-nails of our negroes.

On the morrow, ascending ever higher and eventually attaining 3,000 feet, we reached Benishangul.

Benishangul is a range or, it would be fairer to say, a cluster of mountains crowned with villages. The population of the entire area amounts to 10,000 and consists of the negroes of the Berta[3] tribe and the Arabs of the Jaali[4] and Khomed[5] tribes.

The negroes are either slaves or soldiers of sorts, conscripted in case of war; the Arabs are rulers; seeing that the former far outnumber the latter, it often happens that they kill their ruler and appoint another instead; it is always an Arab, however, one of the red ones, for the negroes respect their skin-color. There is constant turmoil and anxiety here, as in any military republic. The word *republic* was not unintentional. Benishangul, as well as all the mountains situated beyond it, are separate republics which live independently, almost deprived of any communication with the rest, and thus are easily destroyed by the raids of any enemy that is stronger or bolder than each of them taken

---

3 An ethnic group living along the border of contemporary Sudan and Ethiopia.
4 Ja'alin, an Arabic-speaking ethnic group in Sudan.
5 Possibly the Abu Homed tribe of Sudan.

on its own; while also being prone to destroy themselves. The negroes of the White Nile, as we shall see, are governed differently; they are the valley negroes.

About two years ago, the tribe of Benishangul was defeated by Mohammed Ali's soldiers, and henceforth, they have been obeying him again—that is, paying their taxes. The government wants no other part in the affairs of the negroes or the Jebel Aali Arabs[6]: let them fight each other to their heart's content—the government could not care less; that might even be for the best, for they would be sooner ready to be conquered. Despite being dependent upon the lawful government, however, the negroes and the Arabs looked upon us with much dislike and even talked of preventing us from going into the mountains, for they knew from experience that, should you give in to the Turks, wherever they passed there would be nothing left but razed ground. Yet all their designs led to nothing; indeed, they were pretty defenseless against some thousand well-armed soldiers, even if their entire population were to stand in the field!

Our own soldiers, and especially officers, were no less tempted to attack the negroes once we were already in the mountains and thus could beat them so easily and yet so profitably. Everyone was willing to obtain a free slave, which would be their lawful property in the time of war. Yet considering that there was no apparent hostile movement on the part of the negroes—who were constantly kept in check by their own Arabs, the latter being well aware of the intention of the Turks—and realizing that a camel injured by them or a stolen donkey were not at all worth demanding that the negroes pay for it with their blood, I strictly prohibited the soldiers from launching any attack or engaging themselves in plunder or violence.

We spent two days in Benishangul, which was rather hard upon the soldiers, for they had to constantly guard the camp while at the same time resisting the temptation that so often presented itself to them.

Upon our arrival, on the very first night, the mountains all round us, as far as the eye could see, got covered with signal flares, which heralded alarm, catastrophe, the invasion of an enemy army. These

---

6 Jabal Awliya, a place next to Khartoum. Kovalevsky refers to the Arabs of Sudan.

signals, being transported from one mountain to another, reach the most distant lands with the speed of the telegraph, letting the natives know whence the enemy is coming; who the invaders are, whether it be the Galla, their own people, or the Turks; and how strong and dangerous they appear. Yet what purpose does it serve? The best they know to do is flee their *tukkels* and hide themselves in some impregnable gorge.

I have only just noticed that, following everyone's example, I get carried away and call Mohammed Ali's government Turkish and his soldiers Turks; that is how they all express themselves here, yet it is not done to show that their ruler obeys the Porte—oh no, far from it! The Egyptians stand by their distinctive nature, or at least so they say, for, as we have already noted, there are almost no Egyptians to be found in the army, nor in Mohammed Ali's government, while Turks of various countries and descents prevail everywhere without exception. As for the negroes, they are slaves, and not even worth mentioning; the army being the only place where they are feared, especially in the mountains: disturbed by the sight of their homeland, of the mountains, so irresistible to those who have spent their early years there, the negroes often desert the ranks and can easily turn their guns against the whites, who scarcely ever amount to one-hundredth in any detachment.

The negroes and the Arabs of these parts, like any population living under the influence of seasonal rains, dwell in *tukkels*, wicker huts made from bamboo, with high conical roofs. Those possessed of a higher station or wit place their huts on tall props to preserve them from being completely flooded during the rainy season; the *tukkel* is surrounded by a gallery, also wicker, but rather more loose so as to ensure the free passage of air inside it. The double fence makes the interior of the *tukkel* dark; but then again, why would these people need light! They do nothing and, moreover, spend most of the day under a sprawling fig-tree in a common gathering, to which women, too, are freely admitted. Not only do they not wrap themselves in Mohammedan veils, but they leave their nakedness quite uncovered, their dress consisting of a single narrow belt tied below the back-bone: a leather fringe decorated with various metal trinkets and ornaments. Some wear even less; yet they are proud of their luxuries and decorations—which consist of numerous necklaces, ivory bracelets, ear-rings, nose-rings, and lip-rings—the other object of their pride being their hair. You cannot but wonder at this naked lot taking so much trouble with the dressing of their heads! The negro is quite naked, and yet his bushy, wavy hair, akin to the fleece of the merino sheep, has several pretty little feathers sticking out of it. The Arabs of these parts shave their hair into a pattern, sometimes leaving only the top, made to stand like a crown, sometimes shaving the top alone so that the remaining hair flows in strands or in locks shaped as rings. Such head-dress comes at a high price. Women are forced to use a forked piece of wood or a little bench instead of a cushion, putting their heads inside it, as if it were a pair of pincers, to preserve their hair. Some negroes, men and women alike, plait their hair into small braids; but there are too many types of head-dress to mention them all. Women tie their fringe-like belt at the back. Men—who use instead a piece of leather, a quarter in length—tie it at the front, so that it is only the backside that is slightly covered, while a single knot sticks out at the front, this being their only dress; although, as I have noted, some dispose of it altogether. The Arabs are less naked, some of them, sheikhs, for instance, even wearing a *ferdeh*, a long piece of fabric draped round the body in a free fashion.

At first the sight of this naked humankind strikes you as barbaric; the coal-black skin-color amazes you; but then, accepting it as some kind of special dress, you become accustomed to it. Were it a white person, you think, then, of course, his nakedness would be disgusting as it would define every part of his body; but he is black, so everything is merged together in a single vague color. Eventually, the very color no longer alarms you, as you find certain charm in this black, greased skin, smooth, tender, and glossy like kid-skin. The mountain people, both the negroes and the Arabs, are for the most part well-built, especially the offspring of the two races crossed; their movements are supple yet mostly frantic, like those of animals. The negroes have limited wit, their minds constantly remaining in a child-like state, and if they do something bad it is mainly done on an involuntary impulse, without thought. Yet they do possess some notion of honesty, manifested more strongly in those more civilized! After a rebellion of negro troops in Walet Medina,⁷ the military tribunal demanded that they name the instigators; one instigator surrendered himself, without any prompting from others. He was shot. Despite such a terrible precedent, another stepped out of the ranks, also voluntarily, and came to the same end; and then another dozen people followed his example. There was no evidence against them, yet they themselves claimed to be no less guilty than their comrades. One must say, however, that life is a most insignificant thing for a negro, who can readily die at any moment.

The negroes are idolaters; or it would be fairer to say, they have no religion except superstitious rituals. The Arabs pretend to be Mohammedans. Yet they have neither mosques nor priests, and all they do by way of practicing their religion is recite the holy prayer: "*La ilaha ill Allah, Muhammad rassul Allah.*"⁸ The Arabs are very tempted by the paradise promised by Mohammed; were it not for it, they would abandon their faith altogether, for it does restrict their freedom somewhat.

A negro from these parts once told me, with child-like simplicity, about his deceased kinsmen: "So many of our people are already gone, God knows whereto. I remember my father going, my grandfather, and my brother also. People say they are dead: good! For they shall return; they cannot lie there buried till the end of time!" His simple speech was met with a chorus of laughter from the Turks, and yet one could, after all, glimpse in it some notion of Resurrection! One of the Turks said, "Indeed! Return they shall; oh yes, they shall come anon."

That might be the reason why the negroes have this custom: they come to graves and, pelting them with stones, say, "Rise, rise!" Yet the dead will not rise.

After a two days' stay at Benishangul, we commenced our ascent from the encampment. Everyone was very glad: both the soldiers, who had been bored with constantly being on guard duty, and the Arabs, who were happy to realize that on this occasion, the clouds had passed over them without a thunderstorm.

---

7 Again, perhaps Kovalevsky has in mind Wad Medina.
8 The Shahada, or the profession of creed: "la 'ilaha 'illa llah muhammadun rasulu llah" (Arabic; There is no God except Allah and Mohammed is His messenger).

The *mek* of the village, an old man the likes of whom I was never to see again, volunteered to accompany me, despite all my attempts to convince him to remain at home—I was worried that he would die on the road. They brought him a white horse with a little bell round the neck, which was to remind us of Russian post-bells throughout the march; having mounted the horse, not only did our guide keep tight, but he also pranced all along the way, and would often gallop ahead at full speed. The bell denominated his high title. Behind him marched 150 or so Arabs and negroes, armed with bundles of spears; yet this was not, of course, the defense that we relied on in case of an attack.

We marched back east but, having reached Geta, turned south and, at about noon, halted and made a camp by the Sorgol, its banks shaded by the bright greenery of the so-called negro lemon-trees. The tree is quite similar to the ordinary lemon-tree in its aspect but much larger and more luxurious; its fruit is the same in appearance; once ripe, it tastes very sweet and refreshing, its flowers, however, being quite different.

We had hitherto seen *tukkels* upon the mountains we had passed and, occasionally, above the *tukkels*, some armed men in a threatening position. Hereafter, everything was deserted. The beautiful land of Kamamil, adjacent to the Toumat, stood completely devastated by the Galla negroes.

Chapter III

Farther into Africa Than Anyone Else

The Galla, a very populous tribe whose habitations stretch from lat. 8° or 7° N. to the equator (or perhaps beyond it), frequently threaten Abyssinia itself, having only recently conquered a part of it and kept it under their control for a few years. The Galla are not much different from other negro tribes; if the Sphinx be a negro type, most likely he is a Galla. Trading Arab tribes, however, wandering all over Africa, brought their traditions here too, having improved the physical aspect of people and taught some of them the original Prophet's prayer. There the education of the Galla ends—except, perhaps, for the art of the smelting of iron ore, which does, of course, require a certain degree of enlightenment. At the Fadasi market, which now belongs to Abyssinia (see map), people gather from all parts of Inner Africa, but the Galla prevail there. They bring horses, honey, iron shaped as short blocks, and spears, so very ubiquitous, although I cannot tell if they make those spears themselves or obtain them from negroes living on the other side of the equator.

The Galla negroes eat raw meat, which has given some an excuse to say—quite wrongly—that they are anthropophagous! The Makadi and

ГЛАВА III.

Мы проникаемъ далѣе другихъ внутрь Африки.

Племя чрезвычайно многочисленное, которое идетъ отъ 8—7 градуса широты до экватора, быть можетъ за него, внутрь Африки, Галла, не рѣдко угрожаетъ самой Абиссиніи; еще недавно овладѣло частію ея, и держало нѣсколько лѣтъ въ повиновеніи. Галла мало отличаются отъ другихъ племенъ негровъ; если сфинксъ есть типъ негра, то всего скорѣе изъ племени Галла. Бродящія по всюду въ Африкѣ, торговыя племена арабовъ занесли, однако, и сюда свое начало, улучшивъ физическую сторону людей и научивъ нѣкоторыхъ изъ нихъ первоначальной молитвѣ пророка. Тѣмъ и кончается образованность Галла, да еще развѣ искусствомъ плавить желѣзныя руды, что, конечно, требуетъ извѣстной степени просвѣщенія. На рынкѣ

Sphinx situated near pyramids

many other tribes living on the confines of the Sudan and in Abyssinia are more civilized, yet they eat raw meat. In Europe raw meat is also believed in some cases to be more wholesome that fried meat, raw ham being preferred to boiled ham. The Makadi and the Galla have learned this hygienic truth sooner. Indeed, they enjoy perfect health and live longer than other negroes, even though the farthest-living of them are under the equator. Ultimately, such is their taste, and that is the end of it! ... Thus at feasts, freshly slaughtered bulls, their blood still steaming, are hung upon a pole among the guests, and everyone cuts off a piece for themselves according to their taste.

The Galla live in *tukkels*, which form villages; dressed not much better than the rest, they are distinguished from other tribes in the battle only by large ivory rings worn above elbows, as well as sheep-skins, or sometimes leopard-skins, thrown over shoulders, hair out; they are armed as everyone else, but while few other negroes in these parts have shields, almost all the Galla do have them, although those are mostly of elephant-hide rather than hippopotamus-hide. What, then, is their advantage over other negroes? Firstly, it is their large number; secondly, their united force. In wartime, they select a commander amongst themselves, who rides in front on a mule, his men obeying him unconditionally; meanwhile, it is during this time that outrages occur in these mountains. Taking advantage of the Galla's incursions into Kamamil, not only do the tribes subjugated by Kamamil provide no assistance to it, but they also rebel against it while neighboring tribes stab it in the back to avenge their latest grievances, until eventually their own turn comes. Thus the Galla have recently reached Benishangul with almost no resistance, having covered 600 or 700 versts[1] in their campaign—and in a short time at that, for they had to hasten back home with all their speed, aware of the danger of the *kharif* approaching. They commence their expedition at the beginning of the *rashash*, a period of moderate rains in early April, usually marching along the Toumat, for water in these parts is the main condition on which any free action is possible—the condition of success and life. They fly like a storm-cloud, yet rumors travel everywhere faster than themselves. They do not bother their neighbors, the negroes of the Berta tribe, including the inhabitants of Shumba and other mountains; whether it be because the latter are their vassals or for some other reason, I do not know; yet even the neighbors tend to tremble during the campaign, no-one hoping for long-lasting peace and many getting out of the way as a precaution. Terrible fluster ensues, as if in an ant-hill: they run from one mountain to another, they ask for help, arm themselves, and kill

---

1 Between 400 and 500 miles.

each other at incessant meets; a horn never stops summoning people from all points, the lights burning all night through, on every mountain. The *mek* of Kamamil gives the *mek* of Benishangul his daughter, he sends gold to Fasdur, and so he is promised help... but here come the Galla, they are already on the mountain... and everyone perishes or is taken into slavery, far away from their native mountains to the land of a people whom other negroes believe to be cannibals. To kill a Galla is a heroic deed, a celebratory occasion here; his corpse is cut into hundreds of pieces, which are carried round the country as if they were trophies and displayed for all to see.

From the Disah we descended straight to the Toumat. No Egyptian had ever been here, to say nothing of Europeans; the army of Mohammed Ali had never penetrated here; the guides from Benishangul did not know the way forward; but we no longer needed them, for the Toumat was to conduct us further on. No-one could even tell how far up the Toumat we were from Kamamil and whether we would be able to proceed with the camels; I halted and made a camp, sending a cavalry detachment to search for a route, having already decided to proceed along the river-bed itself.

Search for gold had usually been conducted here in accordance with the instructions of guides, in those places where negroes had previously worked and where, of course, more gold had been found. It would be forgivable if the authorities did that, for they know no other means; but Europeans, too, did the same. Of course it ended with the guides doing their utmost to deflect the searchers from rich deposits rather than conducting them there, for it was those deposits that constituted the source of wealth that the Turks wished to extort from them. That was one of the many reasons why—despite Mohammed Ali's efforts of 20 years past, as well as immense costs—gold still had not been discovered in the Sudan. I say that from experience: no sooner had we abandoned the guides, no sooner had we followed our own considerations, than we found on the Toumat a significant deposit containing gold, near which we proposed to establish another gold-washing factory.

This point was also of military importance, for it was here that the Galla usually ventured out to launch their devastating incursions into the territory of the Berta. An encampment and a garrison, required to protect the factory, would also protect the new subjects of Mohammed Ali from total extermination; and the settlement, connected with the first factory and the already established encampment, would be included in a line of military settlements in the mountains along the Toumat, a project I had submitted to the Viceroy.

In the evening the detachment that I had dispatched to explore the route returned and announced that in many places, the Toumat was blocked up by rocks across its entire width, and that even horses (let alone camels) were occasionally unable to walk over them. "Can we still walk it?" I asked. "We can!" "Well then, we shall walk."

Having left the caravan in a fortified place, under the protection of 300 people, and having instructed them to explore the gold-mine I had discovered, we set forth. The soldiers carried a supply of *dourra* sufficient for six days or so, the other provisions having been loaded on donkeys, of which there happened to be about 40 in the detachment.

The Toumat is beautiful here, lying in the shade of the bright-green foliage of negro lemon-trees and wild laurel-trees. With giant rocks piled up everywhere, the river must be magnificent when in full flow; the rocks are so high that the waves do not drown them but tear and rush through them with a deafening roar, according to eye-witness accounts. *Asclepias lanifora*, very similar to the jasmine in color and smell, was sweeping over us with its branches from the bank. It is very common here; being completely devoid of leafage and covered with flowers and fruit all over, the plant is extremely beautiful.

A six or seven hours' crossing over sand and rocks, and sometimes over water—for instance, by the mouth of the Sorgol, which never dries out—with heavy burdens and under the white-hot skies, was arduous for the soldiers; in addition, the guides, doing all they could to deflect us from this route, had told them frightening stories of terrible dangers; yet my little black soldiers marched briskly and cheerfully, as though nothing was the matter. An army better able to bear all the labors and hardship of a march would not be easy to find. To go without food for a day or two, or without water for a whole day, is no trouble to the negro. Also, the negro does not concern himself with his choice of viands, always being able to find some potatoes, onions, or edible roots, or even gongoles (the fruit of the baobab), and requiring nothing more; thirst poses the only mortal danger for him in this extraordinary country where for six months one cannot find any respite from water, entire masses of it falling from the sky, while for the next six months there is not a drop of water to be obtained. If these soldiers had good officers, they would be good soldiers in all respects; but the officers are not worth a curse, being illiterate, timid, and avaricious. Their only advantage is their skin-color, which the blacks customarily respect from an early age, recognizing the lawful nature of their own denigration.

Along our route, where the banks were high and hung over the dry river-bed, we could see pits which, protruding far into the banks, were filled with water and seemed deep. They had been dug by negroes, who search for crocodiles under the thin layer of sand, where there are deeper cavities providing permanent shelter to the amphibious creatures until the Toumat is inundated. The negroes know that a crocodile, when confined in a tight space, is not very dangerous, and they kill it with lances alone, predominantly stabbing it in the wide-open mouth or under one of the front legs. This place is occasionally reached by negroes from very remote parts! What attracts them is not the crocodile-hunting alone, but especially the washing of golden sands.

Riding with a vanguard group, I had just passed a pile of stones without noticing anything, when suddenly loud cries behind us made me return. What was the matter? A negro—bewildered, frightened, with a vacuous countenance, and naked, of course—stood there surrounded by the soldiers, many of whom were claiming their right to him, some being the first to have noticed him, others to have caught him. With great difficulty I managed to pacify the crowd and make them explain the matter: it turned out that the wretched man, upon seeing the vanguard group, leapt into a space between rocks and buried himself in the sand. Yet negroes can scent their game from afar, and so they extracted him from under the ground. Some signs betokening that he was from Fandango, they found a soldier who could understand his language (in these parts nearly every mountain has a distinct language); I tried to ask the captive about the route and nearby tribes, but it was all in vain:

he stood before me like a madman! Bored with the interview, I told the soldiers that Fandango obeyed, if only ostensibly, Mohammed Ali, and we therefore were not to take prisoners amongst its people under any circumstances; in addition, our object was something other than negro-hunting—whereupon they let the poor man go. Another time we encountered several negroes; there were five of them or so; had they rushed sideward, onto a bank overgrown with a thicket of trees and shrubs, no-one would even think of chasing them; yet the frightened negroes, like the wild chamois I have written about, ran ahead in front of us, along the river. They were, of course, caught and, after various interrogations, also set free. They themselves found such magnanimity incomprehensible; they thought that we were about to fire a volley at them, if only to amuse ourselves, and so they hesitated awhile, unable to decide whether they should go, and then rushed forward, like an arrow launched from a bow. One negro surprised me. No sooner had they caught him than our Arab guide, having peered at him good and proper, cried that the man was a slave that he had bought some 20 years ago from *jellabs* and claimed his rights to him. We had no time to hold court and dispense punishment in such matters, and therefore, turning to the negro, I announced that he was now free to go wherever he wished; yet the negro, to my great surprise, followed his former master, and an hour later, I saw him again, now loaded, like an ass, with his master's possessions. A sense of abjection, duty, and respect toward the right of power that others have over them is perpetually manifested in the negroes; those feelings, inexplicable and instinctive, reduce them to a most miserable condition.

A two days' march from Kamamil we reached a fork, where one river, known as the Degessi,[2] bent south-west, while the other, the Toumat proper, took us straight down south. The town of Fadasi, constituting the market of Inner Africa, lay not far off on our left, on the frontier between Abyssinia and the Galla land. From thence the bed of the Toumat diminishes in width visibly until it finally becomes a low ravine, at the bottom of which flows a narrow stream of the river's sources, and that only during the rainy season. There we halted, there

---

2 The Didessa River, in present-day Ethiopia.

being nothing more to search for, our aim having been achieved! My negro soldiers rejoiced, having penetrated the land of the Galla as an open force, and they talked amongst themselves, saying that no-one would believe them in Khartoum when they began telling people about the place they had been to. We were still to reach a mound ahead of us: from thence one could observe the entire surrounding country, casting one's eye over a place that so many travelers had attempted to reach, all in vain, many of them having paid with their lives for their unreserved commitment to science. I took with me about 20 soldiers, as well as several negroes and Arabs who knew the area and would be able to explain to me at least something about the blue mountains in the distance; we reached the mound about two hours ere sunset. I looked round cheerfully and proudly. No-one had ever got as far into Africa as we did from this side, which was the most forbidding to travelers. This victory over nature, this primacy of man's conquest of it are not without a certain pleasure; a lofty pleasure that can be experienced only by a traveler who reaches his destination, having endured a series of hard labors, hardships, and trials of his patience and will-power.

Around me, and mostly to the left, there lay a land that had been inhabited 12 years ago or so and was now completely deserted, having lost its very name; the native negroes had been exterminated or taken into slavery by the Galla tribe. This land shall, of course, remain deserted for long, for it constitutes a raised plateau, providing no protection from enemies. It has now been taken over by elephants, which are extremely numerous here, one of our men having seen an entire herd amounting, by his count, to 130 elephants; they roam free here; the inhabitants of these lands, unlike the negroes of the White Nile, do not know how to hunt them; true, there is no water on the surface here, yet the elephant has found a way to obtain it: lying on the bottom of the Toumat, it wallows there until the sand gives way to its weight, whereupon it rises, water appearing in the created pit, in which it remains for several days.

I named this place the Land of Nicholas; a small river (which in the current season was, of course, completely dry) ran across it, a river whose name had been lost, and so I named it the Nevka on my map, which name would point to a European traveler's having reached this place and indicate his nationality.

Further to the east, nearly in the same latitude as we were and even slightly behind us, there lay the town of Fadasi, which we could not see behind a nearby hill, and beyond it rose the giant mountains of Abyssinia. To the west, amongst a variety of mountains, two peaks, Radokah and Fadokah, stood the highest of all; the mountains stretching from them southward and northward.

Down the Toumat, the eye could reach the horizon, scarcely covered with small hills, with thickets and undergrowth in abundance. Yet my thoughts and my eyes were drawn south, to the sources of the White Nile, of which no-one had told me anything yet, despite all my queries.

In the distance loomed blue mountains, which are usually denominated on all the maps as the Moon Mountains, Jebel-el-Khamar,[3] an Arabic rather than a native name, as you can see; as to how it managed to reach these parts, geographers could tell you that. Even here, on the northern side of the mountain-face, where the mountains are most likely to be known by an Arabic name, they are called Souri. At their foot-hills, according to an assumption made by the D'Abbadie brothers, the White Nile, or the Nile proper, should flow, having apparently been diverted south along the mountain range and then forced to make its way through its masses, directly to the west. Yet that is physically impossible; the northern side of the mountain-face gives origin to rivers that flow directly to the north, such as the Yabous, for instance, and even the Toumat itself, which, were the White Nile indeed here, would be bound to meet it along the way and merge with it, while in reality, having run a long distance north, these rivers safely reach their destination—that is, flow into the Blue Nile. Thus if the river discovered by the D'Abbadies does constitute the sources of the Nile, then it should make an abrupt bend, applying extraordinary efforts at its very birth, so to speak, prior to strengthening and enriching itself with extraneous waters so as to be able to tear through the mountains, which, at this bend, would press on it from every direction, in Abyssinia and in the Galla land, in the latitude given by the D'Abbadies. If, on the other hand, one assumes that it

---

3   Jabal al-Qamar.

flows on the other side of the mountains, south of them, and makes its way north after it has circumvented them, then it would be bound to encounter along the way the Gokhob or the Omo, rivers that have been well mapped by Major Harris, and consequently, to flow into them and disappear in the southern direction.

I shall not make so bold as to categorically refute the important—nay, great—discovery made by the D'Abbadies, and yet, having nearly reached the latitude of 8° without finding Bahr-el-Abiad (that is, the Nile proper) nor even hearing of it from any of the natives, while also bearing in mind the above considerations, I now have more than enough reason to doubt the supposed discovery. By the bye, this is what many negroes said, their words being confirmed by those of one of my Arab companions, who used to be a high-ranking official in the time of the former Sennaar rulers—a man who had visited Abyssinia and knew his country, which stretched far south, very well. In the latitude given by D'Abbadie, perhaps subject to a slight variation, there is, indeed, a Bahr-el-Abiad, but that is a small river flowing into the Blue Nile, on your right if you face downstream; it is, however, shown on a map compiled by Caillaud and printed in Paris in 1827; there is also, a little way to the south, a small lake known as Bahr-el-Abiad.

Did D'Abbadie mistake the sources of that river or the lake for the Nile itself?

I repeat: I have cited my considerations and my doubts here, although I hesitate to refute the discovery made by D'Abbadie, a courageous and respectable traveler, as we have heard. However, we shall return to this question, which excited so heated an argument between Ayrton, who defended D'Abbadie, and Beke, who refuted his reasons, the latter being subsequently attacked by Werne too.[4]

---

4 Frederick Ayrton (1812–73), British traveler and explorer of Africa; Charles Tilstone Beke (1800–1874), British geographer, traveler, and biblical scholar; and Ferdinand Werne (1800–74), German scholar, diplomat and explorer. The polemics around the D'Abbadie brothers' discovery of the source of the White Nile occurred in the pages of the *Journal of the Royal Geographic Society of London* in 1848–50.

CHAPTER IV

The Sources of the Nile in Studies,[1] from Herodotus to the Present Day

The Nile, great and mysterious, worshipped by the ancients, who had temples and numerous priests dedicated to it; the Nile that they chose as a symbol of the superior and life-giving Amon-Ra; the Nile that affords life to present-day Egypt and propels it further... Had the famous Albuquerque, the Viceroy of Portugal in the 15th century,[2] indeed put into practice his bold project, diverting the current of the Nile into the Red Sea (which is not as impossible as it is generally thought to be), the entire Egypt would have turned into a desert, with the wind blowing freely and sand-hills racing around. Is it any wonder, then, that this very Nile has been a subject of studies in every age; that all the peoples of Egypt have striven to lift the veil of a river which remains incomprehensible to them; a river that would suddenly, with no apparent reason, at a time when all the other rivers become low, be filled up to its banks, bursting them and reviving the fertility of the exhausted

---

1 In 1863, Jules Verne (1828–1905), renowned French writer widely considered the father of science fiction, published his *Cinq semaines en ballon*, in which he first referred to the study of the sources of the Nile.
2 Afonso de Albuquerque, Duke of Goa (1453–1515), Portuguese aristocrat and imperial statesman.

earth, and then, jubilant after its great good deed, would return to its bed again, its waters reaching their usual level!? People have searched for the place of birth of this river in every age: in the ancient times, for the sake of religion, wishing to erect temples by its very cradle, and in the modern times, for the sake of science or trade; yet in all times, the searches have been equally futile.

This is what one of the most ancient historians, Herodotus, who tried in every way possible to learn something about the sources of the Nile, says: "Not one either of the Egyptians or of the Libyans or of the Hellenes, who came to speech with me, professed to know anything, except the scribe of the sacred treasury of Athene at the city of Saïs in Egypt. To me however this man seemed not to be speaking seriously when he said that he had certain knowledge of it."[3] That was but a lie! Herodotus himself, never believing a word the man said, continued his searches. At Elephantine Island he was told that he was to sail up the Nile for another four months to a place occupied by Egyptian colonists and refugees and that half-way to that place there was Meroë, the capital of Ethiopia. Taking into consideration the difficulty of sailing up the Nile from Elephantine to Meroë, where there are endless submerged rocks and rapids along the way, one cannot but believe this account. Further, Herodotus talks of young Libyan adventurers who were magically transported far south, to a big city inhabited by black people; a large river flowed by the city *from dawn to dusk*, which in this waterless country could be nothing but the Nile. Sweeping aside any magical additions to the tale, we shall see that the account is not too different from those we later obtained from a number of subsequent travelers, including, most recently, d'Arnaud and D'Abbadie. Even more detailed evidence was collected by the scholar Eratosthenes,[4] one of the keepers of the famous Library of Alexandria. Taking advantage of Ptolemy Evergetes's[5] campaign in Ethiopia in the 3rd century B.C., he traveled much farther up and wrote a minute description of the Nile on his way to Aswan, as we know it now, and back.

---

3 Author's note: Herodotus, book II, 28.
4 Eratosthenes of Cyrene (circa 276–195 BCE), Greek scholar and librarian.
5 Ptolemy III Euergetes (284–222 BCE), monarch of the Ptolemaic dynasty in Egypt.

Emperor Nero[6] sent a number of Romans up the Nile, with the particular aim of finding its sources. After a long journey, they reached Ethiopia, whose ruler, upon giving them a very gracious reception, conveyed them to the neighboring kings. Thus they safely reached "wide marshes overgrown with empty bush" whence they could not proceed by land or by barque. "Here," the travelers say, "we saw two large cliffs, a river rushing with a terrible force from a gorge between them." The intelligent Roman centurions would have never mistaken that mountain stream for the sources of the Nile, but as we have noted, they could not proceed any farther. That they were telling the truth about the places they had seen was quite confirmed by d'Arnaud's expedition, which came the farthest up the White Nile; that is, up to those two cliffs—which, in d'Arnaud's account also, follow wide marshes covered with bush—undoubtedly the same rocks as the ones that stopped the voyage of the intrepid Romans. And so it was not until now, following all the efforts and the deaths of many a traveler, that we reached the places which had already been reached by an expedition in the time of Nero.

I shall forego certain negligible attempts made by the Romans to attain the sources of the Nile, for they added nothing whatsoever to the previously gathered evidence. On the contrary, the inner part of Africa was drifting ever farther apart from the civilized world. It was not until the 10th century that the Arabs appeared here, some coming from Egypt, others from the Arabian shores of the Red Sea; they went far up the Nile, all the way to the Sudan, and in such numbers that they were able to establish entire states, of which Ghana,[7] for instance, was famous for the lavishness and wealth of its court. Abyssinia and Nubia remained Christian countries, and the Arabs were forced to enter into trade dealings with them; yet any accounts provided by the Arab geographers and travelers are confused and full of fairy-tales, similar to those in *One Thousand and One Nights*. Generally, they did not contribute much to science, their studies having been predominantly concerned

---

6 Nero Claudius Caesar Augustus Germanicus (37–68 CE), Roman emperor.
7 Also Wagadu, a West African imperial formation (circa 800–1200 CE). Earlier, the founders of the Ghana Empire are believed to have resided in western Sudan, where they formed a kingdom.

with astrology and alchemy, for which the Sudan, the foremost land of miracles, had been famous since the ancient times. They changed many names to suit their taste, thus misleading European geographers in some important questions; hence, the Arabic name of the Nile of the Negroes, which present-day scientists resolutely acknowledge to be the Niger, still remains quite mysterious, and it would be much fairer for it to refer to the part of the Nile proper that goes through the land of the negroes.

One of the Arab travelers, however, is to be distinguished here: for the veracity of his accounts, some of which are being confirmed in practice to this day, as well as to show how curiosity, passion for the new—that omnipotent engine of the traveler—can lead him too far once he has stepped onto the slippery road of wanderings. I am talking of Ibn Batuta.[8]

Abu Abd Allah Muhammad ibn Abd Allah al-Lawati, widely known under the name of Ibn Batuta, went from Tangier to Mecca so as to visit Mohammedan holy men, alive and dead, along the way, being a well-known scholar himself. In Cairo he met Imam Borhan Oddin el-Aaraj, famous in the East for his wisdom and his holy ways of life and even possessed of the power to work miracles.

"I perceive that you are fond of traveling into various countries," al-Aaraj said to him.

Ibn Batuta "had at that time no intention of traveling into very distant parts," yet he hesitated to contradict the holy man. "Yes," he said timidly.

"You must visit my brother Farid Oddin in India, and my brother Rokn Oddin Ibn Zakarya in Sindia, and also my brother Borhan Oddin in China: and, when you see them, present my compliments to them."[9]

Ibn Batuta was astonished by such an assignment, yet how could he refuse the most honorable *effendi* of them all, especially seeing that he himself, Batuta, had expressed his passion for the dangers of travels to far lands? Our traveler gave Oddin his word and kept it most

---

8 Ibn Battuta (Abu Abd Allah Muhammad ibn Abd Allah al-Lawati al-Tanji ibn Battutah, 1304–68), medieval Muslim scholar and traveler from Morocco.
9 Ibn Batuta, *The Travels of Ibn Batuta*, ed. and trans. Samuel Lee (London: Oriental Translation Committee, 1829), 7.

faithfully. Moreover, he would not take a straight, well-beaten path to his destination, how difficult soever the path might have been in those days—oh no! Whenever he heard of some miracle occurring out of the way—for instance, the foot of Moses imprinted in stone; or Bulgarian snows, never before seen, and frosts, never before experienced; or indeed, the lavishness of the Tartar court—he would turn off the road and make his way to those places, even though God only knew how far they were; in a word, he became quite an eager traveler.

While in Bulgaria, he heard a lot about Siberia, or the "land of darkness" as he called it, and was about to set off for it, but other travelers distracted him. Batuta tells many stories about Siberia, about its trade and its sable rides, yet he tells of things he has heard rather than seen, and therefore talks nonsense for the most part. Having never seen any Russians either, he has heard that they are a red-headed, garrulous, and treacherous people. It is a pity that we cannot relate here much of his curious tales and adventures, which a traveler is bound to experience in those countries; we cannot do that for we must hasten to our true goal.

Having visited Mecca three times, seen all the three brothers, and presented each with the holy imam's compliments, Ibn Batuta still was not satisfied; bored of staying at home again, he betook himself to Spain, thence to the coast of Africa, and thence to the Sudan to seek out another of the imam's brothers, Kawam Oddin, which the former had not even asked him to do.

Upon seeing the Nile (not for the first time, of course), he compares it to other big rivers of the world; which comparison shows him as a man knowledgeable in geography, a subject he studied during his travels; yet his account of the upper reaches of the Nile is so confused as to make the scholar Cooley[10] claim that the river in question is definitely the Niger, even though the Nile is clearly mentioned by its name, and the very description of the people inhabiting the river suffices to confirm that the river in question is the Nile. As we have noted, that was not the first time that scholars confounded the Nile with the Niger, for

---

10 William Desborough Cooley (1795–1883), British geographer. Kovalevsky refers to his work *The Negroland of the Arabs* (London: Arrowsmith, 1841).

no serious reason but predominantly owing to the name "the Nile of the Negroes," as if the White Nile was anything but the Nile of the Negroes.

This, by the bye, is what Ibn Batuta says.

Having crossed a wide desert, he reached Abu Latin, the first district of the Sudan. "No one is named after his father, but after his maternal uncle; and the sister's son always succeeds to property in preference to the son: a custom I witnessed no where else, except among the infidel Hindoos of Malabar."[11]

The custom has quite survived to this day in a negro tribe known by the name of Homed, or Abu Homed, living not far from Roseires, near the foot-hills—one could say, at the entrance to the land of the negroes in the East Sudan.

The Arab narrator further adds that, while traveling from Abu Latin to Mali, he encountered trees so enormous that an entire caravan could fit inside one of them. Despite the exaggeration, it is clear that he is talking of the baobab, which, as we have already said, grows in abundance near Roseires and along the route to the White Nile. Following this river downstream, Ibn Batuta saw numerous hippopotamuses in its wide inlet, or in a lake. Here, as you can see, Batuta's route is designated with ever more clarity. He sailed from the White Nile into the el-Ghazal river, which in the past everyone recognized—although nowadays few do—as the Nile proper, its bed being wider than that of the White Nile. The el-Ghazal abounds with lakes. Along it—namely, in its upper reaches—lives a negro tribe of which, incidentally, Ibn Batuta writes that they eat people but only those as black as themselves, the whites, in their view, being still unripe and therefore difficult for the stomach to digest.

Thus Batuta is clearly mistaken when he calls the river he followed the Nile.

From thence Batuta betook himself to Tambuktu[12] via Bornu.[13] Bornu must have been much easier to reach in the past, for caravans and travelers very often took that route to Tambuktu and farther, into Inner Africa and to the Niger.

---

11 Batuta, *Travels of Ibn Batuta*, 234.
12 Timbuktu, a city in today's Mali.
13 Borno, in the northeast of today's Nigeria.

Eventually, Batuta must have felt fatigued after 28 years' wanderings round the world. Having returned to Fez[14] in 1354, he settled there. I have forgotten to say that he did indeed find the brother of the imam in the Sudan and passed on his compliments, naming Fez as his abode. Let us also mention Abd al-Latif's[15] journey to the above-mentioned countries.

Finally, at the end of the 16th century, Portuguese Jesuits living in Abyssinia as missionaries, and especially a Portuguese by the name of Neez,[16] announced with great pomp their discovery of the sources of the Nile. The scholarly society was so glad to hear of their answer to this important riddle, which so many peoples had spent so many centuries trying to solve, that the glory of the great deed was attributed to them without further investigation; later, however, d'Anville,[17] followed by many others, disappointed the scholars, claiming that those were the sources not of the Nile but of one of the rivers flowing into the Nile—namely, the Blue River.

Bruce[18] was to make the same mistake later. An odd fate was to betide the man, showing all the vanity of our fame, all the fickle and petty nature of the public, who would rather laugh at a traveler's idle story or an error than take pride in the fame of their fellow-countryman. It is time the name of Bruce was displayed in the glorious light it quite deserves and cited alongside the names of the most famous travelers of recent years, such as Burnes, Conolly, Lander, Ross,[19] &c.

Bruce had been blessed with the same relentless will-power and the strength of character that allows one to never surrender in the face of catastrophe—the same dedication, quick wit, and patience as the mentioned travelers—but in comparison with them, he was better prepared to accomplish the chosen aim and had more luck; they paid with their

---

14 A city in the north of Morocco.
15 Abd al-Latif al-Baghdadi (1162–1231), medieval Muslim scholar and traveler.
16 A mistake by Kovalevsky; most likely he means Pedro Páez Xaramillo (1564–1622), a Spanish missionary in Ethiopia who described the source of the Blue Nile.
17 Jean Baptiste Bourguignon d'Anville (1697–1782), French geographer and cartographer.
18 James Bruce (1730–94), British explorer and writer.
19 Alexander Burnes (1805–41) and Arthur Conolly (1807–42), British military explorers of Central Asia; Richard Lemon Lander (1804–34), British explorer of Africa; (most likely) John Ross (1777–1856), British explorer of the Arctic.

lives for their unreserved commitment to science or to political projects of their governments, whereas he returned to his homeland . . . only to be greeted with mockery and ungratefulness.

James Bruce was a descendant of a good and wealthy family in Northern England.[20] As a mere school-boy, he would be inflamed at the thought of the sources of the Nile and their discovery, a thought that never left him wherever he went. Traveling in Europe, he aimed all his studies, all his inquiries at the achievement of his goal. He had a sojourn in Holland, where the school of languages was flourishing at the time, and became an eager student of the Arabic language, as well as of mathematical sciences and astronomy. In 1762 he gladly accepted the post of Consul in Algeria, where he hoped to be closer to the object of his explorations and, most importantly, to learn colloquial Arabic and some of the dialects of Abyssinia. Yet haunted as he was by his thought, Bruce did not remain in Algeria for long; having visited Barbary,[21] he went to Cairo. In those days a journey through Egypt was not easy, the principal obstacle being the government itself, untrusting and avaricious; however, Bruce was fortunate in his fight with it and was soon able to set forth. In Keneh he parted with the Nile and traveled to Cosseir through the desert. Alas, here we must forego a great many curious things seen by Bruce. From Cosseir he betook himself to the Emerald Isle,[22] and then to Jedu,[23] from whence he set off for the Abyssinian coast, going to Massau.[24] Despite having letters of recommendation for the governor of the place, he nearly fell victim to suspiciousness, but he was saved by the firmness of his character. Thence his journey in Abyssinia commenced. Having overcome the obstacles presented by the Christian ruler of Gondar,[25] he reached Alata,[26] the second cataract of the Blue River, which he always mistook for the Nile proper, talking of it with rapture. "It was a most magnificent sight, that ages, added to the greatest length of human life, would not deface or eradicate from Mr. Bruce's

---

20 Kovalevsky mistakes Scotland for the north of England.
21 The North African coast.
22 Most likely one of the Brothers Isles (Al Ikhwa Isles) in the Red Sea.
23 Jeddah, a city in today's Saudi Arabia on the Red Sea.
24 Massawa, a city in Eritrea on the Red Sea.
25 A city and a region in Ethiopia.
26 A tributary of the Blue Nile near the rapids.

memory; it struck him with a kind of stupor, and a total oblivion of where he was, and of every other sublunary concern."[27]

Then, upon learning that the Galla had taken over Gondar, he had to go and pay his humble respects to Fasil,[28] the savage ruler of the half-naked tribe. Notwithstanding a bad reception, Bruce managed, however, to procure the patronage and protection of this new ruler of Abyssinia too, and then he resumed the journey to attain his goal, the goal of his whole life. This time, attain it he did, or so he believed, and he was happy—as happy as a man whose hopes and ideas have all come true at last; and it is not mockery that his rapturous description of the sources of the Nile should provoke but rather sympathy. Here is what Bruce is reported to have said, reveling in his triumph:

> It is easier to guess than to describe the situation of Mr. Bruce's mind at that moment—standing in that spot which had baffled the genius, industry, and inquiry of both ancients and moderns, for the course of near three thousand years. Kings had attempted this discovery at the head of armies, and each expedition was distinguished from the last, only by the difference of the numbers which had perished, and agreed alone in the disappointment which had uniformly, and without exception, followed them all. Fame, riches, and honor, had been held out for series of ages to every individual of those myriads these princes commanded, without having produced one man capable of gratifying the curiosity of his sovereign, or wiping off this stain upon the enterprise and abilities of mankind, or adding this desideratum for the encouragement of geography.[29]

A traveler who has endured so many tribulations on his journey, presently standing at the sources of the Nile, can almost be forgiven for delivering such a rapturous speech. True, that was not the real Nile, yet Bruce took it for the real thing, believing in his heart of hearts to have discovered it, while nearly everyone shared his erroneous view at

---

27 Samuel Shaw, *An Interesting Narrative of the Travels of James Bruce, Esq., into Abyssinia, to Discover the Source of the Nile* (London, 1790), 247.
28 Fasil, Ethiopian nobleman of Oromo descent, governor of Damot; important figure in the Ethiopian dynastic crisis of the 18th century.
29 Shaw, *Interesting Narrative*, 280.

that time, and so it is no wonder that he gushed out quite a stream of exaltation. Some, including Cooley, will ask "Why, then, did he keep silent about the sources of the Blue River discovered by the Jesuits?" Firstly, it is possible that Bruce did not know about that, for it had occurred 200 years before his time; secondly, there are so many streams and little rivers flowing into the lake and the inhabitants of those parts treasure their fame so much, proud to be in possession of the sources of the Nile, that it could easily have happened that the Jesuits took one river for the Nile proper, while Bruce took another for it. As for the truthful nature of Bruce's accounts, at least of the principal ones, those concerning his journey through Abyssinia were fully acknowledged by travelers enjoying everyone's trust, such as Lord Valencia and Mr. Salt,[30] to say nothing of the others; and with regard to Sennaar, Nubia, and Egypt (Bruce returned via the Peninsula of Sennaar), I was able to quite convince myself, while traveling there, of the observant and precise nature of the facts related by this learned traveler.

Society seemed not to have noticed these explorations; particularly affronted by one of the stories Bruce told, it mocked him, which alone sufficed to subvert all the merits of the book.

This is how it went. Bruce, having already reached Abyssinia, had scarcely left Axum[31] when he saw three men, half-naked, their aspect provoking extreme suspicion; they were chasing a cow and soon caught up with it; one of them delivered such a strong blow to the cow's head that it fell down, whereupon he grabbed it by its horns, another man, by its front legs, while the third commenced to cut out soft lumps of flesh from under its skin, having made an incision in it. A piece of beef-steak obtained from each side, he covered the wound with skin, applied some soil to its edges, made the cow stand up, and drove it onward.

Such a method of obtaining beef-steak from a live animal is, of course, not quite natural; however, we do not know if the men did not

---

30 George Annesley, 2nd Earl of Mountnorris (1770–1844), known as Viscount Valentia (1793–1816), British aristocrat and traveler; explored the Red Sea region. Henry Salt (1780–1827), artist and amateur antiquarian; Viscount Valentia's secretary on the eastern tour.

31 A city in northern Ethiopia, the historical capital of the Aksumite Empire, which ruled the region from the 4th century BCE to the 10th century CE.

wish to mock the master of the cow or take revenge on him. Bruce merely needed to say a word by way of explanation; yet he—already prepared for such cruelty to some extent, having seen that many in Abyssinia eat raw meat, he therefore perhaps believed there could be some who, possessed of a refined taste, preferred the flesh of a live animal to that of a dead one—he himself appears to have been mistaken. Also, he had already witnessed so many miraculous and incredible things whose veracity he had confirmed by touch, so to speak, that he readily believed this extraordinary folly of the Abyssinian taste, too.

Among the latest travelers to the upper reaches of the White and Blue Nile, the greatest number of facts about these territories and the adjacent lands were provided by Caillaud,[32] who was in the service of Mohammed Ali and took part in the conquest of the East Sudan. He went farther than anyone who had visited the East Sudan theretofore,[33] namely, to the Singhe Mountains.[34] The only one to later approach this point was Russegger.[35] The journey of the latter and that of Rüppell[36] were important in the facts they gathered with regard to natural sciences. Having already mentioned d'Arnaud and D'Abbadie, I shall add to them the name of Werne, d'Arnaud's companion, who contradicts him in every detail, whilst foregoing as irrelevant Pückler-Muskau and others, who never once ventured beyond the lands already explored quite well. However, allow me to pay special attention to a recently published description, written in Arabic, of a journey to the Sudan, by Sheikh Zain al-Abidin, a conscientious and inquisitive man, albeit at times inclined to superstitions—a trait inseparable from the nature of an Arab—which often presented him with perverse notions of things. Indeed, the very object of his journey was to study alchemy in the Sudan, a place generally famous for its magic in the East. His *Journey* was translated from Arabic into Turkish and from Turkish into German

---

32 Author's note: Frédéric Caillaud, *Voyage à Méroé, au fleuve Blanc*. . . , Paris: Imprimerie royale, 1826–27, 4 vols.
33 Author's note: I reached 1.5° farther than he had.
34 The Semien Mountains.
35 Author's note: Joseph Russegger, *Reisen in Europa, Asien und Africa*. . . , Stuttgart: Schweizerbart, 1846.
36 Wilhelm Peter Eduard Simon Rüppell (1794–1884), German explorer and naturalist who visited Egypt, Sudan, and Ethiopia.

by Rosen,[37] the Grand Dragoman of the Embassy of Prussia at the Ottoman Porte.

The sources of the Nile were long confounded with the Niger, many maintaining until very recently that it was the same river. Thus the dutiful and hard-working author of the book *Égypte Ancienne*, Champollion-Figeac, wrote as early as in 1846, "It is believed to be quite true that travelers used to reach Cairo from Tambuktu, a big city in Inner Africa, and since this last is situated near the Niger, it is therefore concluded that either this large river is the Nile itself, flowing from Tambuktu to Egypt, or that there is another river between the Nile and the Niger, yet undiscovered, which serves as a means of communication between the Niger and the Nile."[38]

The discovery of the mouth of the Niger leaves no doubt whatsoever about the unique nature of this river, which has been disputed for so long, first in favor of the Senegal, and then of the Nile; as for the travelers reaching Cairo from Tambuktu, that would only be true if by "travelers" M. Champollion meant very few Arab missionaries or Mecca pilgrims, some of whom do, indeed, come from Tambuktu, although they hardly ever reach Cairo, instead turning off the Nile to go to Sawakin[39] or to Cosseir; we saw one such and conversed with him about the Nile at length. The *hajji* insisted—confirming what I had never doubted, having read about the travels of mediaeval Arabs—that pilgrims go from Tambuktu to Kordofan, via Darfour and Bornu.

As numerous parties strove to reach the sources of the Nile—whether it be governments or expeditions under protection of army detachments or brave individuals, many of whom sacrificed their lives for the sake of their devotion to science—a great many travelers, encouraged by the enterprising and generous London African Society, set forth in various directions from Cairo, Tripoli, Maroc, and Tangier toward the sources of the Niger, which had always been believed to be close, if not related, to the sources of the Nile; alas, very few of them returned! Most

---

37 Author's note: Zayn el Abidin and Georg Rosen, *Das Buch des Sudan: Oder, Reisen des Scheich Zain el Abidin...*, Leipzig: F. C. W. Vogel, 1847.
38 Author's note: M. Champollion-Figeac, *Égypte Ancienne*, Paris: Firmin Didot frères, 1839, p. 9.
39 Suakin, a city port on the Red Sea in Sudan.

perished of fever, while some fell victim to the cruelty or suspiciousness of the natives. The history of their travels is a veritable Odyssey of contemporary times, similar to the history of travels to Central Asia, where, it must be added, the primacy in the glorious field of geographical discoveries does not belong to the English alone. The names of Mungo Park and Clapperton,[40] along with his loyal companion Lander—a comrade rather than a mere servant, who was the first to put the mouth of the Niger on the map—these names shine there with glory as bright as those of Burnes, Conolly, Muravyev,[41] and others do here.

I mention the sources of the Niger not without intention; gathering the facts in the course of my travels there, rereading the accounts of other travelers, contemplating the subject, and considering every possible aspect of it, I have convinced myself from all the evidence that the sources of the Nile are, indeed, not far from those of the Niger; and I propose a new route to the discovery of both, a route that, in my view, is more passable. I say "propose" with sadness, for I myself am unlikely to ever find any relief from the diseases that I have brought from my travels to distant lands, especially contagious African fever, and ... But enough of me! There are many people in God's world who—being courageous, healthy, and capable—know not in which direction to apply their activities; so here is a glorious aim the equal of which you can hardly find in our day and age: an aim that would open up all kinds of prospects, requiring great audacity and courage, patience and profound research. The world would be enriched not only by scientific discoveries but also by an example of heroic dedication. Here is the route I propose.

You have to go from Cairo, via Khartoum and Sennaar, to Fazoglu. This route presents no difficulties except for the climate and means of travel, there being no obstacles from people; you become accustomed to said difficulties; and, when all is done, what are they? The heat attaining 40 degrees Reaumur[42] at high noon, camel rides, the crossing of the Great Nubian Desert, which at any rate can be circumvented by those

---

40 Mungo Park (1771–1806) and Hugh Clapperton (1788–1827), British explorers of West Africa.
41 Nikolai Nikolaevich Muravyev (Karsskii, 1794–1866), Russian officer; made a trip to Khiva in 1819–20.
42 50°C.

who do not hasten to their goal. In two or three months, you shall be at Fazoglu—naturally, not during the rainy season, for you cannot survive it unless you accustom yourself to it in advance. Henceforth, it is a four days' journey to Khassan, where you shall, so to speak, be in the centre of the negro population, strike up relationships with all the *meleks* of the area, and make friends with them by means of small gifts and kind treatment. Then you will turn to *jellab* Arabs: do not become friendly with them, for they are an unpleasant lot; always keep yourself high above them, buying any favors for money only. Among them, especially those who come from Benishangul, you shall find many people who have been to Fadasi. I have already described the difficulties of going to Fadasi, but for a brave traveler, especially when aided by friendly *meleks*, they are insignificant. The most important thing is to decide which of the *jellabs* to entrust yourself to; yet whomever you have decided upon, call someone of the authorities to be witness to your deal: in that case the family of the guide shall, as it were, remain as a pledge of your safety; as for the word of an Arab or his honesty, you should never rely upon it.

In Fadasi you shall find people from all over Africa; introducing yourself as an Arab (you must, needless to say, learn Arabic in advance), you shall meet and make friends with Galla chiefs, thus acquiring some initial patronage and learning their language somewhat; neither task being difficult. The journey thence shall depend entirely upon chance and upon your luck: you shall make your way to wherever friendship, benefit, or the connexions of your patrons shall take you. While the object of the journey may be discussed confidentially, you must use any excuse possible to keep to your chosen direction. Finally, as you wander from one patron to another, and having gone far inside the country—for instance, to Tambuktu—you can introduce yourself as a native of Guiana and then proceed thereto, now quite openly. The title of a *hajji*, a worshipper of Mohammed's tomb, shall bring you some respect from the Arabs, whom you have to fear most of all; as for the negroes, as I have already said, it suffices to acquire patronage in Fadasi, and then they will pass you from one onto another as a welcome guest, especially if you learn their customs. Doubt not, the proposed route is also difficult and dangerous, and yet it seems to me that it is still far easier than all the others. The worst dangers along the way are African fever and dysentery, which no-one new to these parts is able to protect oneself from, but there are medicines that can relieve your sufferings, albeit temporarily; I myself traveled for three months while ill of a fever of a most painful variety, halting only when completely deserted by energy. And yet, what countries you shall visit! The whole of Inner Africa, where even the bravest of travelers have never trodden; this, of course, being the most certain way to discover the sources of the Nile and the Niger, which are too famous among the natives for you not to hear about them, even without any inquiries on your part. Suffice it to recall the numerous countries that Ibn Batuta visited, traveling along the route I have described.[43]

Yet another note: it is Bahr-el-Abiad, the White River—or the White Nile, as we call it, which flows south as far as its course is known—that has recently been mistaken for the Nile proper; yet Bahr-el-Ghazel, which merges with it, is both larger and wider at its mouth than the White River; it has scarcely been explored; its water is too unwholesome and was pernicious for d'Arnaud's expedition, which did attempt to go up this river; its current is so quiet that it is barely noticeable; it sprawls itself in immense reaches and lakes abundant with fish: it is of those that Ibn Batuta must have spoken. El-Ghazel has its source in the mountains of Darfour. So having answered one question—that it is not the Blue River but the White River that constitutes the Nile—one has to answer another: namely, which of the two tributaries is indeed the White Nile, the so-called Bahr-el-Abiad or Bahr-el-Ghazel?

---

43 Author's note: It was not until after my return to St. Petersburg that I learned from foreign journals about a French traveler, one Dr. Raffenel, who decided to cross the African Isthmus, west to east, between lat. 10° and 15°. I have no doubt that everyone is avidly awaiting any news of this hero of science, who follows in the footsteps of so many fallen predecessors with patience, firmness, and self-denying devotion worthy of the glorious object he has dedicated himself to. Following some news sent by him from the peaks of the Senegal in 1846, another letter has recently been received from Koghe, the capital of Kaarta, dated the 3rd of May 1847. Many scholarly societies and the government of France have taken an active part in his enterprise.

Editor's note: Anne-Jean-Baptiste Raffenel (1809–58), French colonial officer and explorer of Africa.

Chapter V

The Second Expedition to the Mountains

Another white horse, a bell round its neck; riding upon it is something like a charred log, bent and broken, or a monkey, but whatever it is, it bears little resemblance to a human being; behind it, more bunches of spears and rows of bayonets; more black bodies, black faces, and black feet, with white rags above the knees, owing to which our swarthy detachment can be mistaken from afar, among the trees, for a flock of cranes; another thicket, also impassable, for we decided, in order to shorten the journey, to go straight across, from one mountain to the next, following no road or path, by sight, so to speak, carrying our provisions upon our backs; acacias and blackthorns of every possible variety, brambles of various kinds, designed for no purpose but to tear people's dress—or, in the absence of any, their skin—bent in the manner of fishing rods and apparently expecting us, attacking with remarkable viciousness and biting bone-deep into our flesh. There was a difference, however, between this and the previous occasions: to our surprise, the sun did not appear in the sky, which was overcast with clouds everywhere, but wherever it was at the time, it must have remembered those living under it, amusing itself at the sight of our sufferings, the air being stifling and heavy.

Yet again the same dear companion, the *samsamieh* by my side, on the pommel of my saddle; yet again the same invariable batman, a loyal negro from the Huli tribe; yet again the same *youzbashis* and *bimbashis*, now changing guard, now joining the vanguard, and the respectable figure of Hassan Effendi, the chief of battalion commanders; yet again the same march, "Marlbrough s'en va-t-en guerre,"[1] calling us to march forth, while the voice of the doctor, who is always fussing and always running late, drowns out the clarion call of the music. However, the soldiers now have a new task to perform at bivouacs: that of erecting *tukkels*, for the *rashash*, the first rainy season, has already commenced. This one is not long, lasting for two or three weeks; it is not until afterward that the *kharif* comes, the season of constant, heavy rains lasting for four months, concluding with another month of intermittent rains.

We came to our first halt quite late and, not wishing to exhaust the soldiers, put up no *tukkels*, but at about 2 A.M. we were awakened by a torrential rain falling on us. Pulling a rug over me and holding its middle aloft from underneath, now with one hand, now with the other, so as to make at least some slope for the water to roll off the top, I contemplated the position of a man suffocating in such a restricted space, and thought, *What is it like? It is like being confined in a coffin alive, lowered into a grave, and buried . . . ? How terrible.* Wishing to free myself from this thought sooner and to convince myself of the opposite, I made to look out from under my confinement: the rain swept over me, and I hastened to hide myself again. The sky, as if caving in under the heavy clouds pressing on it, seemed about to collapse upon the earth . . .

Meanwhile, another catastrophe was about to betide me: the soaked rug was getting ever heavier; I could scarcely hold it above myself, my hands distinctly feeling its moisture from the inside; eventually, several drops percolated through it; having made its way in, an entire stream was now threatening me, and I poked my head outside again: it was dark, there was no rain, and yet I could clearly hear its noise as it splashed in puddles. What was the matter? The soldiers had put up a kind of tent, made from all sorts of rubbish, over me; I was particularly pleased to

---

1 "Marlborough went to war," a popular French song that gained Europe-wide circulation in the wake of the Napoleonic Wars.

receive such attention from black humankind. It was not for the first time, however, that the soldiers and officers took care of me. They seemed to understand the difficulties that I, coming as I did from the North, experienced in the course of this expedition, while themselves bearing great hardship under the white-hot sky on such arduous marches.

In the morning the rain commenced to subside; having ventured out from under the tent, I was amazed by our motley encampment, for even in ordinary times, our men presented a sight that had little order or harmony to it. The line of sentries stood still, of course, but the others, naked for the most part, crowded round the fires in various positions, drying their dress and mocking one another; laughter could be heard everywhere, as if nothing was the matter. The Arab guides did the most prudent thing of all. As soon as the rain began, they took off their *ferdehs*, which was their only dress, and sat on them, naked, through the night; when it stopped raining, having dried and warmed themselves, they put their dress, completely dry, back on, whereas no-one else, including ourselves, had any dry underwear to change into, all our things having been soaked through.

It was not until 10 A.M. that we were able to dry ourselves somewhat and set forth from the bivouac. There were no traces of the rain left on the ground, however heavy it had been; it being the third rain in the course of that summer, the earth, exhausted and scorched, swallowed it like a drop. Only *khors*, or creeks, still expressed narrow streams; by the evening, there was no water there either.

We crossed Hassa, the *khor* where we had spent such an unpleasant night, and another *khor*, Belmeh, into which Hassa flows, several times. The journey was extremely weary; having brought a few donkeys with us, we still walked for the most part, sometimes descending from a mountain, sometimes climbing another, walking over rocks and landslides. At noon we reached Sodah.

The Sodah Mountains used to be very thickly peopled—solely by the Berta negroes, who would never let any other tribe, and especially not the Arabs, come close to their habitation; no-one could pass their land as long as they could get the better of the passers-by; their neighbors had tolerated them for a long time, but the previous year the *Hakumdar* attacked Sodah; he spent three days killing the inhabitants and burning their dwellings, whereupon he retreated, leaving in his wake nothing but ashes and ruins and taking into slavery as many as 1,000 surviving negroes; however, the soldiers also took a beating. The negroes would hide themselves in caves, which are plenty in Sodah, launching sudden attacks from thence on the soldiers, who carelessly engaged in plunder. Besieged in their caves, the negroes would either kill one another so as not to fall into the victor's hands, or put themselves to death by starving, surrendering only when taken by surprise. Women, while being led away by the soldiers as their own property, would attack them suddenly and, clutching them, would often throw themselves off a cliff, taking the enemy with them, too.

There are few inhabitants left in Sodah now, scarcely 2,000, and those were only able to survive thanks to having fled prior to the arrival of the *Hakumdar*. They pay taxes to the Egyptian government in gold and in slaves. The *melek*, having been warned about the approach of our detachment, came to see us; the negroes gathered in a crowd at the very top of the mountain, bundles of spears upon their shoulders, and waited to see what our meeting would lead to. The *melek* was accompanied by several slaves; it was then that we saw, for the first time, people dyed red from head to toe, their hair and even their eyebrows being red. Poor people! Having no hope of becoming white, they wished to imitate a color that was at least semi-aristocratic. According to a negro legend, they were once white also; but the sun, which the majority of them worship, turned its wrath on them for some reason and burned them; henceforth, they have been as black as charred logs.

The *melek*, or *mek*, and his companions, having halted a few steps prior to reaching us, threw themselves on the ground and kissed it; then, having come close, they stretched their arms upward, as if to protect themselves from the bright sun shining upon them and, lowering their eyes, halted again; their movements and poses were extremely theatrical and gracious. Needless to say, little did our negroes know that what they presented us with was a tableau vivant picturing the worshipping of Ramses and other pharaohs by slaves, a scene whose image we had seen repeated so often on the remaining monuments of ancient Egypt.

The two peaks of Radokah—which we had already seen so many times, both from Benishangul and from the Toumat, sometimes resembling barely visible spots, like fleecy clouds on the horizon, sometimes outlined with a crimson-red line, sometimes pale, sometimes blue, as we variously came closer to or farther from them—these peaks now took ever more defined shapes and stood against the horizon, formidable and magnificent.

We halted for the night at the foot-hills of Fadokah. Fadokah is connected with the mountains of Benishangul; Singe, or Singhe; Radokah; and finally, Doul; together they make up a regular, elevated range between the Blue Nile and the White Nile in the East Sudan, or the so-called Peninsula of Sennaar. The mountain range stretches from south to north-east, ending a long way from Khartoum still. The rivers that flow into the Toumat from one side and into the White Nile from the other take their origin in this range.

The population becomes ever more dense as one leaves the realm of Mohammed Ali far behind, deviating west of the Galla tribe, and as the mountains grow more impassable. Vegetation becomes ever more rich. What plants did we not encounter here in their wild state! Wild bananas attain an incredible size, but their fruit, also enormous, is not so tasty, being full of seeds. By the banks of *khors*, there are jasmine-trees the height of our apple-trees; the jasmine is always in blossom, for although it sheds leaves, I have never seen it without flowers, and its smell spreads far in the sultry, hot atmosphere. Wild grapes, wild plumes, trees similar to apricot-trees; giant baobabs, or *Adansonia digitata*; *Sterculia setigera*, which the Arabs call *tertu*; sycamores of divers varieties; *Euphorbia, Bauhinia, Celastrus decolor* (a variety of buckthorn); ebony-trees (*Diospyros ebenum*); as well as many other fruit-trees, creepers, and lianas, a thicket of which we struggled through. What a remarkable variety, what an immense power of vegetation! Here, by the bye, the wild potato grows in the mountains. Poisonous in its primaeval state, it loses its poisonous quality once replanted, all the inhabitants of the mountains consuming it; it also reaches an extraordinary size, one potato weighing up to 15 pounds. Another variety of the so-called potato, to use the local word, is nothing like the ordinary potato; it sprouts the same shoots (we have not seen any flowers), but the fruit is different: smaller than our potato, it resembles chestnuts in taste. I brought with me several tubers of both varieties; but will they take root in our cold soil? The asparagus is excellent.

Lord, what nature, what luxuriousness! As we traveled to Doul—in the middle of April—everything along the way had been burnt by the sun, all-destroying and all-creating in these parts; while on our return journey—which was a week later, after heavy rains—everything was changed! . . .

The reader has now seen whom and what we found in those parts; and given all that, Inner Africa is still believed to be deserted; Inner Africa, where man can live off the fruits of the earth, with no need for ploughing or sowing. I have not told you, reader, about the half of the fruits, roots, and leaves that the negroes eat. I brought with me nearly everything I could gather in different seasons. Perhaps some of these plants can also grow in our country, in the South of Russia.

As one approaches the equator, the population does indeed increase noticeably. According to the evidence I have gathered, it decreases in the same manner, diminishing gradually, as one moves away from the equator on the other side of it; within the confines of the seasonal rains, where wonderful vegetation provides all means necessary for the meagre life of the negro, the population cannot be eradicated; people live here without labor or effort, so what could possibly prevent them from living here? One becomes accustomed to the heat and the rays of the burning sun; and one can, of course, become accustomed to them far more readily than to frosts of −30 degrees Reaumur,[2] common in our land. The sultry African atmosphere does at least have some languor and luxury to it, unless you must work, whereas in our parts frosts make one's blood curdle. I suffered greatly in the Sudan in the heat of 40 degrees Reaumur,[3] but as I recall, the weather had been even harder to bear on the march during the Khiva expedition, when the Reaumur thermometer had no longer told the temperature, the mercury having frozen.

---

2 −37.5°C.
3 50°C.

I repeat: Why would the negro not live here when he can have more than he requires? By the most negligible amount of labor, working a week or two during the rains, he obtains as much gold as he needs to buy a dozen spears or necklaces and decorations for himself and his naked wife. Two enemies abuse him: *civilized* neighbors, who chase negroes as if they were beasts, to catch slaves for themselves; and heavy rains lasting for nearly six months, which one cannot hide oneself from in a rickety *tukkel*. Another concern is where to find water; however, it does not last long, as water remains in *khors* and caves for about three months after the rainy season. Some negro tribes have built tanks in which water is kept all year round; others make do somehow—that is to say, they either bring it from afar, from the *khors* that always contain water under the sand, or take it away from their more prudent neighbors, or finally, drink the bitter-salty water that they extract by means of shallow wells.

Chapter VI

Jebel Doul and Its Entertainments

Sheikh Ibrahim took us to one mountain after another, going round and round the same spot as much as he could, eager to show off our detachment to the negroes and to present himself to them as a very important figure with an army to command at his will, while at the same time doing his dubious business through the *meleks*. My patience finally exhausted by the dealings of this Arab Jew, I ordered the men to put him under arrest. You should have seen the way the other Arab guides stood up for his honor; but I did not relent and hired a negro as a guide, a native, who conducted us to our destination as if along a straight line.

Soon we descended to Doul, a wide *khor*. It flows west prior to merging with the Sobbat, which in its turn flows into the White Nile. Further on the left, Mount Doul rose 3,500 feet above the ground, on the right was Kurmuk-ue-Zerab, and straight ahead, directly before us, stretched a range of less elevated mountains.

Among these mountains, on a raised plateau, the fortress of Doul, the only one in these parts, had been indicated to us, but we had not seen anything yet. Soon a crowd of riders appeared from behind a mountain, all in lavish Albanian dress, followed by several negro outrunners and led by two gallant riders upon excellent Arab horses. They were Osman Bey, the governor of the fortress, and Omar Aga, the commander of the Arnaut soldiers who made up the garrison there. Good Lord, how many memories stirred up in me at the sight of these people! Not long ago, it seemed, in some other mountains, crowning their tops, there had been people dressed and armed exactly the same as these, and those people had been waiting for me, glad of my arrival, and had followed me at my beck and call ... It was not so long ago ... and yet how far away it was ... and how different. And now these people rode out to meet me; but they gazed at us in surprise, having become unaccustomed to seeing white people in their confinement; they had grown heavy and stooped low in their idleness! It takes six months for one-half of the garrison to die, and in two years there is no-one left alive. The old Albanians were almost all gone, which seemed to have been the aim of the government that had sent them here. They had often pestered it with their not too delicate demands that their salary be increased. There were new recruits from everywhere; that was down to the commander of the Arnauts: should he run out of men, they would take away his power and with it his salary. On the other hand, Omar Aga did not hesitate in his choice of men nor in his use of means. Here he had a Tartar who had deserted from the Prut, a Bosnian, a Dalmatian; there was a Serb, a Montenegrin, a Turk, and a Greek, most of them having fled from various persecutions in their homelands or escaped the gallows.

But Omar Aga—the very same Omar Aga who, according to Schœlcher, shot the Governor-General of the Sudan at a dinner, in the presence of guests, on the Viceroy's orders; Omar Aga, born on the frontier of Montenegro and Albania, the perfect type of those lands, which are related to one another not only in the dress of their inhabitants; Omar Aga, resolute, courageous, always gay despite his miserable position in this political exile, with his habit of drinking a bottle of vodka at lunch and another at dinner—vividly reminded me of my old comrades, many of whom he had known personally and of whom he spoke with fascination ... He talked of alliance[1] and of sworn brotherhood; of the bare cliffs of his country; of Scutari, which he called

---

1 The word used in the Russian text is *cheta*, which in South Slavic languages means a group, a band, a commune.

Skadar,[2] as we all once used to call it; of the Prince-Bishop;[3] of our expeditions... Oh, what a happy time that was! We shall never see the similar of it now. I was 25 then, and the Prince-Bishop of Montenegro was 21; back then we were brave in our endeavors to further our ends, armed with our blind faith in Slavonic chance, and that chance was our blind ally... Now we walk timidly and cautiously, feeling and observing each step... but how far can one get in this manner? Certainly it was not our ancestors who invented the saying "more haste, less speed"; rather, it was borrowed from the Germans ("Eile mit Weile"[4]).

What a fortress Doul is! Around it is a shallow moat, a prickly wicker fence, and two little cannons by the gates—that is the entire citadel, impenetrable for the negroes. Inside the fortification everything is clean. Among numerous *tukkels* stand several little clay houses, whitewashed to perfection and thatched with straw, which reminded me of our Ukrainian huts... Serbian overcoats flashed before me; Osman Bey plied us with rakia; everything was familiar, close to the Slavonic heart, and I found it all enormously pleasing. Laugh, reader, laugh! Yet I should like to transport you to Inner Africa and show you anything or anyone that would remind you of the past so strongly, assuming that the past has left you with at least one memory, assuming that you do have a homeland—and thereupon I should like to see your expression and hear your words. Now that you are peacefully smoking your cigar at home, you will, of course, find my effusions ridiculous.

Doul was built about six years ago, with the same object that prevails here, the only one that forces people to resort to every kind of expense and to make most imprudent suppositions. The object is gold, the daemon that has tortured the Viceroy and never left in peace the rulers of the Sudan over the past 20 years. As usual, no gold was ever found, or if it was then the amount was such that would not pay for one-twentieth part of the costs incurred to maintain the garrison. They could not

---

2   The city of Shkodër in today's Albania, near Montenegro.
3   The Metropolitan of Cetinje, de facto theocratic ruler of Montenegro under Ottoman overlordship. Kovalevsky refers to Petr II Petrovich (1813–51), at whose invitation he stayed in Montenegro in 1837 to explore for gold. While there, Kovalevsky took part in military action against the Austrians on the Montenegrin side.
4   "Slow and steady wins the race."

commence their work, having no knowledge at all, and so they were left with nothing but vain efforts, hopes, and fruitless expenses. In the meantime, the garrison, surrounded by unfriendly negroes and situated far from the realm of Mohammed Ali, was enduring much hardship in its life provisions. Scurvy and fevers were fast wiping it off. Mohammed Ali continued to send new men and, despite all the submissions made by the Governor-General,remained adamant and strict in his orders for them to stay in Doul and search for gold. The thing was that he had read in some old Arabic manuscript, preserved in one of Cairo's mosques, that the pharaohs had once obtained several barrels of gold, which, in his view, must have come from nowhere else but Doul. He told me about that himself. If Mohammed Ali does get some idea into his head, he will never abandon it but will pursue it with remarkable persistence and patience, the proof of which can be found in the important monuments to his rule: the barrage of the Nile, the discovery of gold deposits, the digging of the Mahmoud-iya Canal, the conquest of the Sudan, &c. Whatever price he had to pay for those enterprises, considered impossible to accomplish, still he overcame all the obstacles and achieved his goals. One can no longer doubt the success of the Nile dam or the expansion of the gold industry;[5] the gold-washing factory operates very well even under the management of Arabs, gold being produced daily, which cannot be concealed nor created by imagination alone. The barrage is nearing its completion under the guidance of Mujul Bey; we shall describe this immense enterprise in due course. It is only complete ignorance or political upheavals that can destroy the glorious deeds of Mohammed Ali's rule.

Traces of civilization had penetrated Doul itself: in Osman Bey's vegetable patch, we saw a plough which vividly reminded us of the ploughing of fields in both ancient and present-day Egypt: first a camel and a buffalo, then a buffalo and a cow dragging this wooden cutting tool, which scarcely scratched the soil, unable to dig a single inch into it.

---

5 Author's note: Unfortunately, the death of Ibrahim Pasha and the miserable condition of Mohammed Ali raise serious doubts with regard to the continuation of the great enterprises established by the reformer of Egypt.

пріятія, считавшіяся невыполнимыми; но онъ превозмогъ всѣ препятствія и достигъ своей цѣли. Теперь уже нельзя сомнѣваться въ успѣхѣ запруды Нила и распространеніи золотаго производства *): золотопромывальная фабрика дѣйствуетъ даже подъ руководствомъ арабовъ очень хорошо, золото получается ежедневно, его не скроешь, не создашь однимъ воображеніемъ. Баражъ приводится къ концу подъ руководствомъ Мужуль-бея; мы опишемъ это гигантское предпріятіе въ своемъ мѣстѣ. Только одно совершенное невѣжество или политическіе перевороты могутъ сокрушить славныя дѣла правленія Мегеметъ-Али.

И въ самый Дуль проникли слѣды цивилизаціи: на огородѣ Османъ-бея, мы видѣли плуговую упряжку, живо

напоминавшую распашку земель древняго и нынѣшняго

---

*) Къ несчастію, смерть Ибрагимъ-паши и бѣдственное положеніе Мегеметъ-Али заставляютъ сильно сомнѣваться въ поддержаніи огромныхъ предпріятій преобразователя Египта.

Соч. Ковалевскаго. Т. 5.

Egyptian plough

The Viceroy instructed me to explore the locality of Jebel Doul and, should there be no gold there, to withdraw the garrison. Hence they were expecting me there as a liberator. Having set to work on the very day of my arrival, I was glad I did, too, for on the third day, in the evening, it began to rain, and in the course of the night it got worse, the rain turning into a downpour; the thunder roared incessantly, rolling from one mountain to another or breaking out as if right over our heads, shaking our poor little huts like some reeds, the lightning crossing the sky without pause; the thunderstorm did not subside until the afternoon of the following day. That was only the *rashash*; I can imagine what the real *kharif* must be like in these parts! Dol, a *khor* in which we could see not a single drop of water on the eve of the rain, turned into a wide, fast-flowing river, similar to our second-rate rivers; reader, you must be familiar with our second-rate rivers! There were streams in the streets; currents rolled down the mountains, waterfalls cascaded; hollows turned into lakes. It was no time to do business; but the sun rose, even hotter than usual, and over a single day, everything went back to the previously established order, except the *khor*, along which a narrow turbid stream of rain water was still rolling.

The authorities of Doul gave dinners in our honor. Dinners in Doul, with music and various entertainments! The repast itself was not distinguished in any regard; it was prepared by our cooks and partly from our own supplies; for what could one possibly procure in Doul, despite our hosts' every intention to give us a feast? The music was Albanian rather than Turkish, but it hissed, banged, and made noise just as much as Turkish music would: good music! After dinner, they made a little negro boy—there being no monkeys in Doul—drunk, and he fooled around and grimaced no worse than a monkey; after that they summoned two negroes, gave each a cue to hold, and told them to fight; when the negroes bloodied each other's heads, they were calmed down, not without difficulty, for having commenced a fight on their masters' orders, they carried on in eagerness. Then, at our host's beck, 15 or so shackled slaves appeared; the poor things could hardly move their feet, and yet they danced, clicking their fingers, moving in step with the clinking of their shackles, and singing along, which must have been extremely amusing, for the audience took hearty pleasure in it. "Did they shackle them deliberately, so that they could dance with more agility?" I asked, thinking whether it might not be a Doul substitute for the garlands of ballet dancers or something of that nature. "No," the host replied, "these are negroes from the nearby mountains; they are shackled all the time, lest they escape." "Is it their traditional dance, then?" "Not at all!" Omar Aga replied with disdain. "I had an educated boy, so I told him to teach these animals; being a docile lot, they learned it soon." Indeed, all their movements, all their tricks were imbued with cynicism of the harshest kind; they had clearly been put through the schooling by a *very educated* boy.

"So, do you indulge in this kind of entertainment often?" I asked Omar Aga.

"Yes, almost daily. If it were not for this, imagine what we would have done to ourselves! There is no work whatsoever; the garrison duties are no duties at all; the only occasions for the soldiers to go out used to be the funerals of their comrades and officers, but I prohibited that—it does nothing but bring on gloom. Our families are far away, and God only knows what might become of them! We never receive any news. A whole convoy detachment is required to reach us here safely. About twice in six months, a *jellab* might chance upon us, or a caravan with grain and cattle, but even then the passers-by sometimes cannot tell you anything . . . What would we do if we did not amuse ourselves in this fashion?"

"What is it over there?"

"The dead! As you can see, they are going quietly, with no-one but the carriers. Never mind. Leave them be!" he went on, noticing that I could not take my eyes off them and taking me aside. "Let them go on their own way."

"But there seem to be quite a few of them!"

"Indeed. There are as many as this every night. Do tell the *Effendi* to please withdraw us from this place, lest we all die to the last man."

Osman Bey was right: never mind the dead! Let us leave them be while we shuffle along, proceeding on our own way, until the eternal bed-time comes for us, too. Yet what amusements! What a life! And there are so many, especially in our land, in boundless Russia, who are doomed to such a life. One does require great will-power, strength of character, and patience to be able to bear this torture—a prolonged, extremely prolonged torture, for one has to take every day by storm and live through it, minute by minute and hour by hour, and every minute and every hour shall be acutely felt, for here time does not fly on the wings of distraction and pleasure but rather draws slowly, in the manner of a funeral procession.

Neither Osman Bey nor any of his officers have their families with them. Turks are generally quite magnanimous in this regard, never subjecting their wives and children to the dangers of climate or the inconveniences of hardship in remote garrisons. Yet anyone can have several negress slaves and boys. It is so easy to obtain both here: a single successful hunt provides the garrison with these goods. The rich even keep Abyssinian women—who, it must be said, are still cheaper here than in Cairo: a good one can be bought for 200 rubles in paper money, a beauty for 350 rubles, while a plain one costs between 100 and 150 rubles.

Chapter VII

The Negroes

From the sources of the Toumat, from the south-east tip of the Peninsula of Sennaar and the south-west of Abyssinia, reader, I have transported you southward, to the peaks of the so-called Moon Mountains, where all my aspirations have led me. Now being nearly in the middle of the land between the White Nile and the Blue Nile, at the highest point of the Peninsula of Sennaar, whence my gaze penetrates far, far into the country I have already explored, step by step, and where no European has ever trodden—it is from thence that I intend to present to you the Peninsula of Sennaar in all its spacious variety.

In the north, from behind the gentle spurs of the Toumat range, rises the solitary Mount Huli, one of the highest mountains of the Peninsula of Sennaar. By its clearly defined shape outlined against the blue horizon, one could guess its granite formation, which I later was to become quite convinced of. Along with some other mountains, Huli, together with all the negroes inhabiting it, belongs to Idris Adlan as some kind of feoffment, constituting his permanent residence. From thence he sent messengers to invite us to visit him. Being sincerely fond of his son-in-law, Arbab, who had done us favors, I would have willingly accepted the invitation; but the rains were catching up with us—we could think of nothing but our swift departure from the mountains. One can see nothing beyond Huli. Here the peninsula is locked by the two rivers, becoming ever more narrow and ending at Khartoum, at the point of their confluence. This large space constitutes a raised plain, which lowers very slightly northward; despite having little water, it used to be thickly peopled, but now remains quite deserted outside the river-basin. The close proximity of the headquarters is easily felt. On the plain stand Mount Mouil and several significant hills.

In the east one can see the Toumat range, in which the two granite peaks of Radokah appear to be, if not the highest then certainly the most pronounced of all; to the right of them are Singhe, Andou, and Fandango; to the left, Fadokah, Sodah, Khassan, and Tabi in the south-east; on the other, the south-eastern side of the Toumat, are the mountains of Faronya, Falogut, and Fazangoru. Further eastward, one can make out the blue mountains of Abyssinia, although, of course, not as clearly as one can from the peaks of the Toumat.

In the south we could see most of the mountains we had been close to when atop the Toumat; only a few of them stood out against the horizon with their slate ridges instead of granite boulders, these last visible from the Toumat side; other mountains, previously appearing separate, now coincided with the principal range, some of them concealed, others brought forward; in general, all of them had a more vague aspect, being much further away, yet one could not but recognize the old friends by some clear shapes and outlines.

The horizon opened up the farthest to the south-east and to the east. There, a few hours' or possibly a day's journey from Doul, beyond the mountains of Kurmuk-ue-Zerab, lies the plain. Quite elevated (up to 1,600 feet) at the beginning, it lowers eastward and finally, by the banks of the White Nile, gives way to plains overgrown with trees, small and bent, a country meagre in vegetation, extremely unwholesome in climate, and yet, as the reader shall soon see, very populous.

Having seen the land, let us now observe its inhabitants.

The native population of the Peninsula of Sennaar are negroes, its oldest colonists being Arabs. In towns and even in those villages that are situated on the plains, in the northern part of the Sennaar, there are, needless to say, many foreigners from various countries, people escaped from Egypt, *fellahs*, Berbers, and even some Europeans in Khartoum.

The Arabs, being the most numerous group, can be divided into the latest arrivals from Hejaz and the descendants of Israel, which I am ever more convinced of. We shall talk of the Arabs living here when we commence a general study of this people. Presently let us turn specifically to the negroes, the oldest and most prominent inhabitants of the country.

It is not an easy task to name all the branches of local tribes, for every mountain, even if populated by the same tribe as the next, presents a difference either in customs or in language; however, here is a roster I have compiled with difficulty, gathering, it seems, all the tribes (without branches) that live in the vast space between the Blue Nile and the White Nile. Let me begin at the lower reaches of the Blue Nile before going on to the White Nile.

The Jebel Aouin, on Mount Fazoglu: this is a cross between Arabs and negroes.

The Berta: it is spread extremely far along the Toumat Mountains and the rivers that flow into the Toumat, being second to the Shillook tribe in its population; one can count half a million people in it. They tolerate and even accept Arabs, who are all without exception small traders, and sow *dourra*.

The El-Hassani, on Tabi: a garrulous tribe, recognizes no-one's power and lives only by raids upon the territories of its neighbors.

The Fung, predominantly on Huli.

The Houmous, for the most part on the right bank of the Blue Nile: they cultivate land.

The Hamed, upstream from Roseires, on the left bank of the Blue Nile: it differs from the other tribes especially in that uncles have more power in families than fathers do, disposing of their sisters' children—that is, selling them off as they please.

The Amam, on the Yabous.

Next comes the populous Galla tribe, which I have already described in detail.

The Bouroun, beyond Jebel Doul and all the way to the White Nile: a cruel and predatory tribe.

Let us now turn to the White Nile.

The Shillook, predominantly to the left of the Nile and on its isles: a populous tribe, believed by d'Arnaud to have a million people (which number seems to be exaggerated). They live mainly off fishing and banditry, sowing very little *dourra*.

The Dinka occupies places along the Nile upstream from the Shillook, for the most part on the overgrown plains and marshes surrounding the White Nile; they eat roots and seeds of marsh grasses and deal in ivory, sharing the land with elephants almost equally: a weak, bad-looking, though quite garrulous people.

The Nuer is mixed with some of the Dinka tribes; however, they differ in language and rituals.

The Bari occupies rather elevated locations around the Nile: a very tall, handsome people, they smelt iron ores, manufacturing spears (which negroes buy in great quantities), and use bows, applying vegetable poison to arrows. This is the last of the tribes known in the south; it is divided into a variety of clans, such as Shir, Bambar, Boko, and others.

There are some who still, even now, following Monboddo and Rousseau,[1] put the negro on the lowest rung of mankind, the one that serves as an intermediate step between men and apes, an opinion we have only recently seen in foreign periodicals; as the reader shall see, some, overwhelmed with self-respect and pride, are willing altogether to throw the negro off the ladder atop which they have determined their own place. Generally speaking, this ranking of human beings is no prerogative of man, nor is it compatible with the idea of brotherhood bequeathed to man by the words of the Gospels; it does nothing but demonstrate the relentless egotism and complacent fallacy of those who believe themselves to be the privileged caste of mankind.

However, such an opinion must have originated from some source; it must have some grounds, considering that it is so tenacious amongst people. Esquiros[2] claims that providence itself preserves some tribes under the seal of reprobation, so as to introduce them into mankind

---

1 James Burnett, Lord Monboddo (1714–99), British historical linguist; Jean-Jacques Rousseau (1712–78), French philosopher of the Enlightenment.

2 Author's note: Alphonse Esquiros, "Des études contemporaines sur l'histoire des races," *Revue des deux mondes*, 1848, vol. XXI, pp. 992–1002.

a method when buying negroes; on the contrary, he would subject them to a most meticulous examination, as a Remount Service veteran would do when procuring horses; the trader would even, if there happened to be a doctor nearby, send for him to ensure no mistake in the purchase. I can assure you that a negro taken as a child into a European home is as clean and neat as any European servant, of which a living proof can be found in my own negro valet.

I am far from being a blind protector of all negroes; yet I protect a man whose dignity is being taken away from him while at the same time exposing all his vices, inevitable in any abandoned and despised people, for he is less responsible for his vices than those quite aware of their own are.

Negroes are generally very well built; their limbs, when not subjected to any forced labor or violence, develop in a regular, congruent manner; the body, constantly rubbed with fat, has a smooth, matt skin similar to black kid-skin, being tender and firm, like that of a young woman. Men of many tribes, especially those living closer to the equator, are very tall, some of them being true Goliaths; as for fat people, I have never seen any among negroes nor among Arabs. Negresses, once over 20 years of age, are for the most part plain; their limbs, given complete freedom, roughen under the influence of the white-hot sun; their bodies and, especially, breasts sagging and their stomachs drooping; but girls of 10 or 11 years of age are very graceful, this being the period of their full development. I know very well that Prichard, citing a note by Robertson, claims that genitals in females complete their development by the same age nearly everywhere and that human tribes follow the same law in this respect.[10] What I have said is founded upon my personal experience, upon observations made in the places being considered, and upon the evidence provided by many travelers.

One especially ugly feature in negroes is their projecting teeth, which, in turn, make their lips hang down (the reason being, as we have noted, their protruding low jaw). Yet their teeth, regular and white, as if carved out of ivory, except moist; their large black eyes; and indeed, an aspect of quiet contemplation, of meekness, seen in the lower part of

---

10 Author's note: James Prichard, *The Natural History of Man*, London, 1843, p. 483 onw.

Kyrgyz in Russia, and the Mongols—have protruding cheek-bones and, generally, angular features. Our notion of beauty is quite conventional; in this case superstitions and the habit of the eye often mislead us. I do not think myself deprived of fine taste, and yet I have nevertheless found handsome people among negroes. Below the reader shall find a description of their physical qualities.

It is said that negroes, from birth, exude an unpleasant smell which characterizes their race alone, as well as certain animal species. Odd though the claim is, it is nearly always used as an accusation with a view to denigrating or destroying a particular people; thus the very same poor Cagots had been blamed for the same quality since long ago and reduced by constant humiliation to a most miserable state, until civil laws protected them,[8] while the Gypsies and the Jews are still being blamed. To corroborate such an opinion, its proponents cite dogs trained to hunt hapless negroes by scent. I shall forego any discussion of this barbaric habit practiced by European colonists, a business that no negro would dare engage in; let me note instead that the very invention of it required little intelligence: it is easy to teach a dog to recognize a slave, for all negroes rub their bodies with a certain substance containing fat. I used to know a Frenchman who had taught his dog to recognize Jesuits and leap at them at every encounter, that being a somewhat more complicated task. Not only do the dogs of Constantinople know one another, but they also know the inhabitants of their quarter and never attack them; in Cairo, any dog is able to distinguish between a Turk and a European, even at night, attacking the latter. It is claimed that slave traders recognize the quality of their goods by smell.[9] It is indeed possible that they might be able to achieve such a recognition to some extent, for the rich add fragrant substances and even rose oil to the fat they use to rub themselves with, and seeing that rich negroes have had a better upbringing, they are, therefore, of a superior quality to other goods. Yet having seen many slave traders, I can confirm that not a single one of them would be satisfied with such

---

8 Author's note: Francisque Michel, *Histoire des races maudites de la France et de l'Espagne*, Paris: Franck, 1847.
9 Author's note: Esquiros, op. cit.

to replace another and without even mixing with other tribes, eventually acquire a skin-color close to black; yet negroes do not or hardly change even in the North unless they mix with white people by marrying, which explains why some Abyssinian tribes, living in moderate climes, perpetually remain dark-brown rather than black, as Aubert-Roche unjustly claims, struggling to prove a supposition he makes. This last—which Schœlcher,[5] with his usual ease, is willing to accept as fact—is that white and black people could have existed in the primaeval times. But here is a question: What historical arguments can one submit contrary to folk tales and which would be confirmed so accurately by local observations? None whatsoever; and as for the physiological question, it in itself is far from having been researched and requires many experiments to be explained. In this case we usually rely upon the influence of climate alone; yet how do we know there are no other reasons, whether they be local or physical, that prevent the black color from turning into white, a transformation one could reasonably expect. If the higher *social* relations of a people can clearly depend upon the influence of the country's local character, why cannot the *physical* fate of a people be determined by the nature of the location it occupies?[6]

The skull of the negro is compressed at the top, the lower jaw protruding forward—true, yet it does not prove the above conclusion; some negro tribes, such as the Caribs, compress their children's heads, which could have subsequently turned into a distinguishing feature of the tribe; also, whilst not being followers of Gall, we still agree with Abbé Frère[7] in that moral education has some influence on the outline of a human head; yet the amount of brains confined within the skull of the negro is *nearly* the same as within that of the white man.

The angular character of facial features possessed by a people is obliterated only through its encounter with other peoples. Separately living tribes—such as, for instance, the savages of North America, the

---

5 Author's note: Victor Schœlcher, *L'Egypte en 1845*, Paris: Pagnerre, 1846, p. 274.

6 Author's note: See the excellent article by academician K. E. Ber, "On the Influence of Surrounding Nature upon Social Relations between Different Peoples and upon the History of Mankind," published as a pocket-book for the lovers of geography by the Russian Geographical Society, 1848.

7 Author's note: M. l'abbé Frère, *Principes de la philosophie de l'histoire*, Paris: Gaume frères, 1838.

later, as a new element of life. All this, you see, is designed for the benefit of the privileged! Yet we are convinced that providence has no need to resort to such measures, condemning one group of men to eternal suffering: it can renew mankind without them, sending it those moral storms that have often purged the world from prolonged stagnation, those thunders that have awakened man, warning him of danger. Why, then, is it the negroes that this cruel fate has fallen to? Does the reason for such deep humiliation not lie in the people itself, in that the negroes believe themselves to be creatures of a lower breed, as if marked by some higher power with their skin-color, hence submitting to slavery without protest, as if made for it? Our prolonged comparison of free tribes and those enslaved by foreign powers has convinced us that the above is not the reason, but rather the consequence of their constant oppression by people of a different color; we find a similar example in Europe itself, in a most enlightened state, in the south of France, where an entire tribe of Cagots,[3] being cast off in the course of several centuries and oppressed by its neighbors, has been reduced to a state of cretinism.

They claim that the negro's body is imperfect, bringing him rather closer to the ape than to man; this accusation, so crucial and with which an enormous part of mankind is burdened, requires consideration, not solely historical but also physiological.

As the first count of this accusation, of course, they adduce skin-color.

Indeed, the *corpus reticulare Malpighi*, which contains our skin pigment and lies between the epidermis and the skin, is black in negroes, but its structure is the same as in our race. Whether it is an influence of climate or an innate quality remains a question far from resolved. Contrary to the opinion of Aubert-Roche,[4] who makes the latter supposition, we shall note that Arabs, when transported to the Peninsula of Sennaar, acquire a dark-brown color, which makes them little different from negroes. Experience has generally proven that white tribes, when transported to a hot equatorial climate, as one generation comes

---

3 A persecuted caste in France and Spain in the medieval and early modern period.
4 Author's note: Aubert-Roche, "Essai sur l'acclimatement des Européens dans les pays chauds," *Annales d'hygiène publique et de médecine légale*, vol. XXXI, 1845.

their faces—these features conceal the above drawback, which anyhow is not much visible in many.

Negroes are, for the most part, kind and hospitable; unlike any savage tribes, they are not spiteful, blood vengeance being hardly known to them, while their bad qualities result, without exception, from inherent ignorance.

If you catch a negro unawares, your superior skin-color and European weapons shall force him to run away from you, like a wild beast, into the first hole; and if unable to run, he shall prostrate himself on the ground so as not to see a creature whose mere sight is frightening, whereupon you shall never succeed in encouraging him; his perceptive abilities are easily damaged; yet this is an instinctive sense of fear common amongst animals and men. A camel at the sight of a lion shakes violently, prostrates itself, and hanging its head down to the ground, waits for death. The bravest man, whether black or white, involuntarily stops under the charms of some serpents. But if you come to a negro with kind words and deeds, you shall see a completely different man in him. Any primal notions, any primal human ideas are alien to him, and yet, developed under the influence of nature, he knows many of its mysteries, such as the properties of herbs and roots and the movement of some celestial bodies. The negro is accustomed to thought and contemplation; he grasps your question quickly; his memory is bright; he soon learns Arabic, generally being a very fast learner. He remains in a child-like state, and if you behave judiciously with him, you can make much good out of him. We have already seen that negro soldiers learn no worse than other soldiers, even under the kind of teachers they have, their petty officers being deprived *fellahs* and their officers illiterate Turks; they owe their development to their kind nature and inherent talents, which, far from being lower than those of others, are indeed higher than those of many. The negro, even in his savage state, not being alien to any human ideas, shall sooner be reasoned with than a Belorussian in our land or a French peasant living far from the high road and the city.

The negroes have an obscure idea of a Supreme Being; the majority of those living on the Blue Nile worship the sun and the moon. When asked why they did not worship One Supreme Being, they said, "Show us anything that is better than the sun, and we shall worship it"; like children, they need visible objects to admire. Others, such as the Shillooks, have wooden toys in their homes, but those are rather their penates, their amulets, which they love so much as to surround themselves with; some produce images or mere cuts in trees and offer sacrifices to those trees; finally, the Dinka tribes, like the ancient Egyptians, worship the bull—following a certain celebration, the head of a chosen animal, with its immense horns, is placed on a cleared spot, whereupon sacrifices are made to it.

Any religious notions the negroes have consist of some obscure, fragmented myths, resembling in many aspects the religious beliefs of the Egyptians. It has been said that, south of the Bouroun, there is a negro tribe that preserves the bodies of deceased kinsmen from corruption, drying them in the sun and placing them in special caves; moreover, it is familiar with some of the herbs used for mummification. The negroes are not at all devoted to their religious ideas and easily abandon them; and yet the Turks, who hunt them and catch them as if they were wild beasts, do not convert them to their faith on the grounds that a Mohammedan cannot be a slave. Negro soldiers are all Mohammedans, some of them being very zealous worshippers of the Prophet.

Each tribe and each mountain speaks in its own special language, which serves as an even stronger cause for separation amongst the negroes. Their dialects are quite poor; some can only count to five; to express six, seven, &c., they say, "five and one," "five and two," &c., sometimes using their fingers or grains to add another number; the majority of them can only count to ten; a hundred is, in their mind, a figure that is impossible to achieve; they express many things by imitating sounds; thus in some of their dialects, a cat is called "neow-neow," a dog "gow-gow," &c. It is extremely difficult to get any sense from negroes with regard to the structure of their language; however, as far as I was able to learn, most of their dialects seem to have no cases, while many even lack verb tenses; thus they express the present and the past in the same fashion.

The negroes live in wicker *tukkels* made from bamboo, nature itself having given them the idea of this kind of house as the only one suitable for seasonal rains. There are few diseases in their midst, their witch-doctors being rather good healers. I brought with me some of the medicines they use, such as herbs and soil. Smallpox vaccination has been known here, initially among the Arabs, for much longer than in Egypt. Amalgamation and the sale of gold in rings have been preserved here, perhaps since the time of the pharaohs' rule, in the same fashion as it is shown in pictures one finds in ancient temples. The negroes live in families, making almost no distinction between sexes, ages, or even kinship. While children are small, their parents—particularly their mother—look after them, urged by an animal instinct and, when all is done, see them as a property that can be sold. As soon as a son grows up, any relations between him and his parents cease, which leads, among other things, to one of the most terrible crimes—the murder of the old father and, generally, to the eradication of all old men; yet I hasten to add that this bloody custom is not prevalent among all negroes, and I can only mention with full confidence the Bouroun tribe, where it really does exist; secondly, this is more accurately described as voluntary suicide committed by old men, persuaded to do it rather than violently killed. Here is how it is done. They dig a grave human height deep and, working from its bottom sideways, make a burrow of a size sufficient for a man to lie down without difficulty. Then they bring an old man, who, to quote an expression used by the negroes, has already eaten up all the bread due to him in this world—that is, a man who is no longer able to procure food for himself. They kill a bull, bring some beer, and give the victim some food and drink while also eating and drinking themselves. When the old man is completely drunk, they put grains of gold into his mouth, depending on the wealth and magnanimity of those present at the feast; they say this is done so that he has something to pay for his passage into the other world. Then they lower him into the hole and show him the burrow into which the poor man must climb; whereupon they cover it all with soil and . . . dance on the grave . . . The son is the merriest of all, having ridden himself of the burden . . .

A similar custom existed among the ancient Celts, as well as on Ceos, now known as Zea,[11] one of the islands of the Archipelago; some American tribes still practice the suicide of old men to this day.

---

11 Kea, one of the islands of the Cyclades archipelago in the Aegean Sea.

The Peninsula of Sennaar, up to lat. 4° or 5°, can be said to contain about 2,500,000 negroes, for the most part not dependent upon anyone and governed by their *meleks*; if one adds those living near and beyond the equator as well as in Kordofan, Darfour, and Dar Bournou, one can, without exaggeration, determine the number of negro inhabitants of Inner Africa to be 10,000,000. There are many divers religious and other charitable societies in Europe: the society of missionaries, the Pope's Propaganda—a powerful society, proud of keeping at their institute, in Rome, one or two boys from every place in the world even though they are nothing but an object of pride (the children, upon returning to their homeland, if ever they do return, lose themselves in the crowd and abide by its customs, as well as their own former notions, having no strength to act against the mass of the people). Apart from those numerous societies, there are also many private individuals in Europe who aim at achieving the same purpose in their activities . . . Is there anyone among all those societies and individuals who has ever attempted to tell the poor negroes what is good and what is evil? To say the word of faith, of truth to them? No! Definitely no-one until this year; meanwhile, it is very easy to approach some negroes, who cannot wait to see the arrival of someone able to teach them God's word. So how are they to learn what to do and what to avoid? The words of the Holy Scripture, "for they know not what they do," can verily be applied to them. They follow the sense of animal instinct. One can positively say that many animals kill their infirm kinsfolk (it has been said of elephants and of eagles), and so the negroes, having no communication with other people, follow an example set by animals.

Mohammedan missionaries act differently: some of them, putting their life in danger at every step, have penetrated deep inside Africa, preaching the words of the Quran. One cannot but recall here Sheikh Mohammed el-Touns,[12] a learned man of whom the negroes themselves speak with surprise. Is he not a living blame to the Christian servants of the church? To the shame of the latter, scholarly travelers have acted with much more devotion in this field.

---

12 Mohammed ibn Omar al Tunsi (1789–1857), Tunisian merchant and missionary; wrote of travels in *Algemeine Zeitung* (Munich, 1851), 4347–48.

This year, however, as I have said above, a large Propaganda mission arrived on the banks of the White Nile, supported not only by its congregation but also by some royals and many rich individuals from Italy and Austria. It has now been in Khartoum for six months, building houses, yet it is still to commence its business. As far as one can conclude from the Bishop's words, he wishes to establish colonies among negroes and therefore brings Europeans there. What is it, then? A spiritual mission or a commercial enterprise? Both, I hear some say; the spiritual fathers will become small proprietors, as it happened in America; they will show the natives a new kind of oppression and spiritual tyranny. If so, one can immediately predict opposition; firstly, from the negroes and, secondly, from the Egyptian local governors, who deliberately ignore the bounds of their realm, the missionaries therefore being unable to act beyond them—and that is where their mutual interests shall come together. As for religious tolerance, the missionaries can rest assured in respect of both the negroes and the Turks: there is almost no religion in the Sudan, and the Turks are quite indifferent toward their own. Exceptions, such as the present *Hakumdar*, are very rare. Let me repeat: it is the word of faith, of peace, and of moral education, unreserved and self-denying, as it used to be preached by Father Makarii on the remote shores of Lake Teletskoye—it is such a word alone that is beneficial for the land and shall, here sooner than elsewhere, bear fruit, while colonial despotism is unworthy of the servants of the Holy Church. Let us hope that the mission quite understands this.

Many say that anthropophagy exists among the negroes. It does not in the Peninsula of Sennaar; although the local negroes themselves claim that yonder in the upper reaches of the White Nile there are people who eat human flesh. Where precisely is that? Most indicate the Bournou Kingdom, even naming the Beni Neam Nam tribe living on the Bahr-el-Ghazel river, which flows into the White Nile from the left. One can doubt the veracity of this fact, although not quite reject it, considering that most negroes and some Arab merchants talk of it. At any rate, this is an exception; forensic medicine shows us examples of similar animal attraction existing among white people; the negroes themselves talk of the anthropophagous with disgust. Finally, it is a mania, a disease, an unnatural wish, sometimes observed in pregnant women.

Combe[13] unjustly said some unheard-of things about Darfour. Neither Combe nor any other European, except perhaps Browne,[14] has ever been to Darfour, although many pilgrims come from thence, especially via Khartoum, to Mecca, as do some merchants; I communicated frequently with both, and was on good terms with one Ali, a rich merchant who had just arrived from Darfour: they all as one laugh and refute the tale told by Combe; God only knows what stories the latter, who shall be remembered for other things, tells of Khartoum, where no-one knows him anyhow. The thing is that he describes in some detail a ritual whereby the people of Darfour annually offer as a sacrifice to some deity a boy and a girl, stabbing them ceremonially, in the presence of the king and the clergy. This information is quite clearly wrong. The people of Darfour belong to the rare Mohammedans who never waver in their faith, oftentimes reducing it to fanaticism; they are not at all like, say, the Egyptians. What deity can they possibly offer human sacrifices to; what justification for such cruelty can they find in the Quran, that civil and spiritual code of the Mohammedans? Even animal sacrifices are mentioned by the Prophet in a somewhat oblique manner. He says, "Their meat shall not reach Allah, nor shall their blood, but what reaches Him is piety from you."

On the other hand, here is what sometimes occurs in Darfour: the ruler puts his beloved brothers in a cave, whose name escapes me now, and orders his men to guard it most strictly, thus killing the prisoners by starvation, avoiding both blood on his hands and rivals on his throne. This is quite in line with Mohammedan mores; we saw only recently how it was done in Istanbul and still see examples of it in small Mohammedan countries; the aim is clear: troublesome relations bring the ruler's suspicions upon themselves and would not leave him to rule without distraction.

The same merchant, a friend of mine, told me that once in the mountains of Darfour, a certain negro tribe that lives in no other place than the

---

13 Author's note: Edmond Combe, *Voyage en Égypte, en Nubie...*, Paris: Desessart, 1846.
14 William George Browne (1768–1813), British explorer, the first to describe Darfour.

upper reaches of the Bahr-el-Ghazel, wishing to give him a good meal, killed a slave and cooked his flesh for dinner. Allow me to further corroborate my point by citing some facts related by Sheikh Zain al-Abidin, the learned man who published his account of his journey in Africa in Arabic;[15] he reports having seen anthropophagy on his way from Darfour to Wadai, in the mountains, prior to reaching the town of Nergh.

Apart from the above-mentioned cruelties—which, however, are only characteristic of some negro tribes—there is generally little in the mores of the negroes that would fill one's heart with indignation, in which they differ from their Arab neighbors, who are proud of their faith and of their brown-colored skin, for lack of white. Yet the negroes have many rituals that cannot be explained; for instance, children of the Shillook and the Dinka tribes, upon reaching eight or nine years of age, their milk teeth having already been replaced, have, respectively, three or four of their lower teeth knocked out; this is their introduction to society, following which they commence carrying weapons. I have often asked negroes why they do that. Some said, it is so as not to resemble dogs; others that, as the Arabs have circumcision, so they have the knocking out of the teeth instead. Only the *mek*'s daughters avoid this barbaric custom. Consequently, the negroes do understand all its cruelty, since the privileged family of their ruler is spared it.

The negroes of the White Nile feel religious respect toward their *meks*, or rulers; those living in the mountains seldom obey them, being generally inclined to unrest and to bloody fights with one another. The former own large herds of bulls and sheep; the latter trade in gold, although never more than necessary to buy weapons and to pay taxes to the Egyptian government—for those who do pay them—as well as to buy wives; in the mountains a wife costs about seven zolotniks[16] of gold, in the plains of the White Nile, seven or eight bulls. The negroes of the White Nile are generally easier to civilize than the negroes of the Blue Nile and, especially, the inner part of the peninsula.

---

15 Author' note: An account of his journey was translated into Turkish and from it into German; the latter translation appeared in 1847 in Leipzig, under the title of *Das Buch des Sudan, oder Reisen des Scheich Zain el Abidin in Nigritien. Aus dem Türkischen übersetzt von Dr. Georg Rosen.*

16 About an ounce.

The force of habit makes one tolerate customs that appear most odd; never is it more evident than on a journey. Let me ask you, for instance, about our habit of kissing, of pressing our lips together and rubbing them against one another's: tell me, reader, whether this expression of affection and joy at encountering someone is any better than the rubbing of noses against one another's, a habit existing among savages, who rub their noses together, while mocking us. Turks touch one another upon meeting, heart to heart, which seems to me the most expressive manifestation of friendship. Negroes sometimes embrace, but for the most part they shake hands as we do, although it is not from us that they have borrowed this habit. There is a tribe, by the bye, whose people express their feelings in a completely different manner. Known as the Bari, it lives quite far up the White Nile. D'Arnaud, who recounted this anecdote to me, had once invited the *mek* of this tribe to visit him on his barque. Having been warned by his companions, he was not surprised when his guest spat into his face; yet d'Arnaud was not, of course, content with such an expression of special respect for himself, and so rather than claiming his supremacy in the expedition, he announced himself to be a small person of trifling significance, while naming as the principal man a Turk who accompanied him as a military commander. Meanwhile, a great many negroes gathered there, as it usually happens when a barque moors at a populated place; the Turk came too, and the odd scene resumed: the negroes all proceeded to spit right into the face of the *effendi*, who did not in the least expect such a reception. Enraged, the Turk reached for his saber, but they hastened to explain to him that it was no more than the tribe's custom, a token of special respect for him, an expression of friendship and love, and so the honorable Turk, anxious to maintain a peaceful relationship with the negroes—which other Turks, unfortunately, have so little concern for—magnanimously subjected himself to being publicly spat at while in his turn spitting back with all his might, lest he appeared less polite and kind than his honorable guests.

In conclusion to everything that has been said here about the negroes, let us recall what they once used to be. I shall not claim that the Ethiopian dynasty, which gave ancient Egypt three pharaohs, was of a negro tribe—an opinion that, as the reader shall see below, I do not quite share; however, thanks to Champollion Jr.'s researches and by virtue of my own deep conviction, I can positively say that the negroes played an important political part in the time of the pharaohs. Foregoing any discussion of statues and bas-reliefs preserved in Egyptian temples, which bear a strong resemblance to the negro style, let us merely say that, according to Champollion Jr.'s findings, we know definitely that the mother of Amenhotep III—the wife of Thutmose IV, who went by the name of Mutemwiya—was a negress. Champollion saw a portrait of this queen in a tomb in Thebes and dates her reign back to the year 1687 B.C. Let us, further, mention another fact: the tombs of Biban-el-Moluk in Thebes have a whole series of images presenting figures of apparently different tribes. "Examining them," says Champollion Jr., "I was convinced that the intention here was to portray the inhabitants of the four parts of the world, situated in accordance with the ancient Egyptian scheme: 1. the inhabitants of Egypt, which, in the modest opinion of the ancients, constituted one part of the world; 2. followed by the inhabitants of Africa themselves, or negroes; 3. Asians, and finally; 4. (I am ashamed to say that our tribe came last in this series) Europeans."

There is no need to peer closely into the features of the second row of figures, which have, at any rate, been grasped rather precisely: you shall recognize the negroes by the color of their skin; there can be no mistake here. Thus we can see what high regard the Egyptians, at that time the most enlightened people in the world, had for the negroes. Among the Asians the most frequently portrayed figures are the Persians—whom the Egyptians were the most familiar with—in wide dress and with rich black beards. Finally, after everyone else, there follow half-naked figures, a bull's hide over their shoulders, feathers on their heads, and a mace in their hands. Their light-blue eyes are somewhat dull, their reddish beards thin, and the entire aspect wild and unpleasant: these are the Europeans!

Chapter VIII

Our Return Journey

Diseases

Yet another white horse with a bell round its neck and a swarthy, human-like creature on its back; once again, camels roaring, a *kibosh* cracking, people crying and shouting in all languages; this time, however, loud laughter and jokes, more or less amusing, enlivened the preparations and commotion that had previously taken place under a burden of general gloom and harsh severity. It all augured something new, something good now . . . We were setting off on our return journey! . . .

The Turks who accompanied us were especially glad: they expressed their content in a child-like, unconscious manner, talking with affection to our foremen, despite their being able to understand one another very little. The foremen were no less glad, yet retained the serious demeanor of officials; only occasionally could one hear a witticism addressed to an Arab guide or to a camel, such as this: "My dear fellow, would you please move your hump at least a little lower—I might as well be sitting on an awl." Yet the jolly and happy crowd contained two people who looked with sadness upon all the preparations. Having been revived by European life, they now faced the same old dull, dark sequence of days that brought them one insult upon another, one humiliation upon another . . . We had delivered them temporarily from their plight, but now they were about to be abandoned to their fate: a mire of ignorance and superstition opened up before them, yawning ever wider, threatening to drown them. Well, they will accustom themselves to it again! There is nothing man cannot become accustomed to!

I went to bid farewell to the nearby mountains and mountain valleys, where I had halted so often, exhausted with the heat and fatigue. Stark and scorched by the sun only recently, they were now, following a week of torrential rain during which I had not seen them, covered with bright greenery and with myriads of marvelous lilies and irises. Life had sprung up everywhere, appearing from cracks in the dried-out ground, from caves, and between rocks; while only a very short time ago, there was death here! Now a variety of insects and birds filled the air with their cries, songs, and tweets; occasionally some large animal would run past: a wild buffalo or an antelope, fleeing the advancing seasonal rains. If even animals fled them, we had no hope of remaining here!

I hastened to return to our camp. The entire detachment and the Governor-General were waiting for me. I must admit that I jumped upon my horse cheerfully and set off, accompanied by the entire population of Khassan, white and black alike. After half an hour we halted and, following a long exchange of mutual assurances of eternal friendship and fervent love, bade farewell to the Governor-General; I also bade farewell to those of the soldiers who were returning to Khassan, to all those with whom I had grown intimate in a short time, those who had served me loyally and, perhaps, loved me—a final farewell! . . . Drums rolled, and some set off south to Khassan with the Governor-General, while the others set off north with me: to the cold but dear North. The same black creature pranced on the white horse before me; but the peril ahead of us was hidden behind a dark pall; no-one could see it, and therefore we all found solace in the present, which had so rarely revealed itself to us in a brilliant light.

We spent our first halt on the Toumat. The night was beautiful. The full moon shone bright, rain drops glittering like phenacite on the vivid foliage of negro lemon-trees. Here, too, nature had unfolded in all its equatorial beauty; the air was stifling with the smell of jasmine-trees, which covered the entire mountain valley where we had set our camp; enormous fires, lit to guard the camp from the attacks of wild beasts, played with the moonlight, as if willfully, now casting a shadow upon the marvelous scene that had unfolded before us, now shedding a bright light upon it. Exhausted with the heat and labor, we avidly inhaled the mild, moist air, our hearts light and joyful. What a magnificent mystery this forest harbors in its silence; what a picturesque image the immense stump of a baobab-tree reflects against its darkness; how variegated are the foot-hills and, even more so, the camp sprawled over them! . . . Beautiful nature! . . . My soul seemed to grow ever bigger, striving to reach its greatness! . . . One could not even think of sleep—oh no! I saw negroes who, gathered in small groups, sat there half the night, as if they, too, thought it a pity to part with such a beautiful sight.

Reader, I shall not lead you with me, day upon day, along the road back, but shall instead transport you fast, halting only seldom to observe things we have not yet seen, all the way to the place where we shall turn onto a new path, into the Lesser Nubian Desert.

On the morrow, I met a *kawass* accompanied by several soldiers; it was a messenger specially sent from Cairo to give me a letter and news-papers; it was then that I learned for the first time about all the upheavals in Europe. *What is it?* was my initial thought. *A press canard, I imagine?* I soon realized, however, that it was no canard but bitter truth.

On the fifth day, we reached Roseires, which constituted the last mountain terrace. We overtook the rainy season, which had not commenced in the foot-hills yet; here we parted with T., who decided to wait for the rains so as to see the local flora in its full development.

After a short repose, and having bidden farewell to T. and to our detachment, we boarded our *dahabias* and set off down the Nile. Another bell . . . I thought for a moment that I was about to see a white horse and a black creature, but no! The bell hung at the top of a mast, making a mournful sound when swung by the wind. The men on the *dahabia* began an old song:

A little bird flew from Maghrabia,
Flying all the way to Iskagaria.

There followed a couplet full of improvised gallimaufry and then the same refrain again.

We sailed fast, propelled by the current, the wind, and the effort of 12 hands, skillful and strong Barbars, but it was not to last! In a single day, out of the 26 men on the boats, not counting the rowers, 21 fell ill, all with fever or dysentery. We were forced to halt; I suffered the most; the paroxysms of gastric fever lasted for 21 or 22 hours without respite, accompanied by terrible bouts of sickness, which drew my entire innards out of my body.

Before me, objects of bitter reality vaguely mingled with figments of sick imagination; men on the *dahabia* flashing past me, now pale and exhausted, now black and with shiny eyes and teeth, seemed to have come from the other world, summoned to the Last Judgement, with the chaos of the Judgement presenting itself in all its terror. Scientific subjects mingled with images created by my imagination. The white-hot core of the earth expanded and tore through its crust, its lava flowing into the seas and oceans, making them evaporate; the air was filled with fog, in which figures appeared, now dark, now light, and my gaze always beheld one of them and attached itself to this figure, in rainbow dress and with a face so meek, lit up with prayer and full of compassion for my suffering . . . and in such moments I felt better . . .

But what do you care about my illness and my sufferings, reader! Were I to die in Africa, you would still care nothing . . . Onward and onward, you say; onward and onward, I said, too, as soon as I was capable of giving orders: it was clear that, should the rainy season stop us, we would never be able to leave these lands.

I cannot comprehend why the disease suddenly struck us all on the same day. The doctor assured me that each of us had already carried it *in his breast*, our constant activity preventing it from revealing itself; it was only during a three days' complete repose on the *dahabia* that it grew and developed fast. Doctors are generally pretty good at explaining properties of diseases; were they equally good at curing them, there would be no sick in the entire world. Here are the consolations they offered us with regard to the inevitable nature of local diseases.

No sooner had we arrived at Cairo than one of us, to his horror, saw that his face was covered with spots the similar of which had never been seen in Europe. He rushed to a doctor. "Very good," the doctor said, "it means that you are beginning to *take to* our climate and water, your body being receptive and your skin sensitive; you should settle in." What led the reputable doctor to console the patient with such conclusions, I know not to this day; but whatever the truth, I prefer not to take to the Egyptian climate as long as my face remains as it is rather than resembling a Turkish melon.

In the Nubian Desert another disaster struck us. We became covered with large red patches, which cast much gloom over us. To the doctor. "Good, good! It is best for *all this* to come out rather than to remain inside." "For pity's sake, our skin is now more akin to that of a leopard or a striped hyena than to human skin." "So much the better! Let it *all* come out." "But this is the effect of water which even dogs would not drink; this is caused by fatigue and the heat." "Whatever the cause, the results are the same. Your body is purifying itself of all things bad. Excellent!"

The Nile commenced to rise—we were held to account for it, too. My body got covered with a small rash, so much so that there remained, so to speak, not a single good spot to prick with a pin. To the doctor. "Well," he said, "there can be no doubt here; this is a law of nature: the Nile is rising." "But it certainly is no fault of mine!" "It is only the sick who are not afflicted with such a rash; it is good that you have it—it means that you are not ill." "For pity's sake, how can it be good!? I feel as if my body is on fire; it itches as if being stung by myriads of insects, every scratch causing me terrible pain." "The Nile is rising," the doctor said in a consolatory tone. "This is a law of nature!"

Indeed, as I have said, I fell ill of fever. The first paroxysms of the local fever are horrible: it is a veritable hell inside one's chest, and the outer heat, reaching 40 degrees Reaumur[1] in the shade, serves to greatly increase one's sufferings. "Do you know," the doctor said, "that

---

1   50°C.

we have a popular belief that a fever, as it passes, makes one much healthier?" "Go to hell, Doctor!" was my reply . . .

I have no doubt that, were I to die, he would still find some advantage in it, assuming as he would that I could hear him.

As already stated, had well-meaning advice alone been able to help one in trouble, I would have never fallen ill, for I received all sorts of instructions prior to my departure from Cairo. One doctor told me several times, "In the course of your journey, you must abstain from meat and must drink no wine nor anything strong"; another insisted, "Do not alter your habits; eat and drink everything you used to eat and drink previously, and you shall remain well"; a third ordered me to eat and drink as much as possible, claiming that it was the only way to sustain the energy of the nervous system, the function of the stomach, and the perspiration of the body, as well as to protect oneself from fever. "You shall see Turks in the Sudan," he said, "every single one of whom is healthier than Methuselah, the reason being that every single one of them drinks no less than two or three bottles of vodka daily." I know nothing about the health of Methuselah, ancient history having only preserved the memory of his longevity for us; but that the Turks living in the Sudan do indeed drink two or three bottles daily and freely indulge in every excess without exception while enjoying great health—all that I was able to witness myself. I should note but one thing: that in the entire Sudan, including its Turkish population, you shan't find a single old man of 60 or even 50 years of age.

Henceforth, a long chain of sufferings and illnesses never afforded me any respite all along our journey to Cairo, and when they do subside now, it is only for a short time, so as to allow me to come back to my senses before gripping me again with all the might of their claws, like a cat amusing itself with a caught mouse.

We could not even think of repose: the rains followed hard on our heels and caught up with us several times. A distant rumble of thunder constantly reminded us of the necessity to be on our guard; the sky never rid itself of clouds, driven from the south; the sun rarely appeared from behind them, which did not, however, improve our condition, for the air was stifling and the wind just as hot as ever.

Sennaar is justly notorious for the variety and rarity of its diseases; Bruce described them at length, although he was not much believed. Ismail Pasha—for whom Caillaud translated the account of this traveler, one of the first Europeans to have reached these parts—mocked him; yet he was soon to be convinced of Bruce's veracity: out of 4,000 men who were in Sennaar with him, 3,000 went down with disease, and he himself became very ill of fever.

One cannot help mentioning a noble deed by that favorite son of Mohammed Ali. Frediani,[2] an Italian poet who accompanied him in the expedition, lost his mind, afflicted by an exhausting fever and by the strong heat; such things often happen to Europeans here. Ismail Pasha appointed his own doctor to care for the patient; he constantly visited him in person; upon noticing that the unfortunate poet imagined himself to be a great man, Ismail Pasha, very content to be able to satisfy the sufferer's vanity, gave him his own rich dress and his servants; finally, he provided the sick man with linen, despite his own need for it during a prolonged journey in these wild places.

Sennaar harbors another sad memory.

Once upon a time, there was an obscure legend in Europe, embellished with most fanciful additions, about Ivan the Priest, who reigned over some part of Ethiopia (or India, according to some);[3] certain Christian rulers dispatched entire expeditions to discover this imaginary sovereign. King Louis XIV of France, in his turn, sent an embassy directly to Abyssinia, already a Christian country at that time. It was in 1703, and following many travails and adventures, the embassy finally arrived at Sennaar in 1705. It was headed by du Roule, a courageous and industrious man; the scientist Lippi[4] was with him, serving as a doctor and naturalist; the others had died or fallen behind along the way. The King of Sennaar received the foreign visitors, who brought him rich gifts, very kindly, and he also gave them, in his turn, whatever he could; yet soon news came from Cairo that the visitors were dangerous people,

---

2 Ermenegildo Frediani (1783–1823), Italian explorer.
3 Prester John, mythical Christian patriarch who allegedly resided in India, Central Asia, or Africa.
4 Janus de Noir du Roule (d. 1705), French diplomat; Augustin Lippi (1668–1705), French physician and botanist.

on their way to Abyssinia to teach the natives to produce gun-powder and weapons and also, most importantly, to deflect the current of the Nile to the south and thus to destroy Egypt and Sennaar. Upon hearing the news, the black King was overwhelmed with horror. The luxury in which the embassy traveled proved the most perilous thing for them, for it could not help exciting avariciousness in the nomads; it is odd that, having seen many a traveler perish under similar circumstances in remote and poor countries, their followers still fail to learn from their example.

At the end of the month of August, du Roule parted with the King, apparently on friendly terms, and set off on his way; yet no sooner had he reached a market square at the edge of the town than he was attacked by as many as 300 people, who killed him and all his entourage in a most inhumane manner and seized their possessions. Upon learning of this incident, the King of Abyssinia sent his army to Sennaar so as to avenge the demise of the embassy; but his army seemed to achieve little success in Sennaar, once famous for the bravery of its inhabitants.

I have already said that the population of Sennaar consists for the most part of negroes and then of Arabs. These last, as well as the descendants of themselves and the negroes, are divided by the natives into five categories as follows: 1. El-Asfar: these are essentially Bedouin Arabs, with smooth hair, meek expression and yellowish-red skin; it is they, it seems, who are the real descendants of the original Hejaz people, which is proven by, among other things, their pure Arabic dialect, far better than the one spoken in Egypt. 2. El-Amar, red in color, their hair curly and with a reddish hue, their eyes languid and matt: they seem to be a cross between the original inhabitants of the Sudan and foreigners. 3. El-Sudan Azrak, descendants of the Fung, the conquerors of Sennaar: the color of their skin is bronze, their hair curly. 4. El-Akdar, very similar to the Fung in hair and skin-color: these two groups seem to be one and the same people, transformed under different influences of foreigners. 5. El-Kat Fatelobem: yellow in color with a greenish hue, with either curly or smooth hair; they bear a great resemblance to the Abyssinians; like the latter, they are somewhat inclined to the cultivation of land and seem to be related to descendants of peoples whose forebears lived in Egypt in the time of the pharaohs.

Before we leave Sennaar, let us say at least a few words about the hospitable princess of the former Sennaar Kingdom. She has to this day retained a shade of her former magnificence; her palace, if one can apply this word to a fortified group of houses, is the best dwelling in the peninsula, and even the Turkish authorities enjoy visiting her, safe in their knowledge that here they will find rum, vodka, and women! . . . Nasra, for that is her name, was once beautiful, which procured her the patronage of the beast-like *Defterdar*; now she is an old woman. Arbab, her husband as well as First Minister, was my permanent companion and took care of me as much as he could. When parting with me, he asked me to be sure to visit his home, and I was bound by my word; to tell you the truth, it was also my illness that forced me to go there. Nasra received me as a welcome guest. At dinner, which was rather decent, rum and vodka were served; the hostess at first took umbrage at my refusal to drink anything, but my companions appeased her, themselves reaching for the bottles with great desire and frequency, each time insisting that they drank for me, wishing to please the hostess, who would otherwise have been quite offended.

Nasra herself, too, partook of the forbidden drink from time to time. She pretended to be of Mohammedan faith, and yet, probably because the law-making Prophet had forgotten to mention women in his book, she, in her turn, thought little about the Prophet; she was, however, bitterly saddened by the loss of her greatness.

After the repast, one of her servants led me to a little house that stood apart from the rest.

Upon opening the door, I immediately closed it again, willing to return. My guide, embarrassed, assured me that it was the best house in the entire Sudan. "That may well be," I replied, "but it is already occupied." "How could you say that?" he cried. "They are your servants."

I entered.

A number of women of divers colors, yellow, red, greenish, and completely black, their arms folded across their chests, their eyes cast down, wearing traditional dress—that is, the costume worn by their great-grand-mother Eve—stood along a wall in a servile manner. The bed was on the opposite side; next to it was a little table upon which stood various oils, including rose oil, in disgusting little jars. I guessed what the matter was, yet still asked my guide, whose face and voice were not very different from those of the unfortunate female slaves in the room, what it was all for.

"To rub you with oil."

"But who shall rub me?"

"They shall!"

"And what shall follow next?"

"They shall remain at your service."

"But what can they possibly do at night?"

"They shall remain standing there all night—unless you find other things for them to do," he added with an arch smile.

"No! It is too much!" And with that, to the great surprise of Nasra's loyal servant, and perhaps to the even greater surprise of his hospitable mistress, I told him to lead these ranks of Sennaar beauties away, refusing the pleasure of my body being rubbed, as well as various other pleasures.

I can imagine what my fashionable Turks must have done! Despite the fear instilled in them by my person, they would sometimes break out in a little song whose sounds would reach my room, separated from other houses by a whole garden.

It was with a sad feeling that I went past the Kamlin factory. Lord, could it be that the same future should await my factory, too!? Is it truly the common fate of all useful enterprises in the East? The man who has established it is gone, and the enterprise collapses! Yet I can say with certainty that, for as long as Mohammed Ali is alive, the gold industry will grow: there is still much to do here, and therefore the Pasha will not abandon the business until he brings it to the desired end.

I halted at Saba once again. We went ashore and set off to the ruins, but suddenly we stopped, struck with horror: an enormous serpent, the similar of which I had never seen ere, crawled sinuously out of a heap of stones a few steps away from us. It must, in its turn, have been frightened by the crowd, for it quickly disappeared. Our doctor, who was the last to come back to his senses, assured us that fear was very wholesome for us, and that henceforth there would be no slightest sign of fever among us: completely wrong! It tortured us as much as before. I had once seen a leopard very close to me and, another time, a hyena, but they had not frightened me; I had had no time to take fright, obliged to hold my gun at the ready; yet on this occasion, reader, what weapon could I possibly take up against a serpent!? . . .

Saba is the last frontier of Egyptian enlightenment—or, it would be fairer to say, the first one, for I remain convinced that Egyptian civilization was born in the South; the very ruins of Saba presenting not the decadence of an effete and exhausted taste but the infancy of the arts, a state that manifested itself in energy and immensity.

In 1846, Sheikh Zain al-Abidin, that learned man, traveling in the West, saw in Wadai, beyond Darfour, the ruins of a city which, according to his description, had belonged to the ancient Egyptians and still contained vestiges of their creed. Theretofore no-one supposed that it had been so wide-spread.

The very resemblance between the words *Saba* and *Sheba*, this last being so well-known in the biblical history, proves their identity, especially seeing that the sounds *s* and *sh* are often interchangeable in nearly all languages.

It is odd that the legend of the Queen of Sheba and Solomon, preserved in our holy books, is also recounted in the book of Mohammed (Ch. 27), albeit in the Oriental style. Mohammed says that Solomon, sitting at home, talked to the Ethiopian queen—who also remained at her own palace—quite effortlessly, as if they were in the same room.

I met many old acquaintances in Khartoum. The Rome mission was still there: Father Rillo took to bed, gravely ill; Bishop Cozzolani was making preparations to return home, bored of Khartoum, of Rillo, and of the Propaganda; other members of the spiritual mission busied themselves with building and gardening; but still all of them, taken together, had not yet converted a single pagan to Christianity; moreover, they had not yet conducted a single mass.

It was from the missionaries that I learned further news of the world upheavals; it was also here that I heard of Mohammed Ali's illness, although I took every precaution not to reveal the latter news to my companions or to anyone I encountered along the way: the mere name of Egypt's reformer alone serves as a pledge of order and expedition.

The traces of the terrible *Defterdar*'s rule over the country, marked by destruction and desolation, have not been obliterated yet, perhaps owing to the people's wounds being irritated from time to time; such is a custom of the Turks, who adhere to the method of bleeding both in medicine and in politics.

Horrible stories are told of the *Defterdar*; anecdotes about him are passed round like appalling myths, known to everyone but recounted differently by different people. In my turn, I shall tell a few of the more popular local stories, borrowing them from quite truthful narrators.

"Why is the horse limping?" the Pasha asked his *sais*,[5] for the *Defterdar* was fond of horses. "It is someone's evil eye," the intimidated *sais* replied. The Turks think, of course, that any disaster can be caused by the casting of a spell or the evil eye, but the *Defterdar* must have had his doubts about that, and so he examined the horse's hooves; and when it turned out that the horse was badly shod, the Pasha ordered to take the horse-shoes off and to have the *sais* shod.

Once a woman came to him to complain about a soldier who had drunk her milk without paying her. The Pasha questioned the soldier, who swore that he had not drunk the milk. Then the *Defterdar* announced that, if the soldier was the guilty party, he would himself pay for the milk, twice its price, and if it was the woman, he would hang her; to determine the truth he told his men to cut the soldier's stomach open. The stomach was opened and traces of milk found in it; then the Pasha ordered them to satisfy the complainant's debt and to throw the cut-up body of the soldier to the dogs.

A *fellah* in some village had not paid his taxes, and the *mamur* told his men to take away his cow, the last possession of the poor man, and sell it in a public market; but no-one would pay for the cow the amount owed by the *fellah*; then the clever *mamur* summoned a butcher and told him to cut the cow into pieces and sell one to each household for such a price as to obtain enough money to cover the *fellah*'s debt in full. While

---

5 A groom or stable boy.

the butcher did as he was told, the poor *fellah* went to the *Defterdar* to complain. The Pasha summoned the *mamur* and the executioner of his will. The butcher, trembling with fear, told everything as it was. "Why did you do that?" the Pasha asked. "The *mamur* ordered me." "Will you do anything your master tells you to do?" "Anything, *Effendi*! Tell me to do whatever you please." "Then cut the *mamur* into as many pieces as you cut the cow and take the pieces to your fellow-villagers, asking for each twice as much money as you had for the beef, and then return the obtained sum to the complainant."

The butcher did as he was told.

Chapter IX

The Lesser Nubian Desert and Meroë with Its Pyramids

Dongola

My efforts to sail down the Nile through its rapids were all in vain. The water was still low, rocks protruding from the surface like a stockade. We had to go round by land. The thought of the Great Nubian Desert filling me with horror, I was inclined to agree to a longer march rather than to travel on the same road of torture again; besides, I was keen to see the deserts of the left bank of the Nile and to visit one of the most curious provinces ruled by the Viceroy, Dongola. Having decided to cross the so-called Bayuda Desert[1] between Meteme and Meroë, and not yet fully recovered from my illness, I set off on the 8th of June.

During the first three days of our journey, the Bayuda Desert appeared no different from the Great Nubian Desert: the same cliffs of black sandstone, scattered, scorched, and naked, rising above drifts of white quick-sands; the same round-shaped deposits of ironstone on the surface; two wells we encountered on the first day and a few thin

---

1 The eastern part of the Sahara desert.

trees, devoid of foliage and life, being the only features bringing variety to this somber land.

Further on from the Jak Doul well, granite rises from among cliffs of sandstone, a sight similar to that found in the Great Desert, but here it soon disappears, and nature returns to its former monotony. Henceforth, there are more wells along the way; trees grow somewhat larger, although still without foliage; and one often encounters nomadic Arabs; it must also be noted that the seasonal rains, which are sometimes even heavy, come here every year.

The Jak Doul well was built by nature itself in a cliff which one cannot easily reach on camels; the water in it is pure like tears, and despite there having been no rain for nine months, there is still a sufficient amount of it—so much that, should there be no rain at all this summer, it may still last into the next year. Below the cliff there is more water, muddy and unpleasant; this is a watering-hole for camels.

On the fourth day, I could barely stay upright on my horse, but we could not halt, for there was no water to be found along the way. We made it with great difficulty to the Moutouen well. There I lay for six days under a dry acacia bush, suffering from the heat, both outside and inside, tortured by thirst and anguish, that invariable companion of yellow bile fever. Not a single cloud passed over my head during those six days. The sun would scatter its rays over me immediately at dawn; thereupon it would rise high and the Reaumur thermometer would show 43 degrees,[2] even at sunset, until the sun completely disappeared beyond the horizon; it burned as if enjoying my sufferings. All round me was a desert; the *khamasin*, a strong and burning wind, blew the sand around. There was no salvation from the heat anywhere; I lay there under the open skies stretched over an infinite expanse of space, under the dense scattering of the rays, which blinded my eyes, with my head stuck into the thickness of the prickly bush, searching for shade in vain.

Finally, I heard that our supplies were growing scarce and that the water in the well had been scooped out. Something had to be done. I decided to proceed on a stretcher. The Arab porters were only too glad

---

2 53.75°C.

of such a suggestion: firstly, for money they were willing to carry the Devil to their village with all ceremony and make him their sheikh; secondly, they were in dire circumstances themselves, making do alongside us somehow, their own supplies having been exhausted ere ours.

So they carried me.

I was carried for three days. Toward the end of the third day, the desert was the scene of a most desperate struggle against death. Then suddenly, rows of some colossal objects rose in the west, brightly lit by the setting sun: the pyramids! . . . As we approached them, the portico of a temple appeared in a picturesque cliff. There was a pillar, then another, and a number of Sphinxes. The farther my eyes could lead my excited imagination, the farther it ran. Lord Almighty, if these colossi, these live signs of magnificence and civilization, are here, then they certainly must be furnished with suitable accessories, there certainly must be palaces and theaters nearby, as well as comfortable hotels—all that immediately at the edge of the desert! The consolatory hope of repose and pleasure, neither of which I had known for such a long time, flitted before me in all its splendor. Now the strip of the Nile flashed in a distance and soon grew wide, cut between the green banks in the half-shade of the sunset. Beyond it was a thicket of palm-trees! Everything sustained and nurtured my expectations. I was carried onward and onward. Some half-naked people and several men wearing *tarbooshes* huddled together round a single mud-hut . . . There they put me on the ground . . . What had it been, then, a dream? Had I seen it in my sleep, in feverish delirium, or while under some spell? No! Not far from me there indeed rose the pyramids, the pillars, and the temples, and yet they were touched with devastation—death was all round! . . . The village or, as they call it, the town of Meroë continued to live its miserable life, while these remnants of enlightenment and luxury decayed in their magnificent death. In a word, here was Meroë, and there were the pyramids and temples, and never the twain would meet.

However, prior to leaving the Meteme Desert, reader, allow me to draw your attention to one important fact. Ritter, Humboldt, and many others before them note with surprise that the Nile, along its entire vast span, has no tributaries except the Atbarah River; a unique

тельныхъ для глазъ, лежалъ я, сунувъ голову въ чащу иглистаго куста, тщетно ища тѣни.

Наконецъ я услышалъ, что наши припасы истощаются, что вода въ колодцѣ вычерпана. Надо было что-нибудь предпринять. Я рѣшился отправиться на носилкахъ. Арабы—возчики вдвойнѣ были рады такому предложенію: во-первыхъ, за деньги они готовы были торжественно принести къ себѣ въ деревню чорта и сдѣлать его шейхомъ; во-вторыхъ, сами они были въ плохомъ положеніи, потому что ихъ запасы истощились прежде нашихъ и они пробивались кое-какъ около насъ.

И понесли меня.

Три дня несли. Къ концу третьяго, пустыня представляла видъ самой отчаянной борьбы со смертью. Вдругъ, на западѣ возстали, ярко освѣщенные заходящимъ солнцемъ, ряды какихъ-то громадъ: это были пи-

рамиды!.... Ближе въ живописной скалѣ показался портикъ храма. Тамъ колонна, другая, рядъ сфинксовъ. Разгоряченное воображеніе уносилось далѣе, далѣе чѣмъ

Sphinx, near Meroë

phenomenon in the world. The so-called Meroë Peninsula and the Meteme Desert have many *khors*, which are filled during the rainy season, their waters rolling noisily, yet not a single one of them reaches the Nile, losing themselves instead in quick-sands—not one except the Abou Dom *khor*, thus far mentioned by no-one. During the rains it turns into a wide river which carries an abundant tribute of water to the Nile, its mouth being situated somewhat below Meroë. What especially gives me the right to call the Abou Dom a river is the fact that in the driest season it, like the Toumat and other large rivers of Inner Africa, flows under a layer of sand, half an arshin[3] thick or less: it is mostly there that the above-mentioned wells have been dug. Some may remark that the Abou Dom cannot be called a river since its bed does not have water on its surface all year round; but if that be the only property to give us the right to name something a river, then nearly all the rivers of Inner Africa should be erased from geographical maps.

Compared with other towns of the Sudan, Meroë is no better than them; it might even be worse. There we boarded our *dahabias*, which had long been waiting for us; propelled by the current of the fast-rising Nile and impatient to leave the Sudan, we traveled for two days to arrive at New Dongola, the capital city of the province, or *mudirlyk*, of Dongola.

The place had been the stronghold of the last of the Mamluks; then people began settling near them and under their patronage, and the city was named a horde, which word is still used among the Arabs, New Dongola being its official name only. The location of the city is good. It is being much eroded by white ants, that scourge of the Sudan—which, coming after various *kaimakams*, *effendis*, and other *kiboshes*[4] of Egypt, threatens it the most. The ants destroy houses in their entirety, leaving them to stand in the middle of the city like skeletons; no-one dares settle near them, afraid of their dangerous proximity, and so vast wastelands occupy a large part of the city, giving it a peculiar character. On the other side, the Nile washes it away, and there are more half-ruined

---

3 An obsolete Russian measure of length, about 2.33 feet.
4 A *kaimakam* (also *qaim makam* or *kaymakam*) is the title of a provincial governor in the Ottoman Empire. Kovalevsky uses *kiboshes* (whips) sarcastically along with the Ottoman titles.

walls, as well as trees hanging roots-up; if you add to all that several gardens filled with lemon-trees, pomegranates, annona-trees, and jasmines, you shall see clearly that New Dongola differs not only from the old town, but also from many other Egyptian cities. Beware of putting anything on the ground—it would be the same as putting money before a *fellah*: the *fellah* will steal it from under your eyes, while the white ant will gnaw it away from under your feet, whether it be wood, leather, or dress. Stones are placed underneath chests, bags, and everything else; when ants find their way over the stones, the latter are replaced; yet it takes time, for they need to pave the slippery stone path with loose soil and sand, upon which they then crawl to reach their destination.

A day's journey from Dongola and all the way to the most famous cataract, Wadi Halfa, the Nile is spotted with cataracts, across which the *reis*[5] would not ferry us, the Nile having not risen sufficiently yet, while I could not travel by land, on horseback. Negotiations and persuasion commenced. At last, the honorable governor, who served under the *Mudir*, arranged things so that we could travel in the *dahabias* for as long as possible; upon reaching a cataract, the barques would be unloaded and lowered on ropes; for which purpose 30 camels would follow us, and up to 40 men with ropes would wait at each cataract.

And so we set off.

The Nile is wide in these parts—twice wider than the Neva by the Isaac Bridge—as well as being picturesque and spotted with isles. Argo Island, one of the largest along the entire Nile, famous in the ancient times, had been independent and in alliance with Dongola until the recent conquest of it by Mohammed Ali. An old fortified castle that belonged to the rulers of the island is still there, the title of the *melek* still preserved, but now he barely differs from the *kaimakam*. However, the inhabitants of Argo retain some of their rights and constitute the regular cavalry, as do some Arab tribes, being somewhat akin to the Cossacks in Russia. In the evening, we arrived at the Dal Cataract and, having unloaded our *dahabia*, commenced our crossing in the morning. I alone remained on the *dahabia*, together with the crew. The cataract

---

5   The captain of a boat.

takes about three hours to cross, and the *reis* decided to row across it; had they lowered the barque on ropes, we would have lost a whole day.

The view was beautiful! An entire range of rocks, cutting into the Nile, completely obstructed the way. There seemed to be nowhere to pass, yet as we turned, a strip of water revealed itself, making noise and churning as it fell from quite a significant height, beset by the rocks; the barque would slide off it like a sledge slides off an icy hill, and then it would quietly sail onto a wide reach; but here is another range of rocks, and beyond it a second, and a third; the same fears, the same speed of sailing: one cannot help moving from one sensation to another. I was extremely pleased with the crossing. When we cleared it and found ourselves on the wide Nile, the triumphant *reis* spoke to me: not everyone would be able to navigate the Dal so successfully in this season, he noted . . . and indeed, there is hardly anyone capable of doing that!

On the day following there was another cataract; to clear this one, the barque—empty, of course—was lowered on a rope. The rope was attached to a cliff, for 40 people would not be able to hold it when the *dahabia* flew across the rapids. The crossing, about a verst[6] long, took up all morning; the same happened on the third day and again on the fourth; this last crossing commenced in the evening and occupied a whole day. Henceforth, all the way to Wadi Halfa, cataracts are even more frequent. It was clear that even 10 days would not suffice to pass through them; meanwhile, I was already able to ride, and so we proceeded by land.

Not only is Dongola one of the most picturesque provinces of Egypt, but it is also one of the richest: it is a garden, a forest of palm-trees, with the exception of Dar-el-Ghajar (the land of stones), where there is nothing but stones all round. Sokot, in the borough of Dongola, and Ibrim, in the borough of Derah, alone provide Cairo with 850,000 poods[7] of dates. Sokot dates are distinguished by their size, Ibrim dates by their taste.

How beautiful are the islands of the Nile, overgrown with palm-trees, how picturesque the cliffs, protruding from the water so high or else surrounding the Nile, crowned with the ruins of fortifications.

---

6   About 0.66 mile.
7   About 15,350 tons.

There are ruins everywhere in Dongola. Until recently, peoples used to replace one another at a surprising rate here, each leaving traces of tireless defense, which clearly shows how dear this land must have been to them. The ancient Egyptians left the ruins of their giant temples and speoses, which remain untouched by anyone but time, the reason being, of course, not respect, but the difficulty of handling immense stones; Christians left their churches and monasteries, standing fortified on unassailable mountains and fenced with thick walls of raw brick, which have arrow-slits. The Arabs turned the churches into mosques and repaired the fortifications, some of which are still quite intact. Bosnians, Albanians, Mamluks, and Turks destroyed them and rebuilt them. There is now almost no trace of the churches or the mosques, the fortresses being the only ones that remain; what the latest inhabitants of Dongola required was not a tool of peace and placability but strongholds of defense, a tool of oppression with which to terrorize the natives, upon whom these foreigners, coming from distant countries, swooped like eagles from their nests. There are also caves remaining in the impregnable, hanging cliffs where Christians used to conceal themselves from persecution. One can barely see a black spot on red sandstone, so high it is; impossible to reach from anywhere, it has rapids swirling 200 feet below it and a rock half as tall rising above it. No man, it seems, can ever reach it again; but look narrowly: here is a door! A hermit would climb down a rope into this place, as if into a tomb, turning away from earthly matters. Sometimes an entire parish would hide themselves in these caves, but the persecutors of Christian faith would find them even here, and the hermits would die martyrs, their deaths crowning their sufferings. How changed is everything! There is another faith here, which also had its own martyrs once, whereas now one cannot even recognize this faith, nor see any mosques (except in towns), nor see anyone praying, even though a Mohammedan must perform his prayers five times daily. Yet the number of holy men multiplies by the day; things have changed so much that these days one has to but go naked and eat hay to be known as a holy man; men and women wear numerous amulets; it is always so: once faith weakens, superstition comes along.

Among the magnificent temples of the ancient Egyptians, below the picturesque ruins of Christian monasteries and mountain fortresses, there huddle—barely visible above the ground, made from clay and silt—the huts of the Barbars, a half-naked and poor people. There is hardly any trace of Mamluks, Albanians, or Bosnians left: some of them have mixed with the Barbars, while the majority have become quite extinct; it is only by a certain degree of noble aspect and hospitality that one can recognize a descendant of the Mamluks, who reigned here merely 45 years ago. It is a proven fact that Europeans can live in Egypt, but their children become weak and die: hardly 5 out of 100 survive beyond childhood.

The Barbars are the native inhabitants of Nubia; they are proud of their supremacy over the Egyptians, while the latter mock their simplicity; both hate each other. Which of the two peoples is the better? God only knows! Each seems to be worse than the other. Yet there has hardly ever been a people to equal the Barbars, as well as certain Arab tribes, in the cruelty and disgusting cynicism of their depravity. The production of eunuchs—which Egypt is finally willing to abolish, instead procuring expensive eunuchs in Abyssinia, where it is Christians and even Catholic priests who, to the shame of mankind, deal in this trade—this business is less cruel than the torturing of women intended to satisfy the Barbars' overindulged passions. Elsewhere such examples are few and exceptional, whereas here all women are subjected to the operation. Our public language is not so nimble as to allow one to relate an account of it without blushing. The operation is usually performed at the age of 8 or 9 years, when the woman is already maturing in these lands. Its object is to preserve virginity and, later, to avoid adultery, for the husband repeats it every time he leaves home, despite it being accompanied by great pain, lasting 10 days. Yet the pain is negligible compared to what the woman endures during childbirth. In her childhood, pieces of live flesh were cut out of her body; and now it is being ripped this way and that, as if it were a patch of shoe-sole or cheap fabric—whereupon her tyrant of a husband still has the cruelty to subject the unfortunate mother to another torture, so as to return her to the state of virginity for his own pleasures. Let me say to the credit of the

Egyptians, to whose credit so little can be said, that they look upon this disgusting custom with disdain; however, quite a few nomadic Arabs have already adopted it. The circumcision of women is in itself abominable, but it is at least sanctified by local religious beliefs, and moreover, far from everyone undergoes it, while the above-described custom is based on utmost depravity, which suggests a deep moral decline, a fall from a great height—this being one of the many proofs that the Barbars are the remnants of the ancient people of Egypt.

The psychologist and the moralist would find this land edifying. You can see how mankind has declined, step by step, physically and morally, until finally descending to the most miserable state, which the Gourneh tribe is currently in.

Hitherto no-one seems to have paid any attention to this last. Being in the midst of the Barbars, it speaks a distinct language and has certain customs of its own. Its women are better than its men, which is an exception here; the Gourneh are generally dull, short, weak, and poor; their language is polyphonic, like the language of the Gypsies, their women somewhat resembling Gypsy women.

While keeping away from Egyptians and Copts, Barbars enter blood relationships and friendly liaisons with nomadic Arabs—or Bedouin Arabs, as many call them, lending some poetic meaning to the word, which, in essence, is not unlike the term for skillful thief.

Here is an odd and also rather cruel custom, either learned by the negroes from the Barbars or, much more plausibly, by them from the negroes, for while it has some meaning for the latter, it has none for the Arabs or the Barbars, who do not know themselves why they follow it. I am talking about cuts which they cover their bodies and most of their faces with, and which are somewhat akin to tattoos. The operation is quite easy to perform: they use a knife to cut various patterns in one another, or simply make lengthwise wounds, or sometimes burn skin with iron; the sufferer is bleeding, yet he never shows his pain with a single word or gesture; afterward the wounds are rubbed with a stiff rope made of palm leaves, so as to ensure that the scars remain for a long time; and should they begin to lessen, they are reproduced anew. Among the negroes, the enviable right to cut one's body in patterns is enjoyed only by those who have already killed at least one enemy in war, and it is done with solemn ceremony. For them it is a distinguishing feature, an award for bravery, whereas for the Arabs and the Barbars, it is just an ordinary custom—a fancy, as they say here.

The origins of some customs are difficult to explain, especially in a people with no written language and no regard for legends. Tell me, reader, where the following shameful custom could have come from—one that contradicts the laws of Mohammedan faith, is alien to the Arab people, and exists in one tribe only, the Hassanyeh, which wanders from Khartoum up the White Nile, as far as four days' journey or so. Every married woman in the tribe can enjoy her freedom from all observation of her matrimonial obligations on the fourth day of each week; the husband, at any other time being as jealous as any Arab, looks with indifference upon his wife selling herself in public. The land of the Hassanyeh is the Capua of *jellabs* and merchants of all hues, who trade with the negroes. Upon one's arrival here, one only has to enquire whether anyone has free days, and men will themselves bring their wives to him. This custom probably comes from avariciousness, the prevailing passion among the Arabs, who have bestowed the force of tradition upon it, seeking any excuse to justify it in the eyes of their brothers in faith.

Chapter X

Giraffe- and Ostrich-Hunting

Ipsambul[1] and Thebes

Our caravan, full of the sick, moved forward slowly. For the most part we marched at night; during the day, we sought protection from the heat of the sun, the burning wind, and the waves of quick-sands in some ruin or in a poor hut of some Barbar, for as I have noted, the borough of el-Ghajar is quite deserted. It did, of course, provide us with the chance to know the country more intimately, yet I have to admit that, after an arduous march, I would have no slightest wish to pay such a price for this knowledge. Nomadic Arabs would often approach us and then, despite all our precautions, something would inevitably go amissing.

The Arabs of these parts deal in ostriches and giraffes. Live giraffes have recently appeared in Europe; hunting an adult giraffe is not easy—one can, perhaps, kill it but not catch it; usually a giraffe is found at an early age and grown at home. We saw a domesticated one in Dongola: it is, no doubt, the most beautiful of all animals. It wagged its small

---

1 Abu Simbel, a village near the site of the temples of Abu Simbel dating to the reign of Ramses II.

head, similar to that of a chamois and perched on a swan-like neck, with such grace, and its glittering eyes looked round so sweetly that one could not take one's gaze off it. Arabs know the price of a giraffe; *jellabs* asked 2,000 francs for that one.

Ostrich-hunting is very toilsome. Having set off in pursuit of the light-footed bird, they give it chase on dromedaries, but not too closely, so as not to lose sight of it while not exhausting the dromedary; it is impossible to catch up with it in the morning or at night; but when the high-noon heat grows unbearable, they increase the pace of the dromedary and, finally, make it run at full speed. The camel cares nothing about the heat! While the ostrich becomes fatigued, and yet it does not give up easily and often dodges the skillfully launched lance, straining what energy it still has left; then they employ another trick, driving the ostrich to a thicket of shrubs, and unless it be very experienced and shrewd, it becomes entangled among the branches, an easy prey to its pursuers.

Ostriches are readily domesticated. In the Sudan and Dongola, many keep ostriches in their households, sometimes riding them, although one has to be extremely agile to be able to keep one's balance in the narrow space between their two wings, which they usually spread when running, especially at full speed; then no horse is capable of keeping up with the ostrich. My landlord in Dongola had an ostrich—the poor thing was used to carry water.

During our journey, I often heard about an English sailor, one Captain Horton, who had passed through these parts in 1822 or so and, as one can see, left lingering memories. Firmly resolved to reach the sources of the Nile, he taught himself—beforehand, on his way to them—to bear any hardship, any changes of climate, going half-naked, as all Arabs do, and being as indefatigable as they are; he could swim like a fish and easily absorbed the customs of the natives and even their language, while also, in addition to all that, being brave as befits a true sailor! And yet nothing could save him from the perilous climate of the Sudan: he died of fever! . . .

In the wake of the profound studies conducted by Lepsius, who spent three years in the country, and of the descriptions provided by

Drovetti, Belzoni, Salt, Norov,[2] and finally, Champollion Jr., I dare not describe the ruins of ancient Egyptian monuments so as to create from them the kingdom of the pharaohs or, at least, a chaos of hypotheses; many have already labored over that; and yet anyone is bound to do as I did, stopping involuntarily before the giants of Ipsambul, which seem to have come out of a cliff and remained there, waiting for us.

Four colossal statues, each 65 feet tall and 25 feet across between the shoulders, are carved in the cliff, and so is the temple itself, which they sit leaning against. They had been buried under the sands of the desert, the very entrance to the temple remaining out of reach despite all the efforts of travelers wishing to penetrate inside; but then Lepsius managed to open it. The interior of the temple, hermetically sealed theretofore, is well-preserved, and even colors in some spots remain very vivid. Among its many images and hieroglyphs, I was struck by some hieroglyphs carved in relief next to the ancient ones, still bearing the traces of their recent birth: it turned out that they had been inscribed by Lepsius and had not had the time to merge with the rest. Our offspring, however, shan't be able to distinguish between them any more, and it may well be that one of their future decipherers will read them thus: "Thutmose, blessed by the tutelary sun, the beloved son of Lepsius, the slayer of the Persians and the Ethiopians, returns to Berlin in the year 1844," &c. Imagine what comments he will make thereupon.

Having come out of the temple, I halted once again by these colossi: their immensity oppresses rather than elates you; this lack of finesse, these small figures barely reaching up to the knees of the colossi, representing their wives and children, cast gloom as one reflects upon their pettiness.

The same unloading and reloading of our baggage took place by the *first cataracts*, but now my companions were working full swing: everyone hastened to return home, and we were extremely glad to find, upon our arrival at Aswan, a steam-boat sent to fetch us, the very same

---

2 Bernardino Michele Maria Drovetti (1776–1852), Italian-French officer and diplomat; became a well-known antiquarian and collector of Egyptian artifacts after taking part in Napoleon's invasion of Egypt. Giovanni Battista Belzoni (1778–1823), Italian antiquarian and archaeologist, one of the pioneers of European Egyptology. Avraam Sergeevich Norov (1795–1869), Russian writer and explorer; traveled to the Holy Land and Egypt.

one that had recently been prepared in England for Mohammed Ali's voyage: the luxury of its rooms appeared somewhat miraculous to us, coming as we had from the deserts of Nubia.

We halted near Thebes and went ashore at ancient Necropolis.

According to Champollion Jr., pharaohs of the 18th and 19th dynasties are buried in the valley of Biban-el-Moluk, or ancient Biban-Uru. Today it is a field, dug up, spotted with hillocks, deserted, and desolate. Burial chambers made in a nearby sheer cliff are strewn with ballast and sand; tombs have been toppled over, taken away, or destroyed so far as human weapons can be used to conquer these stone monoliths; in a few places statues and drawings, glittering with colors, have been preserved. But let us transport ourselves to this field of death as it was 3,000 years ere our time, in one of its solemn moments.

In Egypt—where the clergy used to enjoy enormous privileges and where the military, being the defenders of the homeland (although acting more by the right of the powerful), also appropriated many advantages for themselves—it was the people that shouldered the entire burden of state duties. But when Menes entered a close alliance with the people intending to overturn the power of the priests, which was supreme in the state, it seems that he granted the people the right to elect kings. It has at least been historically proven that during the whole time of sovereignty in Egypt, the people enjoyed the right—a formidable one, bearing in mind Egyptian religious beliefs—to pass judgement upon deceased kings.

If there ever was a people of whom it could be said that they lived for death, it was the Egyptians. As soon as a citizen came into his rights, as soon as a king was enthroned, his first concern was to build himself a dwelling for eternal rest, which he extended over his entire life, adorning it with drawings and statues until, finally, the hand of death halted him in his work, which had cost more than his earthly home. Now imagine what the thought of losing this dwelling must have meant to him! . . . The assumption made by many—that the Egyptians hoped to be summoned again into the same life several centuries later, as long as their bodies were preserved intact—this can be readily believed once you have reflected upon their care for the security of tombs and upon their rituals related to burial. Let us presently turn to the valley of death. The King is dead. The people are in deep mourning. The heads of men are sprinkled with ashes; their luxurious belts replaced by ragged pieces of rope. The wives and daughters of the King are covered with mud. The lesser priests are busying themselves by the corpse, preparing it for embalming. The high priests are composing a burial ceremony, which must exceed in its lavishness any celebrations that took place in the King's life-time, how profligate soever he may have been. People everywhere are obliged to pray and observe lent for the deceased, and rich sacrifices are being offered to gods. Finally, the time required by law—72 days—has passed. The King, resting on a lavish bed which costs several hundredweights of gold, is solemnly placed at the threshold of the burial chamber that he has built whilst alive, where he remains until the people's judgement is passed upon whether or not he deserves his burial. In a portico covering the entrance—a fine portico in the Doric order, which existed for millennia before appearing in Greece—42 selected judges sit, gathering opinions and votes. Necropolis is full of people, yet there is silence and awe everywhere; everyone understands the holy nature of the place.

The deceased, whilst alive, knew how to show his virtues, how to flaunt them, dazzling the people with the generosity of his kindness and with the ceremonial offering of sacrifices to gods; but his inner life is not known to the people, the depth of his soul being a mystery they cannot penetrate, and therefore the people demand a ceremonial burial, avid for spectacle as ever. True, sometimes there would rise the voice of an orphan who had not been admitted to the King to complain about unjust judges; at other times the cry of a widow or a beggar would be heard—only to be drowned by the vox populi. When that, too, fell silent, a high priest came on a raised platform and uttered a speech, whose rapturous expressions conveyed all the great deeds and virtues of the deceased, which deeds were presented in pictures and inscribed in hieroglyphs on the lavish sarcophagus carved out of a single piece of pink-grained granite as well as on the walls of the burial chamber. The priests were envious of the important right of the people and wished to guide the masses with the power of their own eloquence—all in vain, for the Egyptian people, already developed and matured, were able to decide upon their own opinion. This time the priests and the people agreed in their opinion. The court was ready to pass judgement, when suddenly the crowd wavered and parted: "Another vote, another vote!" people shouted as an old man approached the coffin. Tall and gaunt, he had deep-sunken eyes, which bore witness to prolonged and terrible sufferings. He would sooner be taken for a visitor from beyond the grave than for a living man.

"Wait!" he cried. "An unjust judge is swayed to the wrong side by the weight of gold, usually belonging to someone else or acquired by evil means. The deceased King swayed you to his side by the glitter of virtues that had been borrowed, invented, that had cost him nothing. His heart, possessed by vice, was not in them. He committed good deeds in public while committing evil deeds in secret; the former he did out of fear, the latter out of passion. Listen to my words. At high noon, when even the busiest streets of Thebes become empty, I lay exhausted, dying, tortured by the mortal heat and thirst, in a deserted alley. Nearby, under a canopy, stood a cup of water, put out by charitable people for passers-by, yet I was too weak to approach it and thus unable to avail myself of the blissful moisture, nor of the equally blissful shade of the canopy. Their proximity only tried my patience, increased my thirst, and made the torture worse still. At last I saw a man coming out of an obscure little house; he wrapped himself tight in his thick sheet, clearly attempting to make himself unrecognizable; but when he turned his face to a woman who remained at the door, recognize him I did: it was the King! You say he performed good deeds under a veil of secrecy, content for them to be witnessed by gods alone, as befits a wise man; but now you can see how much good his nefarious soul contained. He who performs a good deed rejoices in his heart when he has a chance to perform another afterward; he who returns from a place of vice is bound to push away a hand reaching out to him for help. I thought of the King the same as you have done hitherto, and therefore I addressed him, as I would have addressed one of you, asking him, begging him in the names of gods, who protect the powerful and the poor in equal measure, to help me up and walk me to the canopy where the water was. What did he do? . . . You shall be horrified, you shan't believe it . . . He pushed me away with his foot, for my outstretched body was in his way!"

A wave of horror, clamor, and disbelief agitated the crowd, which was able to remain calm in the most frightening moments.

"Who will believe it? . . . How can one believe in such an inhuman deed? . . . Where is your witness? . . ."

"He is over yonder!" the old man said, pointing to the sun, and the sun, covered with a stray cloud, the similar of which appear so rarely in the blue skies of Thebes—the sun came out from behind the cloud in all its dazzling shine. The people, taught by religion itself to see truth in images and symbols, cried in terror at the sight of this formidable testimony. The body of the deceased was toppled from the lavish bed and onto the ground, and the people—just, law-obeying, and moderate even in their feelings of revenge—were satisfied with these signs of disgust, and so they dispersed, filled with fear and awe, having witnessed heavens take part in their judgement. The judges proceeded to fulfill their duties.

They walked along a dark corridor to a small chamber, which served as the ante-chamber to the splendid temple where the sarcophagus stood. Then stone-masons proceeded to wreak terrible devastation. Some destroyed the walls of the room, where the great deeds of the deceased were depicted in images they themselves had toiled over for many years; others, unable to destroy the sarcophagus, erased the images of the King carved in it. Meanwhile, the judges threw out of the sarcophagus three coffins, nested one inside another so as to preserve the body. These coffins, destroyed and desecrated, were taken outside, to the field of death, for everyone to see. Nor did the formidable judges stop there. Wherever the name of the King or its image appeared, be it on monuments or public buildings, it was chiseled away, erased, or defaced. Moreover, the pages describing his deeds were torn out of the very annals of history, and the name of the pharaoh was preserved by the priests alone, and later the just Manetho[3] conveyed it to posterity in his chronicle.

---

3 Likely an Egyptian priest of the Ptolemaic era who lived in the early 3rd century BCE; believed to be the author of *Aegyptiaca*, a history of Egypt written in Greek.

The body lay in dust, as if no-one wished to touch it for fear of defiling himself or provoking the wrath of the people. It was not until late at night that the wife of the deceased came to the priests and persuaded them, by begging and offering them money, to place the corpse in the defaced sarcophagus, which had been toppled over and now lay amid the rubble of the all but destroyed temple . . .

As we stood on a sheer range that used to serve as a tomb for the aristocracy of Thebes, we embraced the entire ancient city, which, due to its enormous size, truly deserved its name: the City of a Hundred Gates, as Homer had called it, although in reality the city could have hardly had any gates as we know them today; it probably had not even been surrounded by a wall; whatever ancient historians say, such an immense mass of stones would have left some traces behind, as happened in Babylon and in any place where a wall had once been; yet here no-one had seen any signs of it. If by the word *gates* Homer meant "pylons"—objects akin to truncated pyramids, whose walls, set at a more right angle, have no steps and are covered with various images and hieroglyphs—or if he meant "rows of pillars," which indeed formed entrances to palaces, &c., then it is possible that there were indeed an entire hundred of them, for many survive to this day.

Two enormous statues—their faces being pensive, silent witnesses to millennia—reign over the ruins and the valley of death, bestowing great significance upon this lifeless desert. One of them, situated on the northern side, used to be famous as the Colossus of Memnon, which made sounds at sunrise. The veracity of this evidence is recorded in 72 inscriptions, Greek and Latin, made by those who used to come here to listen to and wonder at the Colossus of Memnon; among these inscriptions, by the bye, are those made by Emperor Hadrian and Empress Sabina.[4] Such a miraculous phenomenon had long been argued about, until the opinion prevailed that the rays of the sun, as they appeared, drew moisture out of granite grains of the statue, which produced a rustle akin to the sound of a human voice, sometimes a painful groan, as can be seen from the evidence of some of the

---

4 Publius Aelius Hadrianus Augustus (76–138 CE), Roman emperor from 117 to 138 CE; Vibia Sabina (83–136/37 CE), Roman empress, his wife.

inscriptions. Yet as far as I can judge, this opinion is not substantiated. The fame of the Colossus of Memnon is known to have spread during the reign of Nero[5]—namely, soon after it had been broken by an earthquake. Septimius Severus,[6] unsatisfied with its unclear sounds, believed that if a broken statue was able to make a sound, then upon being fixed, so to speak—upon being re-created and put back in its place—it would, no doubt, commence to speak properly; however, the opposite occurred—the statue lost its gift. Why, reader? The effect produced by the rays of the sun upon granite remained unchanged, ditto the surroundings; indeed, why has a similar phenomenon never been observed in granite cliffs? And if it has been, then the observations are so far-fetched that one cannot help but doubt them.

The Greeks called it the Colossus of Memnon, although it, as well as the one next to it, had been erected by Amenhotep III, both depicting him.

Farther downstream along the Nile, one can see the tops of the Memnonium, half-buried in silt. Beyond the statues, scattered pillars, pylons, and propylons can be glimpsed, sometimes standing there in all their splendor, sometimes humbled into the dust; farther down there is Gurnah, which deserves little attention, and finally, the Ramesseum;[7] this last, even in the proximity of Karnak, is marvelous. It may lack in grandiosity and have no forest of pillars surrounding it, but its pillars are of finest quality. What makes it remarkable is this: it had long been thought to be the tomb of Ozymandias;[8] the Greeks, inspired by the priests' tales, relayed the miraculous stories of this imaginary tomb to us, in the words of Diodorus Siculus;[9] according to them, there was a library nearby, famous for an astronomical circle, extraordinary in size and made of pure gold.

---

5 Author's note: Letronne et al.
    Editor's note: Most likely Kovalevsky refers to Antoine Jean Letronne, *La statue vocale de Memnon considérée dans ses rapports avec l'Égypte et la Grèce: étude historique faisant suite aux recherches pour servir à l'histoire de l'Égypte pendant la domination des grecs et des romains* (Paris: Imprimerie Royale, 1833).
6 Lucius Septimius Severus Augustus (145–211 CE), Roman emperor from 193 to 211 CE.
7 The memorial temple of Ramses II on the site of Thebes, across the Nile from Luxor.
8 The Greek name of Ramses II.
9 Diodorus Siculus (1st century BCE), Greek historian.

"J'espère que, dans ce siècle éclairé des lumières de la critique et de la philosophie, l'immense cercle d'Osymandias et l'observatoire de Bélus trouveront peu de croyance,"[10] Montucla writes; another long-standing belief is thus destroyed.

Among the pillars of the Ramesseum, there lies in the dust an enormous granite colossus, which once depicted Ramesses the Great.

Finally, farther beyond the river rise giant ruins, known as Luxor and Karnak, now poor Arab villages.

I must admit that as far as art is concerned, I have never seen anything greater than Karnak; I was about to complete the description I had made upon seeing these ruins for the first time, but the impression they produce upon one defies any systematic manner of description. The readers would, however, find much pleasure in reading the accounts of Karnak and, generally, of Thebes in the findings of Champollion Jr., Rosellini,[11] Wilkinson, and finally, in the latest studies by Lepsius.

---

10 Author's note: J. É. Montucla, *Histoire des Mathématiques*, Paris: Jombert, 1758, vol. 1, p. 54.

    Translator's note: "I hope that in this age, enlightened by critique and philosophy, the enormous circle of Ozymandias and the observatory of Belus will find little credence."

11 Ippolito Rosellini (1800–1843), pioneer of Italian Egyptology.

Chapter XI

Return to Alexandria

Mohammed Ali, Ibrahim Pasha, and Their Families

Objects, faces, circumstances, news, each sadder than the last, each more striking than the last, changed before us at a great pace, presenting themselves through the black prism of illnesses and sufferings. Finally, Cairo appeared before our eyes—the very city that we were so impatient to see. But alas, Cairo herself, as if in accordance with the sad reality round us, seemed deserted and gloomy, having borne the heavy burden of cholera.

How beautiful is the legend of the construction of old Cairo. While the city was besieged, a dove made a nest on Amr's tent; the conqueror of Egypt, who had destroyed cities and decimated thousands of men, dared not destroy the nest of the dove as he set off to conquer Alexandria, and so he left his tent there, and a city grew round it, named Misr al-Fustat.[1] Europeans deduced the name Cairo from the Arabic adjective *el-kaherah,* meaning victorious, with which the Arabs named this as well as many other cities.

---

1 Author's note: *Fustat*: tent.

The court and consul-generals were all in Alexandria, but Clot Bey remained in Cairo: he had nothing to do in the service of the old Viceroy... It was the end!... Clot Bey said that the choice had been between the life and the mind of the sick man, and that strong measures had been inevitable: Mohammed Ali was indeed cured, but he had lost his mind!... God only knew if it would have been better for him to die... Did he himself think the same in his rare moments of self-knowledge, when he—he, Mohammed Ali!—could see all his nothingness and humiliation... Or did the world require yet another living evidence of the vanity of earthly greatness!?...

Ibrahim Pasha had not yet been invested by the Porte, but he ruled Egypt, presiding over a council that consisted of people who had been previously selected by Mohammed Ali, and were distinguished by their intelligence and activity. Mohammed Ali used to know how to choose his ministers. Nevertheless, Ibrahim Pasha ruled independently.

On the way from Cairo, we had cholera on board, its first victim being our engine operator, an Englishman. Anyhow, we reached Alexandria.

Upon our arrival at Alexandria, I hastened to introduce myself to Ibrahim Pasha, whom I had not yet met. The house occupied by the new governor of Egypt was no different from the houses of private persons of average means, and much worse than those the Pasha rented out. It was empty and poor inside. We were obliged to search for the host ourselves. Fortunately, the voices we could hear from afar served as our guide in the matter, and having walked along several passages and climbed several staircases, we found ourselves in a large oblong room, the only furniture in it consisting of a few *divans*. On one of these *divans* sat a man of about 60 years of age, wearing a short frock-coat and close-fitting white trousers; he sat there European-style, his legs hanging down rather than crossed; the only difference between him and other Europeans who sat next to him being a long, snow-white beard. I was very surprised when the Consul introduced me to this person, his words clearly indicating that the man was Ibrahim Pasha. He rose, bowed European-style, and invited us to sit down. I am describing all these details here since they made a drastic contrast to the commonly

очутились въ большой продолговатой комнатѣ, въ которой нѣсколько дивановъ составляли всю мебель. На одномъ изъ этихъ дивановъ сидѣлъ человѣкъ, лѣтъ 60, въ короткомъ сюртучкѣ, въ бѣлыхъ брюкахъ въ обтяжку,— сидѣлъ по европейски, свѣсивши, а не поджавши ноги; только длинная, бѣлая, какъ лунь борода отличала его отъ другихъ европейцевъ, которые сидѣли тутъ же рядомъ съ нимъ. Я очень удивился, когда консулъ представилъ меня этому лицу въ выраженіяхъ, которыя ясно показывали, что это былъ Ибрагимъ-паша. Онъ всталъ, поклонился

по европейски и просилъ насъ садиться. Я описываю всѣ эти мелочи, потому что онѣ, составляли рѣзкое отличіе отъ принятыхъ пріемовъ, въ то время занимали собою всю Александрію и Каиръ и служили общимъ предметомъ разговора. Въ остальномъ Египтѣ всѣ еще были убѣждены въ томъ, что страною правитъ Мегеметъ-

Portrait of Ibrahim Pasha

accepted manner, being at that time the subject of everyone's attention in Alexandria and Cairo, and much talked about there. Elsewhere in Egypt people were still convinced that Mohammed Ali ruled the country. A poor *fellah* cannot reconcile himself with the idea of ever having another ruler in Egypt except Mohammed Ali; it would be fair to say that, were the old Pasha to die upon bequeathing his beard to Egypt, they would obey it unreservedly, too.

This time traditional Turkish greetings, enquiries about health, &c. were soon over, for Ibrahim Pasha seemed impatient to hear about the success of our expedition; having embarked upon the subject, he was quite taken by it and spent two hours or so questioning me about it, having completely forgotten that there were other visitors in the room who might not be interested in our conversation. We could not help marveling at the speed with which he performed mental calculations, multiplications and divisions of most complicated numbers, announcing one result after another, so that we could barely follow him, let alone check his calculations. One could see extremely good skills in practical arithmetic. I poured out before him the gold I had brought from the established factory; Ibrahim Pasha sank his hands in it with visible pleasure, then poured the gold from his hands onto paper; the gold was good indeed—large-grained and bright-yellow in color, which proved its high quality.

Despite all the fascination that our interview about the establishment of gold-washing factories held for him, Ibrahim Pasha still touched upon my discoveries in the fields of natural history and geography and was extremely pleased to hear that I had reached so deep into the wild lands beyond his rule, under the protection of his negro soldiers, thus spreading the glory and fame of the sovereigns of Egypt. If only he knew what the arrangement of the expedition had cost me. Talking to him, however, I could not help praising the indefatigability of his soldiers, of whom I had previously written to Mohammed Ali; Ibrahim told me that he had decided to form a negro battalion in Cairo, assigning to it negro officers and even a negro commander. I doubt very much that they could accustom themselves to the climate and the land of Lower Egypt: hitherto, at least, all such attempts have been unsuccessful; tens of thousands of negroes, extracted from their native mountains of Sennaar and Kordofan, paying for these novelties with their lives. Ibrahim Pasha was especially interested in my proposal to establish a frontier line of military settlements and encampments in the Toumat Mountains, asking me to submit this project, which he promised to realize.[2]

I do not think it would be appropriate to relate here the entire interview, which was rather long for a first meeting; eventually I bid the Pasha farewell, hoping to see him several more times, but it never came to be. Cholera spread in Alexandria as quickly as it had done in Cairo, and Ibrahim Pasha hastened to leave for Rhodes, whereto I delivered the information which he required from me.

Ibrahim Pasha, as we have already happened to note, was not fond of Oriental opulence, setting his suite a striking example of moderation himself. He tried to free himself from the indispensable customs of the East, which only served to satisfy worldly vanity, as much as he did from the influence of politics or, it would be fairer to say, of the diplomatic agents of the West, who had recently extended their influence across the threshold of the *harem*, formerly unreachable for any foreigner.

Recently people could see, to their extreme surprise, Ibrahim Pasha walking round Frank Square; like a mere mortal, he entered a shop and bought some trifles—candle-holders I think. The Governor on foot, the Governor in a shop, buying a candle-holder! It was a miracle unexpected by people, who had been accustomed, from time immemorial, to see Mohammed Ali in a coach drawn by a tandem horse team and surrounded by a crowd of servants, on foot and on horseback. By the time Ibrahim Pasha emerged from the shop, a great many people had gathered outside it. He stayed awhile, spoke to those he knew, and left.

Upon taking the reins of the government, the first thing Ibrahim Pasha did was to intensify the works carried out to build fortifications in Alexandria, followed by the recruitment of battalions, which

---

2 Kovalevsky clearly follows the tradition of establishing Cossack settlements in Russia's borderland regions.

had not been done for several years. He justly enjoys the fame of a brave and experienced general. Military fame of any kind holds the most attraction for Ibrahim Pasha, which can be seen from his entire past life; I shall forego any description of the latter here, for it is well-known.

Ibrahim Pasha was born in Kavala in 1789, and rumors about the legitimacy of his birth are not worthy of a discussion. He does not have the same brilliant mind as his father did and is far from being possessed of equally lofty feelings; yet he is a good man of a similarly strong and uncompromising will; even if he fails to provide future development for Egypt, he will certainly hold it.[3] Once cruel, his heart mellowed with age and experience; once given to passions, he was changed for the better by his illnesses, which he still suffers from.

What shall become of Egypt when he is gone? It is difficult to predict. He has three sons, two of whom, both men of great promise, were educated in Paris, yet it is not his children who shall inherit from him, but rather *the eldest in the clan*—that is, his nephew Abbas Pasha, the son of Toussoun Pasha,[4] 35 years of age.

Abbas Pasha was brought up—or, it would be better to say, matured—in traditional old ways, and he will certainly find himself protectors...

Out of Mohammed Ali's many children, the other surviving sons are Seid Pasha, educated in the French manner; Halim Bey, who also studied in France; and finally, Mohammed Ali,[5] his favorite, whom he has always kept close to himself, bestowing his affections upon the young man even now, in his infirmity—that he recognizes his son I need hardly say, for he recognizes all his nearest, whatever the rumors about his insanity. Mohammed Ali also has two daughters: one, the widow of

---

3 Author's note: It was only recently that we learned of the death of Ibrahim Pasha, which will inevitably have unfortunate consequences for Egypt.
4 Abbas Pasha (Abbas I, 1812–54), grandson of Mohammed Ali and nephew of Ibrahim Pasha, the successor to the latter as the ruler of Egypt. Tusun Pasha (1794–1816), the eldest son of Mohammed Ali.
5 Mohammed Said Pasha (1822–63), fourth son of Mohammed Ali; the ruler of Egypt from 1854 to 1863, succeeding Abbas Pasha. He was educated in Paris. Mohammed Abdel Halim Pasha (1794–1854); Mohammed Ali the Younger (b. 1836).

обыкновенной личности, которая невольно приковываетъ къ себѣ вниманіе.

Мегеметъ-Али получилъ Египетъ съ 2.500,000 и оставилъ его въ 5.000,000 жителей, — такъ показала нынѣ окончившаяся ревизія. На него нападаютъ особенно за угнетеніе народа чрезвычайными налогами; правда, онъ довелъ ввѣренный ему судьбою край, до того, что Египетъ даетъ теперь слишкомъ 100,000,000 рублей асс.,

изъ числа которыхъ поземельныхъ сборовъ 54,000,000 и личныхъ 10.000,000; остальные заключаются въ продажѣ хлопчатой бумаги, гоми, сенѣ, индиго и разныхъ произведеніяхъ земледѣлія, которое создалъ Мегеметъ-Али, также въ таможенныхъ и другихъ сборахъ. Изъ этого вы видите, что сборъ собственно съ народа не великъ; важны несправедливости, которыя допускаютъ мѣст-

Portrait of Mohammed Ali

a well-known *Defterdar*, is said to greatly resemble Mohammed Ali in character; the other is married to Kamil Pasha.[6]

Alexandria was quite empty of people, some having fled to the islands, others having locked themselves in their homes, voluntarily putting themselves in quarantine so as to avoid cholera; it was empty except for funeral processions, which flowed to cemeteries in a continuous stream, and for Mohammed Ali, who, not quite aware of what was happening around him, appeared on the deserted streets of Alexandria every day, at the usual hour, in his splendid coach and with the same grandeur.

Let us behold once again, prior to parting, this extraordinary personality, who cannot help but attract attention.

When Mohammed Ali took over Egypt, its population was 2,500,000, and when he retired, it was 5,000,000, as shown by a recently completed census. He is particularly criticized for his oppression of the people by means of extreme taxes; it is true that he brought the land entrusted to him by fate to a state in which Egypt makes more than 100,000,000 rubles in paper money, of which land taxes constitute 54,000,000 and personal taxes, 10,000,000; the rest comes from the sales of cotton, *gomi*,[7] *senneh*, indigo, and various products of agriculture—this last practice having been created by Mohammed Ali—as well as from customs and other duties. As you can see from the above, the taxes levied on the people themselves are not great; the important thing is the injustices permitted by local authorities, yet Mohammed Ali certainly did not encourage their development but rather attempted to stop them as much as possible. Further, was it not for the benefit of the people and the country that Mohammed Ali used all the income obtained from Egypt? Having been its omnipotent and unaccountable governor during his 40-year-long reign, he retired without keeping a penny for himself, so that, should his successors refuse to keep him at the state's expense, Mohammed Ali, miserable in his old age, would end his days in near poverty.

---

6 Hadice Nazli Hanem (1799–1860), wife of Mohammed Bey Khusraw; Zeynab Hanem (b. 1824).
7 Gum (Arabic).

Let us now bid our final farewell to this extraordinary man, who has left indelible memories in my mind.

There are no regular boats running between Alexandria and Jerusalem, and therefore I was very grateful to Ibrahim Pasha for providing me with a steam-boat. I left Alexandria, the hand of fate already weighing upon her, with sadness, and a few days later found myself in another city, which presented a no less doleful spectacle—in Jerusalem.

Addendum

Geographical Aspects of the Basin of the Nile

Gold Deposits of Inner Africa

To proceed with our description of the formation the Nile's basin, we must transport ourselves into what for its native people was a prehistoric time. According to Herodotus, who gathered the legends of ancient Egypt from the priests, even before the Delta of the Nile had been fully formed and the sedimentary layers covered with deposits of silt, man took possession of the country, continuing to fight the Mediterranean Sea to conquer his land from it, assisting the natural process with his own labor. That period is dated in Egyptian legends and chronicles to beyond our chronology, and I shall therefore not dwell on it, not wishing to increase the number of hypotheses, already numerous, especially with regard to this subject. Instead, I shall immediately proceed to describe the basin of the Nile in its present condition or as we find it in times that are within reach of geology or history, which terms are here understood in a narrow, more definitive sense.

The Nile is an extraordinary river, unique in the world, presenting as it does some peculiarities pertaining to it alone; its character drastically distinguishing it from the other rivers of the globe. The Nile—concealed in its every action behind a veil that the ancients found impenetrable, not knowing or daring to lift it, afraid of insulting the mystery of the river they deified, and dedicating temples and numerous priests to its worshipping—the Nile has not been quite discovered yet. Despite all the efforts of travelers, its sources have remained unknown since the time of the pharaohs, and many people perished along the way of discovery, sacrificing themselves to science, which silently devastates the ranks of its acolytes. It was not until recently that we learned the reasons for the rising of the Nile at the time when other rivers return to their banks and for its subsiding at a time when other rivers flood their banks. Other rivers flow in a valley that forms a kind of hollow, serving as a natural cradle for them; on the contrary, the banks of the Nile are elevated, sloping not toward the river-bed but away from it, to the sides, toward the deserts; therefore the Nile's waters and silt, having just risen to the height of its banks, soon inundate them and flow beyond, bringing fertility to the country. The ancients said that the Delta is the gift of the Nile, which can be proven by geological facts.

The Delta—that is, the space on the ground formed by the mouths of the Nile River in the shape of the Greek letter Δ (delta)—is clear proof of that; its shells belong to a fresh-water variety, while the layers of the Nile's deposits bear witness to however many centuries they worked to transform an immense swamp that, according to Herodotus, used to stretch down to Lake Moeris. A scientific expedition that accompanied Napoleon to Egypt calculated that the elevation of the continental part of Egypt due to the amount of silt distributed annually by the Nile equals 126 millimeters in every century. In my opinion, this calculation cannot be precise: firstly, the elevation of the banks of the Nile depends not only upon its silt deposits but also upon the deposits of nearby sands, which, despite being obstructed by the mountains, still reach the banks of the Nile, as if attempting to obliterate any beneficial effect due to the joint labors of man and the Nile (which fact is clearly shown by the quartz sand of the desert, whose layers often replace the layers of silt at a significant depth); secondly, the deposits of silt quite depend upon random circumstances which cannot be calculated, such as the scale of inundation, natural obstacles encountered by the floods in different spots, the tide-rips of the river, &c. Peering closely into the layering of the banks, I found that in certain years the Nile had washed away precisely the entire layer of the previous year, replacing it with a new one of the same thickness, thus renewing the soil and making it fertile without changing its level.

The Nile's deposits are of the following composition:

1. three-fifths of alumina;
2. somewhat more than one-fifth of carbonate of lime;
3. about one-tenth of free carbon;
4. six or seven-hundredths of oxide of iron, which communicates the red color to its waters during its inundation;
5. two or three-hundredths of carbonate of magnesia; and
6. several atoms of silex.

The view of Egypt during the flooding of the Nile, when it appears to be an enormous archipelago, with treetops, mountains, and villages scattered around elevated parts coming out of them as if they were islands—this view is indescribably beautiful. It is now reliably known, and we can confirm it as eye-witnesses, that inundations are caused by seasonal rains, which fall in whole masses of water, resembling enormous waterfalls, during four or five months near the sources of the Nile.

Two mountain ranges accompany the Nile, protecting it from the sands of the desert, which threaten to devour it as they advance, and keeping the waters of the Nile in its valley, not letting them any farther, and thus sparing them any waste of fertility. The so-called Arabian Mountains, running along the eastern side, come closer to the Nile and in some places invade its bed; the elevation of the range increases as it moves south, and yet its highest point, not far from Thebes, does not exceed 700 meters. In the north, near Cairo, this range forms a group of mountains called the Mokattam Hills, which barely reach a height of 200 meters. To the west of the Nile stretch the Libyan Mountains. These last are nearly the same height as the Arabian range, while also being equally deserted, black, broken, and scattered. As it leaves the Nile behind, going into the desert, the range becomes significantly lower until it finally merges with the sands completely, while the Mokattam Hills rise as they deviate toward Suez, forming elevated groups of mountains near the Red Sea. Thus the entire basin of the Nile—that is, the entire Egypt—constitutes an area that slopes significantly from east to west.

Nubia, with its Great and Lesser Nubian Deserts, has almost the same aspect, the only difference being in that its elevation toward the south, near Sennaar, is much more pronounced. The Sudan and Abyssinia—that is, the space between the countries of Inner Africa that are barely known by hearsay and the Red Sea in the east, stretching to the confluence of the White and the Blue Nile in the north (which includes the countries we have explored)—these lands are very different in form. Here the ground rises abruptly and significantly from west to east, changing from 800-foot-high mountains in Wadai to immense, snow-covered mountains in Abyssinia, which reach 10,000 feet and more above the sea level.

Those who believe that the interior of Africa—beyond the equator, on the other side of the so-called Moon Mountains—is a depression are mistaken, their opinion appearing as wrong as the previously held one, that this part of the continent is quite deserted. Enough information has now been gathered about these countries to allow one to positively say that the interior of Africa is much inhabited; as for the absence of any significant depression, this fact is corroborated by the rivers that flow out of it at a significant rate, which suggests the sloping of the continent in the same succession from east to west.

Having described the exterior aspect of the lands which form the basin of the Nile and which it irrigates, giving them life and vegetation, I shall say a few words about the river itself and then go on to describe the geological formation of its basin.

I have already expressed my opinion of the sources of the Nile in the above account of my journey to Inner Africa. At any rate, the Nile proper consists of two merging rivers, the White and the Blue, or Bahr-el-Abiad and Bahr-el-Azrak. The waters of the former come out of marshy plains and therefore flow slowly, being muddy, unwholesome, and white in color; the waters of the latter, rolling off the high ground of Abyssinia, are clear and blue in color; the natives think them salutary, and indeed, the Blue Nile's water is the best water for drinking. The two rivers merge near Khartoum, in lat. 15°37′10″ N. and long. 30°17′30″ E. Thence the Nile flows solitary, in meanders, two of which are so large that they nearly embrace the entire enormous space between the Great and the Lesser Nubian Deserts; frequently obstructed by cataracts between Shendi and Aswan, the river, as if against its will, rushes sideways, seeking a new outlet for itself. Linant Bey calculates the amount of water carried by the Nile in every 24 hours to be, at low water, 79,532,551,728 cubic meters for the Rosetta branch and 71,033,840,640 cubic meters for the Damietta branch and, at high water, 478,317,838,960 and 227,196,828,480, respectively.

Humboldt and many other scientists have noted with surprise that the Nile is the only river in the world that, along such a great stretch, lets in only one river, the Atbarah, which flows into it from the right. I have now succeeded in discovering another river which flows into the Nile, from the left, and which the Arabs call the Aboud: it runs through the Lesser Nubian Desert, merging with the Nile somewhat below Meroë (a detailed description can be found in the second part of my *Journey*).

I have already described the composition of soil in the Delta of the Nile. The prominences closest to the mouth of the river, which subsequently turn into the Mokattam Hills, are composed of tertiary sandstone, marl, and limestone, all of them abundant with the following fossils: *Nummulites sp.*, *Voluta sp.*, *Cardium protractum*, *Fusus sp.*, *Nerinea sp.*, *Trochus sp.*, *Mactra sp.*, *Madrepora*, *Nummulites polygratus*, *Dentalium sp.*, *Solen sp.*, *Turbo sp.*, and *Crassatella sulcata* (see the collection of fossils submitted to the Institute of Mining).

Let us trace, if only briefly, the formation of the Nile's basin from thence to the places that are to be the subject of our special study.

The low, lifeless ranges of the Libyan and Arabian Mountains stretch along the Nile's banks with remarkable uniformity, composed of tertiary limestone and marl, which between Suez and Cairo are replaced by a narrow strip of sandstone, also tertiary, this last turning in places into chalky limestone (between Keneh and Esneh) or giving way to quartz sandstone (between Esneh and the cataracts of Aswan). It is from this last that granite and granite syenite rise, forming the cataracts of Aswan and Elephantine Island, as well as enormous quarries near Aswan, which in the time of the pharaohs provided Egyptian cities and temples with giant pillars, obelisks, and statues. One can still discern a colossus in one the cliffs, barely carved, not yet sawn off, remaining there since the time of the pharaohs, as if to indicate the method by which ancient sculptors carved their works of art. The above-mentioned sandstone is occasionally covered with molasse; in my opinion, and contrary to Russegger's claim, it can never be classified as a greensand formation.

The strata of marl, clay, limestone, and sandstone—which combination constitutes, for the most part, the basin of the Nile in Egypt and Nubia—cannot be classified as *Zechstein* in the German notation nor as lower sediments of *New Red Sandstone* in the English one. They are, in my opinion, more recently formed than both of those and differ in their fossils. There is a chalk formation, composed of several strata of greyish chalk, marl, and sandstone; we encountered no new fossils in it except those already known and typical of the chalk formations of Europe: *Belemnites micronatus*, *Terebratula carnea*, *Catillus*, &c. Above the layers of white chalk we occasionally encountered nummulite limestone. Generally, the lower strata of tertiary soil (*période cocène*) are less developed than the other two (*miocène et pliocène*).

We left the Nile behind at Korosko to go ever deeper inside the country, into the Great Nubian Desert; as we went farther from the basin of the Nile, we left behind its formations, which in many respects are unique and pertain to it alone, and hence shall be called the Nile system hereafter. On the surface of the mountains, which grew somewhat higher, quartzite appeared, in places turning into clay slate containing grantolite, often cut through by traprock and subsequently interspersed with limestone; I therefore believe that plutonic effusions must have happened after the deposition of grantolite slate, during the formation of the lower strata, and that they made no influence on the elevation of the Nile's basin, being regularly interspersed with raised sedimentary formations.

Farther on, one encounters crystal rock formations in a much developed state. A day's journey to the wells of el-Murat, strata of talcum slate are broken through by fissured diorite and aphanite, which in their turn are replaced by porphyry, blue elvan, and syenite; the mountains gradually rise and, being scattered one by one or in small groups here, merge into a range in the east, near the Sea of Reeds, separate and rather elevated, where crystal rocks prevail. On the other side of the wells of el-Murat, mica and chlorite slate dominate, cut through in many places by transparent quartz veins or by masses of layered quartz rock with solitary grains of quartz and feldspar, which appear to be clay slate transformed by granite, for nearby there are strata of granite, perhaps forming a granite axis that runs here. At the foot-hills we encountered dolerite, and finally, as we left the desert behind and approached the Nile, we entered once again the *system of the Nile's basin*, to use our term. A narrow edge coming close to the Nile is covered with strata of alluvial foliar clay, which forms a fertile strip, although hardened in places (where it awaits new silt deposits to be brought by the Nile), which occasionally contains impressions of plants.

Mountains that stand apart from one another, scattered around the boundless plain, their aspect and, finally, numerous ferruginous boulders, hollow or with ferruginous ochre inside and partially wind-eroded—these features gave Russegger reasons to suggest their volcanic origin.

Prior to arriving at el-Murat, we had another occasion to convince ourselves of the validity of a remark made by Murchison regarding the fact that the appearance of volcanic rock proves the presence of metal-bearing deposits—especially in the spots where the former touch sedimentary strata, through which they are effused outside. This connexion between certain plutonic and sedimentary strata and precious metals also applies to the occurrence of gold-bearing deposits, which originate from the erosion of lodes. Having collected, in accordance with the above indication, some sand, we washed it at the wells of el-Murat and obtained signs of gold.

Along a stretch of about three days' journey to Khartoum, as well as between Khartoum and Roseires (two weeks' sailing), the banks of the Nile and the space embraced by its two tributaries—the White and the Blue Nile, or Bahr-el-Abiad and Bahr-el-Azrak—which space is occupied by the Peninsula of Sennaar, is a plain sloping toward the banks of the White Nile, rising in Abyssinia, and covered with marl and conglomerate. The banks of the Nile are not sheltered by any mountain ridge; protection from the advance of sands is no longer required here, for we are already in the belt of seasonal rains, where permanent vegetation serves (if not all year round) to consolidate the sands and prevent them from producing a destructive effect. Conglomerate is for the most part bound by limestone mass and reveals, when broken, grains of quartz and numerous fresh-water shells, among which we noticed the so-called *Etheria caillaudi*, *Unio*, *Iridina*, and *Anodonta*.

Toward foot-hills Nubian sandstone appears again, sometimes accompanied by hematite, and finally, the foot-hills themselves emerge at Roseires in separate small groups, consisting of north-inclined strata of clay slate and crossed in many places by veins of wind-eroded quartz. The group of Moe Mountains, standing separately, is much more significant and consists of granite very similar to that of Aswan; we shall turn to it later.

The banks are overgrown with vegetation, which becomes the thicker and wilder the closer one gets to the foot-hills; the date-palm, *Phoenix dactylifera*, begins to disappear; while the *doum*, *Cucifera thebaica*, still grows in abundance; soon a third variety of the palm-tree appears, not yet described by anyone, as far as I can judge, and known locally as *douleb*—I have written of it in my *Journey*; there are plentiful *Acacia heterocarpa*, *Acacia nilotica*, *Acacia gummifera*, *Mimosa habbas*, as well as several kinds of cassia, among which we noticed *Cassia acutifolia*, *Cassia senna*, and *Cassia sabun*;[1] also widespread are *Tamarindus indica*, *Bauhinia tamarindacea*, *Clitoria ternatea*, *Glycine moringaeflora*, *Vernonia amygdalina*, *Inula undulata*, *Ethulia gracilis*, *Eclipta erecta*, *Cynanchum heterophyllum*, *Asclepias lanifora*, *Strychnos innocua*, *Sorghum vulgare*, *Sida mutica*, *Sterculia setigera*, *Ficus sycomorus*, *Ficus platyphylla*, *Ficus glumosa*, *Nauclea microphylla*, *Heliotropium pallens*, *Cordia*, *Celosia trigyna*, *Acanthus*

---

1 It is unclear which species of the genus Kovalevsky has in mind.

polystachyus, Rucelia nubica,[2] *Sesamum orientale, Tribulus terrestris, Tamarix orientalis, Ziziphus purvifolia, Pistia stratiotes, Terminalia psidiifolia*, and *Balanites aegyptiaca*. Finally, let me mention the annona fruit, previously unknown to me, and the *hokan*, as they call it in Sennaar, prior to concluding this brief inventory with that giant of vegetation, the baobab, *Adansonia digitata*, which I have described in detail in my *Journey*.

The ground rises almost imperceptibly from the Mediterranean Sea and the mouth of the Nile to the very confluence of the White Nile and the Blue Nile, near the city of Khartoum in the East Sudan, so that across the immense space between Alexandria and Aswan the Nile valley barely rises by 170 Paris feet,[3] and between Aswan and Khartoum, by 870. Meanwhile, Roseires, situated at the foot-hills, lies at a height of 1,600 feet already, the mountains rising quickly from thence.

Prior to entering the mountains, which constitute the subject of my study, I must define their significance in relation to an immense range (wrongly named the Moon Mountains) which runs through southern Africa, its western extremity crossing the equator, the Moon Mountains making up only the spurs of the range. This subject—so obscure until now, having been the aim of researches conducted by different people, from Herodotus in the ancient time to the D'Abbadies, d'Arnaud, &c. recently—certainly cannot be explained positively and completely by my own explorations, which bold thought I am too far from entertaining; yet nevertheless, some facts gathered in the location, others related by people familiar with those parts (albeit ignorant), and finally, rocks delivered from the vicinity of the equator give me the right to report here my suppositions based on such a large amount of information.

The central axis of the range commences in lat. 12° N. and long. 39° E. and runs to the south-west, gradually lowering and inclining toward the equator, which it crosses perhaps near long. 18° or 19° E.

Thus this mountain range replaces the waters of the Blue Nile, which flows south at first but, upon encountering this impassable obstacle, describes an arc, deviating westward, toward the foot-hills, and then, having been obstructed here also, seeks a passage in the range's very

---

2 Again, it is unclear which species of the genus is referenced here.
3 One Paris foot equals 1.06575 feet.

slopes, using them as a natural incline for its waters, and flows out to the north. Farther on, two or three insignificant rivers take their origin in the range's northern declivity, followed by the Yabous and the Toumat, and finally, by two or three tributaries of the White Nile and by its sources themselves. Between the White Nile and the Toumat, a less significant mountain range intrudes, its waters flowing into the White Nile on the western side and into the Toumat and the Blue Nile on the eastern side: it is this chain that we shall call the Toumat range hereafter.

The following rivers have their source in the southern side of the central axis of the Inner African range: the Wabah or Wabi or Hainis; the Gojeb; the Omo; and possibly the Niger at the south-western extremity.

Thus the principal mountain range of Inner Africa presents a visible water divide, *divortium aquarum*, waters hardly ever crossing it anywhere; in this it differs from the Alps and the Urals. The only exception is a small stream flowing down across the western slope; yet its banks, their exposed parts revealing broken, over-steepened strata of rock, prove that this rock crevice was formed earlier, by ancient tremor and the tearing of the Earth's crust, and thus constituted a bed ready for the effluxion of waters rather than being broken by them in later times.

At its beginning, the range sometimes reaches significant heights, crossing the snow line; thus, as Rüppell indicates, the mountain range rises to a height of 13,000 to 14,000 Paris feet in Abyssinia, in the province of Gojam, south of Lake Zana, or Dembea; the Selah Mountains reach 12,000 Paris feet; Mount Bua-Gat,[4] the highest in the Semien range, is 14,000 feet above the sea level; the mountain valley of Voghera lies at a height of 8,500 feet; and that of Gondar at 6,500 feet.

According to my observations, the source of the Toumat is situated at a height less than 3,000 feet, while the nearest separate mountains reach 4,000 feet. The part of the principal mountain range of Inner Africa visible from thence—or, it would be better to say, its separate peaks, clearly outlined—cannot be more than 7,600 feet in height, while the

---

4 Mount Bwahit, in the Amhara region of Ethiopia.

mountains seen from the upper reaches of the Nile by d'Arnaud, being in my opinion a continuation of the same range, hardly reach 6,000 feet.

The spur of the principal mountain system of Inner Africa which runs between the Toumat and the White Nile, closer to the former—the one I have named the Toumat Spur—was the subject of my geological research. One can say almost certainly that the north-facing edges of the principal range of Inner Africa are composed of chloritic and talcum slate, cut through with gneiss and syenite, the latter being its most recent elements. My opinion is corroborated by streams issuing from this declivity, especially during seasonal rains, which bring with them broken pieces of the above-mentioned rocks. The Toumat ridge, which breaks away from the central mountain chain, also reveals in its sides talcum and mica slate, topped with diorite and diabase in the mountains of Dohosh, Fasadur, and Doul. Here, as well as in the Urals and the Altai Mountains, greenstone rocks are the most reliable indicators of the location of gold-bearing deposits. At the foot of the mountains, in the west, talcum slate is often displaced by thin-foliar chloritic slate and eventually by sandstone, or greywacke slate, similar to many Silurian and Devonian strata.

High-rising separate groups of the mountains of Falogut are composed of gneiss, those of Fazangoru of chloritic slate veined with white, wind-eroded quartz, just as the gneiss of Falogut is full of thin layers of feldspar; the mountains of Fazoglu, Dassi, and some others are very similar in their formation to other separate groups of mountains, their tops being composed of gneiss and their foots of chloritic slate, visibly broken by the effusion of crystal rocks. Hills of quartz run along the Adi *khor*, constituting the river-bed itself.

Generally, the same phenomenon can be observed here as in the Urals: as the central ridge rose, the formations emerging near it suffered the most from strong and constant vibration and tension in the Earth's crust, therefore growing quite disordered, their strata bent and broken; yet as one moves away from the center of these forcible cataclysms, the formations are deposited more systematically and wider until eventually, far from the central axis, the crystal rocks disappear altogether; chloritic and mica slate are transformed into flagstone, quartzite, conglomerate, and psammite; finally, granite and syenite as such do not appear in rock masses but as deposited boulders or in eroded transitional state. Farther south, Paleozoic remnants are closely related to lava rocks, which are very likely to be their contemporaries; erupted rocks have changed any original features—transformed them, so to speak—to such an extent that it is nearly impossible to determine the general line of these highly perturbed, torn, and over-steepened ranges of sediments.

Commencing to describe my explorations of gold-bearing deposits, I am very glad not to be obliged to begin with refutal of discoveries made by my foreign predecessors in the matter, discoveries so brilliant that they dazzled the Viceroy at first; as we shall see, they have already been proven wrong by factual evidence. Thus they reported to Mohammed Ali that at the Adi *khor*,[5] 1,000 hundredweights of sand (about 2,500 poods) produced between 160 and 240 lots of gold,[6] with the richest sand producing 251 lots . . .[7] They also added that, although the deposits were not as rich as those in Siberia, they were nevertheless *reliable*. I would hope they would be reliable if indeed they were so rich; as for the comparison with Siberian deposits, those who say that their composition is richer still than in the above-mentioned examples know very little about them. As I have written in my *Journey*, despite the remote location of the country and the difficulties of traveling there, Mohammed Ali himself and an entire commission, consisting mostly of foreigners, went there in order to explore and verify these treasures—there turned out to be no gold at all! . . .

Above the spot explored by them, there is indeed a small layer of sand, although quite deep, which contains up to ½ zolotniks per 100 poods, but their prospecting pits missed even that layer; thus all the great preparations for the proposed works, as well as the entire supply of mercury (their intention having been amalgamation) were abandoned. It was quite disappointing.

---

5   Author's note: *Khor*, a local name for a gully made by a stream of water during seasonal rains.
6   Author's note: Russegger, op. cit., section 11, pp. 739, 757.
7   The highest yield is 1.25 ounce per 1,000 pounds. The figures mentioned below are all significantly lower.

I commenced my explorations near the Khassan mountains, having seen exposed blue elvan and greenstone porphyry there for the first time, and soon discovered a deposit that occurred along a dry *khor* flowing into the Toumat on your right as you look downstream (see map), at a rather significant depth (up to one and a half sazhens[8] below the surface). The layer visibly deviated to the slope of the nearby mountains, where it came ever closer to the surface, its gold becoming larger in grain size and richer in composition—so much so that on one of the slopes its concentration sometimes reached 2 zolotniks per 100 poods, while the gold-bearing layer occurred no deeper than two or even one quarter[9] below the surface. It was average in thickness, about one arshin;[10] the entire deposit, according to an approximate calculation, contained up to 25 poods[11] of gold.

Bearing in mind, on the one hand, the cheap cost of the workers assigned to me—negro soldiers who cost the government about a piaster (six kopeks in silver) a-day and who were to be settled in a place where any reliable deposits would be discovered—and on the other hand, the impatience and urge of the Viceroy, who wished to obtain results as soon as possible, as well as the short length of time and the proximity of the rainy season, I wasted no time in commencing to build a factory near the Toumat, for there one could always find water under a thin layer of sand (where it tends to occur) beyond the rainy season. The distance from the deposit was about 1½ or 2 versts.[12] The road to the factory ran along a slope and was rather convenient for the transportation of sand.

Having entrusted the construction of the factory to workmen brought from Cairo under the supervision of a Russian foreman, and having left some of the detachment's men with them, I proceeded, accompanied by the rest, further into the interior of Africa.

The reader of my *Journey* will be familiar with the direction I took and with all the circumstances that accompanied me along the way;

---

8 Approximately 10.5 feet.
9 Approximately 1.75 feet.
10 Approximately 2.33 feet.
11 Approximately 900 pounds.
12 Between one and 1.3 miles.

the exploration of gold deposits and other intended objects forced me to go deep inside Africa, to places that had never been reached before, neither by European travelers nor even by Mohammed Ali's soldiers, these last having been driven not so much by their desire to conquer the authorities of the Sudan as by their avariciousness or by negro-hunting. I shall describe here only my geological researches conducted along the way.

We followed the dry bed of the Toumat, with no other guide but the river and the compass. During the rainy season the Toumat is a large and fast river, which we were to witness subsequently with our own eyes; but at the beginning, it was only at occasional spots that a horse, stepping through the layer of sand and burying its hooves in it, would reach water. The banks were cliffy and gently sloping; the mountains stood in a distance. The soil touched by our pits was, for the most part, composed of eroded granite and syenite; it was only at Kamamil that the pits descended onto diorite, the concentration of gold in a deposit resting on the latter being quite significant—namely, up to 1½ zolotniks per 100 poods.

Had I discovered it earlier, I would have chosen this mine over the first for the works, given its regularity and the span of its stratum; yet now it was no longer possible to proceed to build two factories simultaneously, for we lacked experienced men suitable for the business, having been unable to split our resources at the very beginning. However, I proposed that, as men learned the business, we should establish another gold-washing factory, with an encampment attached to it, which was to form a part of a line of military settlements in the Toumat Mountains, intended, among other things, to keep the negro lands under control and to defend them from the raids of the Galla and the Abyssinians.

The deposit—composed of broken diorite, talcum slate, and quartz, bound together with eroded iron clay—is also abundant in ferruginous concentrate; occurring in a hollow, it is quite deep there, up to two sazhens, but toward the bed of the Toumat, it comes out straight onto the surface; the dry river-bed provided us with a means by which to examine the deposit, and we obtained up to ¾ zolotniks per 100 poods. The gold becomes richer near the slopes of the mountains, and even the most mountainous area of Kamamil has a thin stratum of sand, composed of broken quartz mixed with a small amount of eroded clay, resting on quartz soil and apparently formed at a later time, originating from the erosion of a quartz rock seam running along here.

Moving farther up the Toumat, we encountered crests of granite, which form the cataracts of the river at high water. The granite is dense, fine-grained, and crowns the tops of the mountains that run from west to south-east, quite parallel to the central axis of the principal range of Inner Africa, as if dependent on its elevation or effused simultaneously with it.

Farther up the Toumat, a third gold-bearing deposit occurred, contained in eroded granite and poor in composition.

Even before that, at the very foot-hills of the Toumat ridge, we discovered a rich deposit of ironstone and iron clay; and in the upper reaches of the Toumat, we found a wonderful deposit of lodestone.

Having come to the upper reaches of the Toumat, we found ourselves on the south-west extremity of the Toumat ridge. From thence our gaze could reach the foot of what is denominated on the maps as the Moon Mountains, Jebel-el-Khamar, a name unknown among the natives; the reader will have noticed that we have referred to it as the principal mountain range of Inner Africa and will have understood our reason. Later we visited Doul, the western extremity of the Toumat ridge, thus criss-crossing it, so to speak, in every direction.

At the foot of Mount Doul there are gold deposits known to the negroes from time immemorial; they are not rich but embrace an extremely large space, not only in the hollow of Doul but also in most of the hollows of nearby mountains. The deposits in these parts are notable for most regular crystals of gold occurring in them, particularly cubic in shape; also for dual crystals of gold, particularly cubic in shape; as well as for dual and triple crystals of sulphur-ore.

As I have noted in my *Journey*, Mohammed Ali read in some Arabic manuscript that the ancient pharaohs of Egypt had obtained gold from Doul. The terrain here is so dug-up, over-steepened, and cluttered with waste-dumps, already overgrown with colossal trees, that I am almost prepared to believe the manuscript, especially since I found an ancient tool here, a kind of stone pick (of blue elvan). The deposits might have been richer in the past but depleted back then; the ancients might have been satisfied with their richness, for they were able to succeed, if not by their skill, then by the mass of their men, being in possession of innumerable numbers of slaves used to build the pyramids and ancient temples; the present-day rulers of Egypt, too, overcome seemingly insuperable obstacles thanks to their vast number of workers, who are paid so little for their labor. The following, of course, is a mere a supposition: the negroes could have also produced gold since ancient times. At any rate, ancient Ophir,[13] whence they obtained gold in the time of Solomon, could be located here, in Inner Africa, rather than in India—especially considering historical evidence, which brings my supposition so close to the heart of the matter; whatever the truth, it could never be situated in America, as Montezinos[14] believes, very skillfully replacing Peru by Piru, then by Phiru, and finally, by Ophir. Nowadays, they may well commence to search for ancient Ophir in California.

Having observed the Toumat ridge in all its directions, I was convinced that the bulk of the gold deposit on this northern side of the principal range was contained in the basin of the Toumat and mostly on its left side.

Upon our arrival at Khassan, I completed the construction of the factory and the installation of four machines with rakes and iron sieves attached to their heads, designed for the grinding and washing of sand. In order to avoid any future rumors or misunderstandings, I invited the Governor-General of the East Sudan to attend the opening of the factory, as well as to keep—jointly with myself and two German-educated Arab officers who managed the factory—a daily work log, the original of which log I later submitted to Ibrahim Pasha, the former Viceroy of Egypt, while also submitting a copy issued by the ministry to my own superiors.

At first the works progressed slowly: the negroes took a long time to understand the operation of the machines, using which they washed

---

13 A wealthy city port, the source of gold and other riches, mentioned in the Bible. Starting in the 15th century, various European explorers attempted to locate Ophir in India, Africa, Asia, or America.

14 Antonio de Montezinos (Aaron Levi, d. circa 1650), a Portuguese traveler; claimed to have found in present-day Ecuador Native American people aware of the Judaic tradition.

barely 300 or 400 poods daily, whereas in Russia workers do 1,000 poods; by the end of the first week, however, they began accustoming themselves to the work, achieving 700 poods now. The total composition in a week's work turned out to be one zolotnik per 100 poods of sand. I brought the gold to Ibrahim Pasha. A calculation showed that it would cost the government 68 kopeks in silver per zolotnik. The gold from the works was tested in the Laboratory; being of varying quality, it is generally good, marked 81 to 92.

Ibrahim Pasha, who quite understood the importance of the development of gold-mines in his country, embarked on the matter with all his fervor, but then his industrious life was cut short.

Will the production of gold take hold in the Egyptian lands? Will other giant enterprises established by the reformer of Egypt take hold? It is difficult to say; but generally, it is very doubtful, especially bearing in mind the close-minded stubbornness and superstitions of the present-day Governor-General, Khalid Pasha, who is able to destroy but not to create. Mohammed Ali, who dreamed of the discovery of gold (that favorite idea of his whole life), who spent several million piasters on the business over 20 years, undertaking a most dangerous journey to the Sudan, where he was struck by an illness due to his complete disappointment in the success of the matter—Mohammed Ali was not destined to see this enterprise realized, even though he still talks, dimly and unconsciously, of the search for gold.

On our return journey, we crossed the Lesser Nubian Desert, situated on the left side of the Nile. Its formation is very similar to that of the Great Nubian Desert, the mountains of both, as if related to each other, running from west to south-east, parallel to the central axis of the mountains of Inner Africa. In the Lesser Nubian Desert, it is only sandstone, especially that occurring at the entrance and exit to it, that is composed of narrow stony bands, so similar to trachyte in their glass-like fracture and outer aspect that I am prepared to take them for trachyte, its deposits being displaced in their open pits by foliated stone and trachytic tuff.

Table of Barometric, Thermometric, and Psychrometric Observations

Month, year	Place name	Day of the month, new style	Hour of observation	Barometer	Reaumur thermometer, t'	Thermometer, t	Black-ball thermometer for the determination of the highest temperature	Notes
JANUARY 1848	Steamboat, near Cairo	20	12	751.0	8–2	15–2	18.6	Wind mostly N. Clouds rare. Quite still on the 25th.
	Sailing up the Nile, Benisuef to Minya	21	6½	758.0	2–1	5–3	8.8	
		–	7	–	1–8	4–1	7.5	
		–	8	759.1	5–8	8–6	11.9	
		–	9	760.0	7–8	13–1	16.6	
		–	10	760.1	8–2	14–8	17.9	
		–	11	760.1	11–0	18–2	21.7	
		–	12	759.1	13–8	20–0	23.5	
		–	1	760.2	12–4	21–0	24.5	
		–	2	759.0	11–1	19–0	22.5	
		–	3	–	10–7	15–8	18.9	
		–	4	–	9–7	15–7	18.9	
		–	5	780.5	9–9	14–	17.0	
	Minya to Siut	22	7	710.9	5–4	8–	10.9	
		–	9	762.0	7–6	13–2	16.5	
		–	11	759.0	9–8	15–8	18.9	
		–	12	760.0	11–2	17–2	20.5	
		–	1	760.5	12–6	20–	23.1	
		–	2	761.7	12–2	19–6	22.9	
		–	3	757.0	10–2	17–4	20.7	
		–	5	754.0	9–0	13–9	16.9	

TABLE OF OBSERVATIONS

Month, year	Place name	Day of the month, new style	Hour of observation	Barometer	Reaumur thermometer, t'	Thermometer, t	Black-ball thermometer for the determination of the highest temperature	Notes
January 1848	Siut to Keneh	23	12	750.0	12–8	20–6	23.5	Siut located in lat. 26°12'19", long. 23°38'0".
		–	1	749.0	12–6	21–4	24.3	
		–	3	747.0	11–8	20–2	23.1	
	Keneh to Aswan	24	12	731.1	8–2	12–8	15.8	
		–	3	737.2	8–8	13–8	16.8	
		–	4	738.1	7–5	12–8	15.8	
		–	5	739.1	7–6	12–4	15.8	
		25	9	760.4	7–6	12–8	15.7	
		–	12	760.0	10–8	16–	19	
		–	2	761.5	12–	19–6	22.5	
		–	5	759.0	8–8	12–	15.1	
	Aswan to Korosko, on the Nile	26	12	760.9	19–1	23–4	26.6	Aswan located in lat. 24°4'44". Wind N. and N.E.
		27	10	756.7	18–4	22–5	25.4	
		28	10	756.8	17–1	21–	24.8	
		29	10	758.8	19–0	23–	26.1	
		30	10	759.4	20–1	24–1	27.8	
		31	A.M.	–	–	–	–	
		–	6	760.1	9–0	15–8	9	
		–	12	762.0	24–1	27–5	32.1	
		–	6	761.1	19–2	23–1	19.2	

TABLE OF OBSERVATIONS

Month, year	Place name	Day of the month, new style	Hour of observation	Barometer	Reaumur thermometer, t'	Thermometer, t	Black-ball thermometer for the determination of the highest temperature	Notes
FEBRUARY 1848	Korosko, on the Nile	1	10	757.9	10–8	15–8	18.9	Strong wind.
	Great Nubian Desert	2	10	757.9	19–1	23–1	26.9	
		3	11	758.4	20–5	23–8	27	
		4	12	757.1	31–1	34–	38.1	
		5	12	755.8	31–6	34–7	38	Slight wind, clear sky.
		6	12	756.5	25–4	27–8	33.4	
		7	10	757.2	25–	27–1	33.2	
		8	10	760.2	29–1	31–	34.5	
		9	12	760.4	30–	32–2	37.4	
		10	10	762.1	26–5	28–1	32.8	
	Abu Hammet, on the Nile	11	10	759.5	26–0	29–1	32.4	Wind constantly N., being the strongest at high noon; more still toward evening.
		12	10	758.6	26–1	29–3	32.1	
		13	10	755.5	26–3	29–5	32.8	
		14	10	746.9	25–1	28–	31.1	
		15	11	765.9	27–1	30–4	34.4	
	Berber	16	10	764.0	19–2	23–4	26.1	
		17	10	762.6	18–1	22–	25	
		18	10	762.7	15–1	28–7	30.6	
		–	P.M.	–	–	–	–	
		19	6	762.0	8–8	15–1	9	
		20	6	761.2	8–7	15–2	9.1	
		21	6	762.0	10–1	16–3	11	
		–	A.M.	–	–	–	–	
		22	10	763.4	19–8	22–1	25.2	
	On the Nile	23	12	731.2	26–	28–8	34.7	
		24	10	761.6	21–1	27–7	33.1	
		25	10	760.2	20–2	27–	34.4	
		26	10	769.3	19–1	26–1	33.5	
		27	11	755.2	20–1	27–2	34.4	
		28	10	731.1	18–4	25–1	34.2	
		–	A.M.	–	–	–	–	
		29	6	741.2	8–0	16–6	8.1	
		–	10	742.1	17–1	24–1	32.4	
		–	12	744.4	19–1	24–6	35.1	
		–	P.M.	–	–	–	–	

TABLE OF OBSERVATIONS

Month, year	Place name	Day of the month, new style	Hour of observation	Barometer	Reaumur thermometer, t'	Thermometer, t	Black-ball thermometer for the determination of the highest temperature	Notes
		–	6	740.6	15–1	21–1	36.1	
MARCH 1848	From Khartoum, on the Nile	1	10	752.2	14–	21–4	29.8	Khartoum in lat. 15°37'10", long. 30°17'30". Wind N. and N.E., occasionally changing to S.
		2	10	755.7	17–2	23–	29	
		3	10	754.2	17–3	23–1	29.1	
		4	10	751.6	17–4	23–5	30.1	
		5	10	749.0	18–5	24–	31	
		6	10	735.4	19–	25–1	31	
		7	10	737.0	19–1	25–	31.2	
		8	10	742.1	19–4	25–5	32.1	Sennaar located in lat. 13°36'50", long. 31°24'33".
	From Roseires, at foot-hills	9	10	755.4	19–8	26–	33.1	
		10	10	755.8	20–8	27–1	33.1	
		11	10	–	21–1	28–	32.8	
		12	10	759.9	20–1	27–4	34.4	
		13	10	759.4	22–1	29–1	36.1	S. wind often commences, heralding seasonal rains.
		14	10	757.9	25–1	31–	35.8	
	Khassan	15	10	–	25–1	31–1	35.6	
		16	10	–	25–4	31–5	27	
		17	8	–	16–	22–1	23.5	
		18	9	–	18–2	23–1	32.1	
	Sojourn at Khassan	19	10	–	21–1	27–1	31.8	Wind mostly S.; cloudy.
		20	10	760.3	21–	27–4	–	
		21	6	763.4	5–	–	–	
		22	6	759.7	4–9	–	–	
		23	6	764.5	5–1	–	–	
		24	10	759.8	18–	26–1	32.2	
		25	12	761.9	29–	35–	Beyond measurement	
		26	10	760.3	25–2	32–1		
		27	11	758.8	28–3	34–4		
	Leaving Khassan	28	10	763.0	19–1	27–	33.2	
		29	10	764.6	10–2	26–1	31.1	Heavy rain.
		30	10	766.8	22–	28–3	34.3	

Month, year	Place name	Day of the month, new style	Hour of observation	Barometer	Reaumur thermometer, t'	Thermometer, t	Black-ball thermometer for the determination of the highest temperature	Notes
MARCH 1848	Benishangul (in the mountains) and further into Inner Africa	–	A.M.	–	–	–	–	Reached lat. 8 degrees.
		31	6	765.3	5–1	–	–	
		–	10	766.0	18–2	25–1	31.1	
		–	12	766.4	29–3	36–		
		–	P.M.	–	–	–	–	
APRIL 1848		–	6	764.1	20–	26–	31	Singhe in lat. 10°29'44", long. 32°20'30". Wind constantly S.; cloudy.
		1	10	760.5	20–6	28–	33	
		2	10	762.4	19–1	27–1	32.1	
		3	10	758.6	23–8	30–1	36.1	
		4	10	756.6	24–1	30–3	37	
		5	10	764.3	24–	30–1	36.8	
		6	10	763.1	25–1	31–	38.1	
		7	10	762.4	25–4	31–3	38.4	
		8	10	761.7	25–1	31–1	37.8	
		9	10	760.4	24–1	30–2	36.1	
		10	10	760.3	25–	31–1	37.4	
		11	10	758.6	23–1	29–2	35.1	
		12	10	762.7	25–	31–2	37.3	
		13	10	761.4	24–2	30–	36.8	
	Journey S.W. into the mountains	14	10	758.4	23–1	29–	34.8	Rain.
		15	10	756.3	25–3	31–1	37.8	
		16	12	–	29–1	37–		Cloudy.
		17	12	Last spare barometer tube broken, no more observations made	30–	38–1	Beyond measurement	
		18	12		30–4	39–		
		19	12		31–1	–		Heavy rain; wind constantly S
		20	12		31–1	–		
		21	10		25–1	30–2	38.6	
		22	11		24–2	29–8	38	
		23	11		29–1	35–	42.1	

TABLE OF OBSERVATIONS

Month, year	Place name	Day of the month, new style	Hour of observation	Barometer	Reaumur thermometer, t'	Thermometer, t	Black-ball thermometer for the determination of the highest temperature	Notes
APRIL 1848	Journey S.W. into the mountains	24	11		29–1	35–2	42.4	Cloudy.
		25	10		29–1	36–	42.3	
		26	11		25–2	31–1	36.4	Last thermometer and psychrometer left with Mr. Tsenkovsky at Roseires, on our return journey, for the observation of the weather during the rainy season. Moreover, I was no longer able to make any observations myself, owing to a grave illness.
		27	11		25–1	31–	36.1	
		28	10		24–8	30–1	35.8	
		29	10		24–8	30–1	35.8	
		30	10	Last spare barometer tube broken, no more observations made	24–7	30–2	36	
		–	–		24–8	30–4	36	
		31	6		5–4	–	–	
		–	10		20–1	25–1	29.1	
		–	12		20–4	35–1	43	
		–	7		20–1	25–	28	

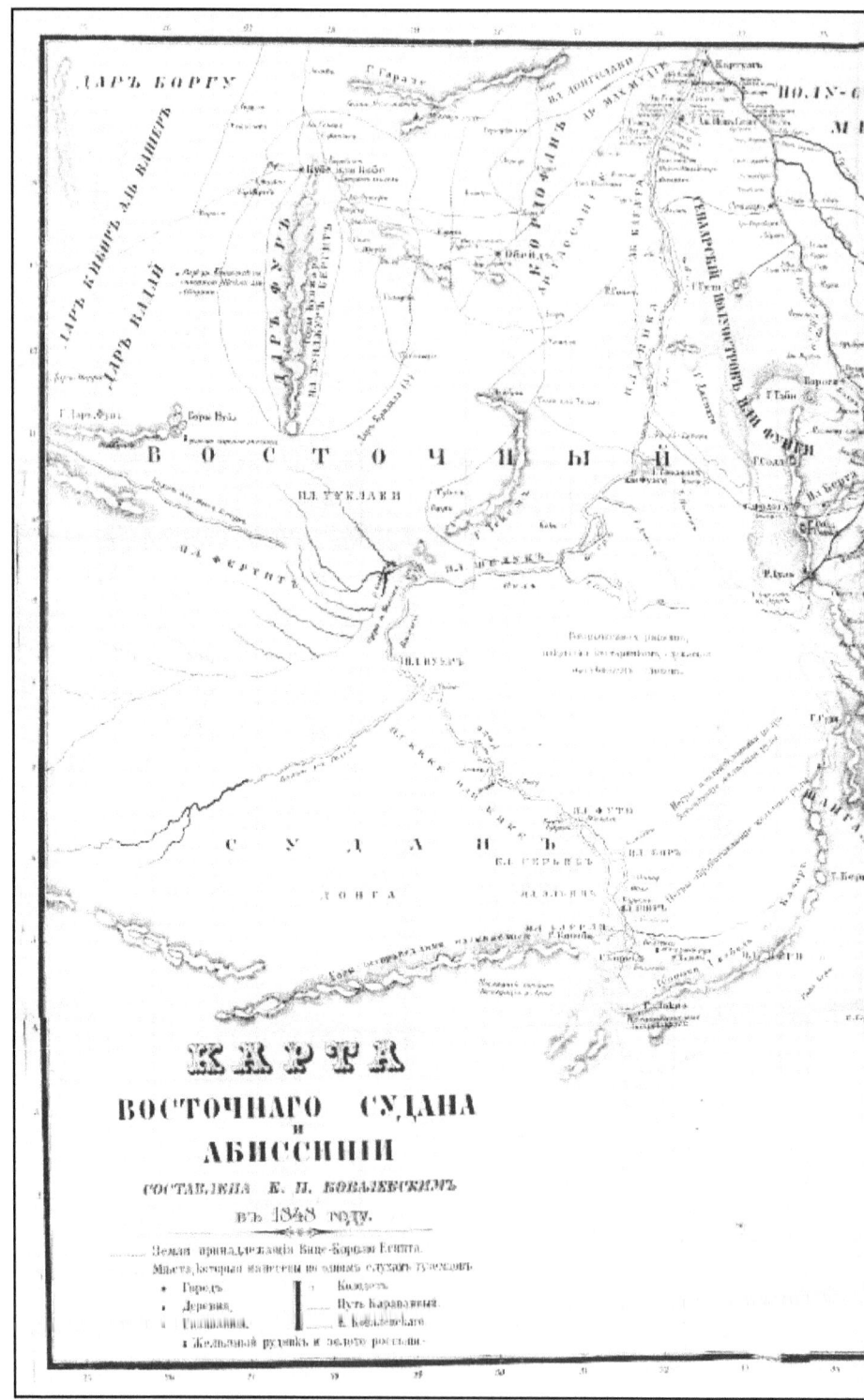

Map of East Sudan and Abyssinia
Compiled by E. P. Kovalevsky in 1848

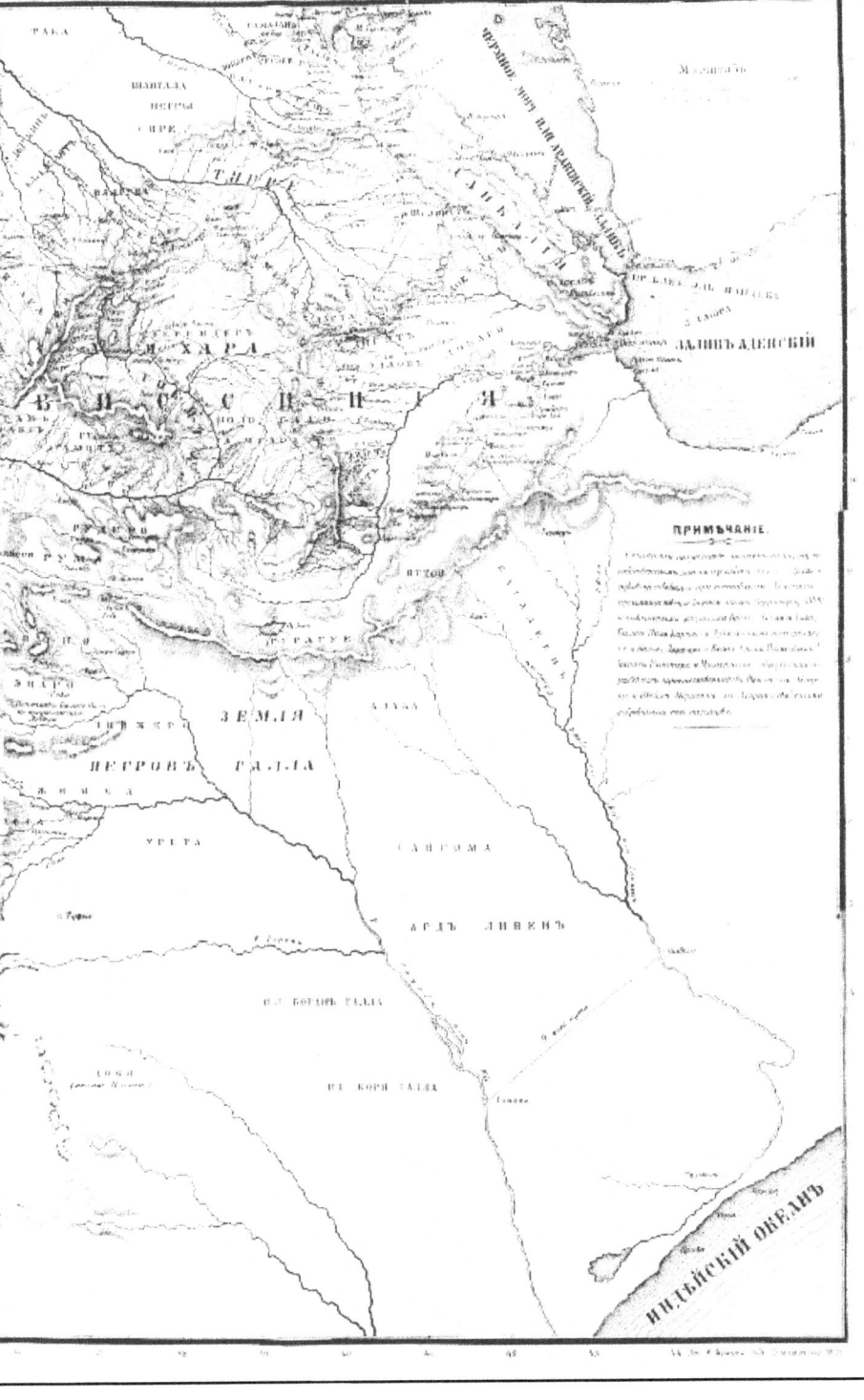

www.ingramcontent.com/pod-product-compliance
Lightning Source LLC
Chambersburg PA
CBHW070606170426
43200CB00012B/2607